MACHIAVELLI
and the Nature of
Political Thought

EDITED BY

Martin Fleisher

ATHENEUM

New York 1972

Preface

T HE ESSAYS CONTAINED IN THIS VOL-
ume were, with one exception, presented at meetings
sponsored by the Conference for the Study of Political
Thought. The conference itself was organized a number of
years ago to encourage and stimulate research in the general
field of political thought primarily through the organization
of regional working seminars throughout Canada and the
United States and the convocation of occasional larger meetings.

The first such meeting, held at York University, Toronto,
in 1969 on the occasion of the five hundredth anniversary of
Machiavelli's birth, was fittingly devoted to his political
thought. Most of the papers presented at this conference enjoyed the benefit of written comments by discussants and,
where available, these have been included in the present
volume.

Those of us who attended the conference will not soon
forget the warmth and consideration of our hosts at York.
It helped to create an atmosphere completely conducive to
the free and easy give-and-take which is so essential to a conference if it is to be something more than simply the occasion
for the formal presentation of papers. It is a further pleasure
to acknowledge our particular indebtedness to Professor Neal
Wood of York. He organized the conference on Machiavelli
and therefore must shoulder primary responsibility for its
success. Finally, there would have been no meeting, there
would have been no Conference on the Study of Political

Thought without the work and dedication of Professor Melvin Richter, its first secretary.

The Conference for the Study of Political Thought has been supported, in part, by a grant from the Chancellor's Fund of the City University of New York and the publication of this volume affords an opportunity for the Conference to thank Chancellor Albert H. Bowker. The meeting on Machiavelli was made possible by grants from the Canada Council, York University, and the Conference for the Study of Political Thought.

Contents

MACHIAVELLI
and the Nature of
Political Thought

Introduction

T HE STUDIES THAT CONSTITUTE THIS
volume cluster about two topics: the nature of political
thought and Machiavelli's contribution to the solution of this
and other problems in political theory. Thus we are reminded,
once again, that whatever else it may be concerned with, and
its concerns frequently appear to be bewilderingly varied, political theory is perennially concerned with itself. It would be
strange if this were not the case since the impulse to turn in
on itself comes naturally to thought or consciousness—reflection is its mode of existence. All political theorizing
then is, to some degree, self-conscious.

In the instance of Sheldon Wolin's essay one may say
that this self-consciousness in the form of an inquiry into
the activity of political theorizing constitutes the very subject matter of the paper. In it the theorist seeks to elucidate
what is implicated in theorizing. In this sense "Political
Theory as a Vocation" is the most consciously self-conscious
of the papers appearing in this volume. Moreover, the self
of which it strives to become conscious is cast in a large
mold, being at least as big and vital as life itself. Wolin conceives of political theory, then, not as one (mere) mode of
knowledge but as a way of life. And that way is itself
broadly conceived. Insofar as the calling is to the life of

political theory, for which Wolin so felicitously revives the name *bios theoretikos,* it encompasses more than the theoretical life as many of the ancients understood it. This may appear paradoxical: it does stand to reason that the life of theory embraces more than the life of political theory. But this turns out not to be so since Wolin's particular linking of the political and the theoretical undercuts the ancient dichotomies of the *vita contemplativa* and the *vita activa,* thus allowing political theory to include practical life.

If, for Wolin, the consciousness of the political theorist is characteristically comprehensive or totalizing in the way it understands, it is also inescapably intentional in its attitude and thrust. The life of political theory is therefore doubly a political life. Its subject is political and it also finds that it must make choices and decisions which have practical as well as theoretical consequences; it is unavoidably engaged with the world. Political theory's perspective, therefore, cannot be professional in the narrow sense—no social or academic division of labor can a priori determine its scope. Rather, the reverse must be the case. All institutions and practices are obliged to submit themselves to the scrutiny and critique of theory. Otherwise we are eternally trapped in the tyranny of the world as it is—the reign of positivism and the worship of the given qua given.

For Wolin this tyranny over consciousness is, in its modern form, embodied in the vocation of the 'methodist' and in his program which proclaims the primacy of method. Dating from Descartes' construction of a method for the regulation of consciousness which explicitly exempted moral and political concerns from its operation, the identification of consciousness with a set of technical procedures turned mind into a *logos* of *techne* while simultaneously transforming its object, the world it can know, into a technology. The triumph in social science, most especially as practiced in the United States, of this consciousness is signaled by what Wolin

4

calls the "behavioral revolution" and its *vita methodi.*

Thus in the contemporary era the *bios theoretikos* defines itself partly in terms of what it opposes—the *vita methodi.* It does not, of course, take its stand against method per se but against a particular version of method and its accompanying ideology. It refuses to identify itself with the role technological society assigns to it or with the distorted image reflected back to it by behaviorism. Unlike the latter, it remains responsive to questions about "the quality, direction, or fate of public life." It has a political subject matter. But it also is committed to a theoretical consciousness in which it finds room for the creative and imaginative powers, a developed sense of context and appropriateness, and the historical dimension of its existence, to all of which the *vita methodi* tends to be indifferent if not outright hostile. The theoretical vocation, then, has at its disposal powers and resources never dreamt of in the impoverished philosophy of the methodist-behaviorist.

Further, to judge from the style of Wolin's essay, the *bios theoretikos* neither seeks to deny the realities of struggle and conflict nor to flee these by the route of transcendence. It adopts an invigorating polemical tone as it confronts social science behaviorists and the contemporary celebrants of consensus.

Alan Ryan would appear to be in substantial agreement with Wolin on the nature of some of the crucial defects of political science and political theory as recently practiced. He too decries the poverty of its notion of the self and its attendant drastic narrowing of the scope and goals of political life. He locates the defects by means of a division which like Wolin he roots in a historical tradition, but which runs along a somewhat different axis than Wolin's. His division "lies between the adherents of what one might call an 'economic' or 'market' account of social life on the one hand and the partisans of a 'participant' or 'self-development' account on the other." Neither does it reach back quite

5

as far in history, dating from approximately the time of the two Mills, James and John Stuart.

But perhaps the most significant difference between the two divisions is that Ryan locates both halves of the pair, 'market' versus 'participant' society, *within* the domain of political theory proper whereas, in the dichotomy *bios theoretikos* versus methodism, Wolin unequivocably places methodism outside the pale. Wolin would seem to be saying that, at best, method may be recognized as the handmaiden of political theory. However, the escalating claim of method, first to be part of political theory, then to be its most relevant component, and finally, to be its only valid component, bears witness to the general tendency in modern civilization for the instrumental and technical to gain dominance over and choke out the very life it was originally intended to serve. This Frankenstein reaction spells the death of the *bios theoretikos*. In such grave circumstances it is hopeless and wrong for the life of theory to embrace a politics that seeks adjustment and accommodation with the *vita methodi*—hopeless because the monster will insist upon being master and will not live and let live; wrong because it implies acceptance of a monstrous life as one possible prototype of human life. Hence Wolin's politics of a clear-cut choice between mutually exclusive alternatives, based on a sharply defined and deep-running ideological difference and the pressing need for decision.

In contrast, the politics of "Two Theories of Politics and Democracy" can be more mild and conciliatory because, while James and John Mill differ, neither the father nor the son challenges the very grounds for the existence of the other; neither, that is, questions the legitimacy of the theoretical enterprise itself. Thus Ryan's politics can even entertain the possibility of full reconciliation since he is not prepared entirely to rule out the absorption of one into the other. The opposition may therefore be correctly viewed as

6

a wholly loyal opposition. There is a common heritage, many shared values. Indeed, it is, after all, a family quarrel within a highly civilized bourgeois family; so we are safe in assuming differences will not be allowed to overflow the bounds of propriety.

Ryan presents James Mill as the theorist of a political democracy based on the economic model of the market society. Always true to himself, utilitarian man remains the calculating consumer even when he is transposed from the sphere of civil society to that of the state. Thus his participation in public life and the goals of that life come to be evaluated and judged by the elder Mill not on their own terms but as part of the cost accounting system that the utilitarians designed to measure private sources of pleasure. The realm of communal goods, public spiritedness, and political activity—the realm, that is, of *res publica* as the arena of human development and fulfillment—is afforded little if any independent basis for existence by this political theory. This view of the political domain as yet another market in which individuals and groups pursue their self-interest through the usual bargaining processes is, according to Ryan, characteristic of present-day pressure group, pluralist, and consensus theories of liberal democracy. Such theories barely recognize the legitimacy of activities of self-realization; they place little positive value on political participation as such. We find them elaborating democratic theories in which political activity is envisaged primarily in terms of the expenditure of effort, as something negative, a cost to be measured against and subtracted from the goods it yields. In this utilitarian perspective, political activity is a mere means; it possesses no inherent value. It is on this issue that Ryan sees the son parting company with his father. J. S. Mill insists on the fundamental value of making one's own choice —the specific choice is always less important than the act of choosing. This is the essence of self-development, and self-development or realization is the essence of human life. From this flows the intrinsic value of political participation.

Thus differing theories of human nature—the utilitarian philosophy of the father and its dramatic alteration by the son in the direction of a continental idealism (Rousseau, Kant) which in varying degrees celebrates the autonomy of the self and the supreme value of its own realization, a process inevitably involving the other—yield dissimilar theories of political democracy. Clearly, these are not solely of historical interest: Ryan contends that much of the present confusion about the nature and ends of democracy stem from the fact that democratic theory over the past century and a half has operated with these "two not obviously compatible views" of human nature.

Thus Ryan has probed and assessed the generational gap between the Mills, père et fils, in terms of different theories of human life and their concomitant differing notions of political life. Since he suggests the differences are still with us it would appear that succeeding generations of Englishmen have muddled along, reliving these differences without striving for or attaining clarity as to their nature or discovering a way to compose them. Ryan makes it perfectly clear that as far as he is concerned this is a task of some urgency. Indeed, he feels it has been an urgent matter for close to a century and a half, yet liberal democratic theory has thus far failed to pose the issues in a clear and decisive fashion just as liberal democratic politics has shied away from making the decisive institutional choices.

While Ryan shares Wolin's dissatisfaction with this state of affairs, the differences between the two are significant. The overwhelming feeling of urgency, the compelling need to choose—we must decide and decide now—and the utter incompatibility of the options—the choice between a free and human life and the living death of a prefabricated role—convey a sense of deeper crisis in Wolin's "Political

8

Theory as a Vocation." Despite this, and despite the fact that for Wolin the scales are now heavily weighted in favor of methodism, *techne,* and a purely manipulative and instrumental scheme of life, the essay communicates a solid confidence, absent in Ryan, in the ability of political theory to provide the vision and political will to summon the energy to confront and overcome the opposition. "Two Concepts of Politics and Democracy" is critical of the present state of liberal democratic politics and theory, but it candidly confesses it has no ready resolution of the theoretical issue, and indeed it is even hesitant to indicate the general direction which such a solution might take.

It is tempting to account for this difference between two theorists who, after all, have a good deal more in common than a common enemy, by reference to differences between the United States and England. For one thing behaviorism and methodism are so much more deeply rooted in United States civilization; as a result, among their opponents the threat looms larger to theorists on this side of the Atlantic. For another, the decline of British power must partially sap the sense of urgency and crisis in political thinking—the stakes no longer seem as great as they used to be, the decisions to be made no longer seem earthshaking. Contrariwise, the sense of enhanced power in the present-day United States heightens both the sense of possibility and the critical significance of each decision. Context, sensitivity to which Wolin tells us is to be assiduously cultivated by the *bios theoretikos,* is plainly identified by him with the political power of the United States and the fatefulness of its decisions for all mankind. This may help to explain why Wolin is at the same time both more disturbed by the opposition confronting the *bios theoretikos* and more confident in its resources to overcome this opposition.

The *bios theoretikos* constitutes one of these resources by reconstituting its own history. It looks for itself in many places including the past, choosing to recognize this image or that reflection as real and authentic. As it picks and chooses its way, then, it simultaneously identifies its ancestry and discovers itself. To deny the theoretical vocation this way of finding itself is to arbitrarily restrict and impoverish it. In the life of consciousness to select our spiritual fathers and more distant forebears is part of the process of choosing ourselves. We may rebel against them, remain their docile children, or disclaim them and go in search of others, but it should be observed that the identification of ancestors as a way to self-consciousness commits us to no one particular philosophy of history. Parenthetically, however, the identification does require us to acknowledge the issue of the relation to and uses of philosophical ancestors as itself a genuine philosophical question, something the analytic school of philosophy, for one, is frequently reluctant to do.

Of the essays dealing with Machiavelli in this volume, the majority were presented at a conference celebrating the five hundredth anniversary (1969) of his birth. This may be taken as evidence that among many contemporaries who are concerned with political thought a turn toward Machiavelli seems perfectly natural, even for people who hold widely differing views of Machiavelli and of the nature of political theory. It is certainly not out of a sense of filial piety that they choose to celebrate Machiavelli. There are more respectable and honorable figures that one might choose as a worthy ancestor or father image. Yet even those who despise Machiavelli acknowledge his importance to vital theoretical issues. Whether he is held up as a patron saint of modern political science or denounced as the progenitor of a modern *Machtpolitik,* it seems impossible for contemporary thought to ignore him. Most of the political institutions of his day have long since disappeared but he is very much with us. In an age which, on the one hand, is characterized by the methodist's horror of history, and, on the other, expresses its own desperate desire to make a new beginning by labeling so much of contemporary culture, let alone the study of the past, as irrelevant to the task, Machiavelli is among the few political thinkers who is not automatically relegated to the dustbin of history. He remains a vital medium through which, by one means or another, present-day political thought seeks to come to consciousness: to locate and define its subject matter, its characteristic mode of proceeding, and its fundamental tasks and goals; and—yes, even this—to recover and renew its sense of vocation, for, as Wolin reminds us, we are dealing with a way of life and not a mere new technique.

The theme of life forms the leitmotif of the essay "A Passion for Politics," which plays on the related images of birth, vitality, longevity, *virtù,* and renewal so often evoked by Machiavelli. Perhaps it was inspired by the occasion, the celebration of Machiavelli's five hundredth anniversary. Be that as it may, the intimation is that there is a relation between Machiavelli's natural vitality or *virtù* and his notion of the vital nature of the human psyche. And this, in turn, it is argued, is crucial to the understanding of his conception of politics and the political.

In brief, for Machiavelli, the human soul is not capable of finding or realizing its own peace or harmony. It has no inner principle of integrity or unity. Both its restrictions and its goals lie outside itself—in the public arena and its relation to others. Like life itself, the characteristic movement of the soul is growth understood as self-aggrandizement. Since this aggrandizement is both public and relative to others it must be political in nature. It follows that true knowledge, Machiavelli's *vera cognizione,* cannot be found by turning inward in an examination of the self. The true reflection of the world of men is not to be found in the soul but in the political experience of peoples. This is the source of political knowledge, for Machiavelli the highest form of human consciousness.

It is his idea of the political and the absolute primacy he

accords political life that distinguishes the world of Machiavelli from that of his humanist contemporaries who wrote on political matters. It also sharply sets him off from the dominant world-views of the ancients, be they of Platonic, Stoic, or Epicurean origin. Thus when Machiavelli proclaims that he is seeking a new way and turns to ancient political experience to find it, what he finds is genuinely new despite its being couched, for the most part, in a language borrowed from the Romans.

It may be said, with perhaps a touch of poetic license, that both Martin Fleisher's "A Passion for Politics" and J. G. A. Pocock's "Custom and Grace, Form and Matter; An Approach to Machiavelli's Concept of Innovation" present us with a Machiavelli who exemplifies the *bios theoretikos* in Wolin's sense of the term. Of greater interest, all three agree that one important value of the vocation of political theory, one to which it should always be receptive, is innovation, and that Machiavelli exemplifies this *virtù* to a very high degree. Moreover Pocock makes it quite explicit that this is no accident. Indeed, his paper is not primarily concerned with this or that particular innovation which is credited to Machiavelli but moves to the theoretical level to raise the issue of the concept of innovation itself.

Employing the method of analyzing the nature and changes in paradigmatic linguistic structures as a qualitative measure of change, Pocock first isolates two such late medieval linguistic paradigms. These, he finds, can give effective voice to certain problems in political thought but are each severely limited in the way they can render the relation between particular and particular, or between the time-bound and the time-bound. In the first paradigm, rooted in a providential idea of history, the ultimate significance of particulars and the pattern of their relation is held to be inscrutable to human reason. This notion gives rise to two perspectives on time-bound events: one, the apocalyptic raises one particular event to the level of the unique and exceptional on extrarational grounds; the other, the perspective of fortune in effect contends that reason cannot penetrate the realm of the time-bound. In the second paradigm there is a discernible pattern, existing not between particulars as such, but as a result of man's repeated experience of particulars. Repetition builds up patterns of usage or tradition and, in this fashion, man acquires a second nature. A correlate notion of community is incorporated in each of these paradigms: community is either apocalyptic and grounded in grace, or traditional and rooted in experience.

In terms of these available paradigms, Pocock next examines the situation confronting Florence and Machiavelli at the time of the restoration of the Medici regime, the very eve of the writing of *The Prince.* He proceeds to demonstrate a specific effort on the part of Guicciardini and other optimate writers to see the Medici as exemplars of innovative, in contrast to traditional or inherited, rule. In *The Prince* Machiavelli generalizes the problem. It is, therefore, a work *"de innovatoribus:* a typology of political innovators."￼ In the course of pursuing this investigation and in working out the implications of innovative rule, principally the need for *virtù* to overcome the traditional mode of rule, Machiavelli is moved to alter the classical meaning of virtue, "to employ the concept of *virtù* in its purely formal sense of that by which order is imposed on *fortuna."* This, Pocock stresses, is Machiavelli's breakthrough. It is further generalized in the *Discourses,* yielding a new paradigm of political community distinct from the traditional and apocalyptic versions, grounded in the realities of innovation and *fortuna.* As a political theorist, then, Machiavelli's innovation is to establish innovation as fundamental to political reality and to indicate some of the conditions and implications of so doing.

One of these implications, the acceptance of the positive consequences of social conflict, the view that such conflict is not necessarily antithetical to communal existence, is Neal Wood's chief focus in his "The Value of Asocial Sociability: Contributions of Machiavelli, Sidney, and Montesquieu." Another subject of political theory brought to the fore by Machiavelli's approach, the nature and function of party, is intensively investigated by Harvey Mansfield, Jr., in "Party and Sect in Machiavelli's *Florentine Histories*." Still another, the notion of time, is reconstructed in a systematic fashion by Robert Orr in "The Time Motif in Machiavelli."

In light of what Wolin has said about the nature of the theoretical vocation, it is interesting to note that Orr takes pains to inform the reader that he has turned to Machiavelli as one of a group of writers "whose thoughts carry a subtle interrelatedness which invites philosophy." Machiavelli's writings, then, if not systematic enough to be considered part of philosophy proper, have another and perhaps greater virture for Orr, the virtue of inducing others to take up the theoretical vocation. In this instance the theoretical task is to make explicit Machiavelli's "distinctive way of looking at man in his universal setting." Orr proposes to construct a generalized schema of Machiavelli's *Weltanschauung* by means of an examination of its central feature, the time motif.

The essential reality of both man and the world he inhabits is their temporality. Man is a creature immersed in the stream of events having to make choices which "turn" events in his favor. Hence his need of foreknowledge which, in turn, is responsible for a particular orientation toward the future. The only way to live is to live in the future but since such foreknowledge can only come from knowledge of events passed, a particular notion of the past and of one's relation to it is also implied. The art of (successful) living, then, is to choose a course of action which results from the correct identification of "emergent possibilities" with past events. The virtue of the exceptional life, the life made for statecraft, is to possess this gift of foresight to a high degree, to be capable of "long foresight" and hence, we may add, remembering Pocock, of political innovation.

The agreement to be found in these essays on the importance of temporality and contingency in Machiavelli's political thought may give rise to uneasiness in the reader. This uneasiness may well turn into resistance when it is discovered that these last essays bring forward yet another general agreement on the purport of Machiavelli's thought, this time on the importance and function of party conflict in the life of a people. Is there a tendency to make Machiavelli more modern and relevant by discovering interests in his writing that should be properly recognized as peculiarly the concern of later, and especially, twentieth-century political thought? If this is so we can then summarily conclude that here is yet another instance of the anachronistic fallacy—of the time sense gone awry. Or, more positively, the uneasiness will turn on itself and hopefully the reader will become critically aware of the time sense rooted in his own *Weltanschauung* and of the way it affects, among other things, his conception of such fields as political philosophy and the history of political philosophy and the relation between the two.

To turn now to the theme of social conflict, the question of Machiavelli's idea of the nature and cause of social division is taken up by Mansfield in his examination of the *Florentine Histories*. He holds that the key to the understanding of that work lies in the distinction between party and sect and the association of the latter with religion, particularly Christianity. "To understand the *Florentine Histories* one must make the importance of Christianity explicit." And this he proceeds to do.

Machiavelli, Mansfield suggests, grounds not only his interpretation of Florentine history but also the remedies he offers for "the disease of modern politics" in his other works, upon the distinction between (natural) party and (Christian) sect. Ancient politics was based on a natural division within a people between the nobility, motivated by the ambition for honor, and the plebs, desirous, above all, for security in their persons, family, and possessions. The struggle between these two parties was by no means inimical to the furthering of common, in contrast to private, ends such as the glory of the whole people. The ancient party system then, incorporated the idea of a public "based on the common good of two disparate orders of men who happen to inhabit a locality together." In the modern system, under the dominant influence of Christianity, parties have become sects no longer united in a common good by common foreign enemies. Now party loyalty is "ideological rather than territorial," "foreign rather than domestic." Mansfield feels that for Machiavelli "the dispute between Pope and emperor was the prototype, as well as the origin, of the modern parties." Christianity obscured the ancient distinction between public and private, domestic and foreign, realms in the name of the supernatural and the universal.

Having made explicit the importance of Christianity for the interpretation of Machiavelli, Mansfield turns his attention to the author's motive in writing the *Histories*. In brief, Mansfield concludes, that "in this conspiratorial work Machiavelli tries to show Italian princes how to regain control of the supernatural." Since the obstacle to the reemergence of the ancient party system is the control of the popular party by the Christian sect, the princes must be enabled to entice popular leaders with the honors of this world.

The theme of social conflict is treated from a different perspective and with different ends in mind by Wood in his "The Value of Asocial Sociability." First, Wood utilizes the theme to demarcate Machiavelli from previous political thinkers: the Florentines' use of it constitutes "a radical break with past thought." Classical political thought accepted harmony or concord as the fundamental condition and end of political life. There was never a question but that social conflict was harmful and abnormal—a social evil to be guarded against at all costs. The depth of Machiavelli's break with this tradition can be measured by the fact that he holds social conflict, as embodied in the clash of popular and noble parties, when properly institutionalized, to be the very basis and guarantor of a thriving, independent political existence. Second, Wood uses the social conflict theme to link Machiavelli with subsequent political thought. The innovative break with one tradition of political thought turns out, in retrospect, to be the founding of another, equally influential tradition. This characteristically modern tradition is distinguished by its acceptance of an egoistic view of man and the welcome it extends to party (and individual) conflict as socially and politically beneficial. Wood traces its lineage from Machiavelli through Sidney and Montesquieu to Kant. In its later forms it is generalized into a theory of society and, at Kant's hands, into a philosophy of history in which the principle of antagonism becomes the necessary means whereby men develop their faculties, lawful social order is established, and mankind moves from barbarism to culture.

In reviewing these essays an editor may be pardoned for seeking out common features or discernible trends. There is, for instance, ample evidence of a very critical attitude toward the behaviorism which informs much of contemporary U.S. political science including its methodological insistence on a rigid separation between the method and subject matter of a discipline, and between what it designates as empirical-descriptive, normative, and historical political theory and philosophy. It is just these delimitations of fields and boundary conditions that beg for philosophical investigation and reexamination. To move across the Atlantic, it is probably equally accurate to say that in a body these contributors reject, implicitly or explicitly, the extreme positivist stance of Wolin and his generation of philosophical analysts who called into question the very possibility of political philosophy as a discipline. Of course this is also the case among the present generation of avowed partisans of the school of philosophical analysis. But if these analysts have arrived at their present position by a process of backing away from the more extreme formulations of their school, some of the contributors represented in this volume envision the scope, subject matter, and methods of political philosophy in ways that reflect other philosophical traditions.

At this point, as is to be expected among a group who may share a common opposition but who do not share a common philosophical position, we are already alerted by the qualification "some" to the observation that areas of agreement begin to narrow. Thus while they are critical of U.S. behaviorism and the more extreme forms of philosophical analysis, several contributors, Pocock to name one, have obviously been influenced to some degree by the general approach of the analytic school, and they employ particular distinctions native to it. But it is still the case that many of the essays in this volume are set off from this school by their refusal to restrict themselves to the analysis of individual and separate concepts as the main, if not exclusive, task of political philosophy. Instead, they choose to see and understand these concepts not solely in splendid isolation, but as they relate to and qualify each other as parts of larger wholes and broader philosophical vistas. In contrast to Anthony Quinton's indictment of the "great tradition" of political philosophy as being, in general, "too all-inclusive" in its treatment,[1] the contributors to the present volume seek clarification and definition of political thought through the use, for example, of a *Weltanschauung,* a leitmotif, a *bios theoretikos.* It is interesting that as they become concerned with *gestalten* and more inclusive structures, their language, like their thought, diverges from the Anglo-American of the analyst and takes on a decided continental accent.

1. See his introduction, Anthony Quinton, ed., *Political Philosophy,* (New York, 1967).

Other examples to be found in this volume of the tendency to challenge the limits imposed by the philosophical analyst upon the discipline of philosophy in general and political philosophy in particular, and to redraw their boundaries, involve the rejection of a division of labor which assigned to political science the description of political actions and institutions, to ideology the prescription of political goals, and to political philosophy the analysis of terms and arguments of the substantive disciplines (to draw once again upon Quinton's epitome of the analyst's position). Both Wolin and Ryan insist on the importance of recognizing the complex way a political thinker's analysis of institutional political life may both condition and be conditioned by his idea of human nature or his philosophy of history, among other things. What is involved here, of course, is a further challenge to the cut and dried way many of the analytic school set up the fact-value distinction. But more is at stake. One generation's liberating insights may become the next generation's confining dogmas. Orr in the name of the activity of philosophizing (certainly the precondition for all philosophy), Ryan in the name of the centrality of an idea of human nature to political philosophy, Wolin in the name of the theoretical life and the commitments it entails—all seek once again to widen the concerns of political philosophy, to break out, and to make it, if not "all-inclusive," at least less exclusive than some analysts would have it to be. But it is not only a matter of widening the domain of political philosophy to include subject matter previously held to be outside its ken, but also of an invitation to rethink the relation between political philosophy and other disciplines and also between the various subparts of which it is comprised. The notion of it as a second-level discipline completely distinct from substantive disciplines is no longer automatically accepted as self-evidently the case.

If one listens closely to the many voices raised in this volume it is difficult not to conclude that we are living in a period in which the concept of "breakthrough" and related notions are felt to be critical to this age's self-description and delimitation. Every essay in this volume that discusses Machiavelli chooses to interpret him in terms of one kind of breakthrough or another. Now the history of Machiavelli interpretation will reveal that this is by no means as obvious or as universal a mode of understanding Machiavelli as might be suggested by the unanimity of the contributors to this volume. Instead, such an interpretation says something about the hopes and fears of our times and the people we turn to and hold up as relevant. The notion of breakthrough is obviously more easily joined to the notion of revolution than evolution. While many of the contributors to this volume may welcome revolutions in science, some revolutions in political philosophy, and even a few political revolutions, what one can sense in this volume, regardless of differing political attitudes among the contributors, is a growing concern with phenomena like impasses and breakthroughs, conflict and revolution, political commitment and political action, not only as subject matter for political theory but, as is intimated in some of the pieces in this volume, as intrinsic to the very enterprise of political philosophy as well as politics. What this could possibly mean is suggested in Wood's idea of the liberating and educative function of a dialectic of conflict, Ryan's notion of politics as an end in itself, and Wolin's vision of theory not merely as a narrow academic discipline but as a complete human way of life.

There is no question, then, that with many of these writers the notion of philosophy itself differs significantly from that of the analysts, even those of a modified persuasion. To sum up briefly some of these differences and to hint at their implications: first, they have something in common with a nineteenth-century tradition, and its twentieth-century continuations, which sought to combat positivism and scientism by resorting to the idea of philosophy as *Lebensphiloso-phie* and *Kulturphilosophie* and by devising methods for practicing this philosophy which did not do violence to its nature or ends as so conceived. Certainly the methodist-behaviorist's insistence that his idea of method is the only valid one is vigorously challenged. Nor would most of our contributors necessarily agree with that test of methodological purity that leads to such statements as "The works that make up the great tradition of political thought are methodologically very impure." [2] Second, many of the contributors exhibit a marked propensity to politicize philosophy in the senses which have been briefly illustrated above. All this is in contrast to the tendency of analytic philosophy, true to its name, to cut up what it treats into small bits and pieces, to subject this matter to intensive and rigorous examination, and to view its own activities in highly technical and value-neutral terms, thus giving rise to the paradox of insisting that philosophy deal only with the analysis of ordinary language but that it deal with the ordinary in some extraordinary ways.

Lastly, the contributors do not seem to be about to accept the contention of most behaviorists and some analysts that political philosophy and the history of political philosophy constitute two separate and essentially unrelated disciplines. Though for the most part the problem is not attacked head on in this volume, the reader will find repeated suggestions and indications that the enterprise of political philosophy and the study of previous political philosophers are not patently unrelated undertakings. There seems to be no rush to close off the philosophical question of the relation of political thought to the history of political thought. Just the opposite. There are repeated invitations to explore freshly questions either ignored or ruled out of order by the philosophical tradition recently dominating the Anglo-American scene.

2. *Political Philosophy,* p. 1.

The *Methodenstreit* is thus renewed. There is no reason to assume that it will abate. In the light of the struggle, and of Machiavelli's vindication of the revitalizing effect of party strife, perhaps there is no reason why one should want it to abate—it has been quite productive. To go back, with Wolin, no further than the humanist attack on medieval logic, we may follow the conflicts raging around the search for a method throughout the sixteenth century involving, among many others, Petrus Ramus, Jean Bodin, and Francis Bacon. There is a pause in the struggle after the triumph of the *via geometrica* and the hegemony of the Cartesian method. But dissent soon reasserts itself with Vico's attack on Descartes and his argument that a method distinctively different from that used to achieve knowledge of nature must be employed to understand human culture and its products. In the eighteenth century the procedures of Locke and Hume, which begin with analysis, with breaking down experience into its separate and individual impressions, and for which, as a result, what has to be accounted for is how the individual elements become associated or bound together, stand in contrast to those of Kant and Hegel, who insist on the primacy of synthetic methods and also on the inextricable way method and subject matter determine each other. In the nineteenth-century debate on the nature and relation of the natural to the cultural sciences, and the methods appropriate to each, is the inspiration for much philosophical work.

Polemic has been very fruitful. Its relative absence in the Anglo-American world during the last few decades, due, perhaps, in part to the all-too-complete triumph of one idea of method and its apotheosis as the one and only way, and to a relative intolerance toward alternative views of the nature and methods of political philosophy, may help to explain why political philosophy lapsed into a quiescent state which some take for death. Renewed strife gives promise of renewed life.

Political Theory as a Vocation

SHELDON WOLIN

T HE PURPOSE OF THIS PAPER IS TO
sketch some of the implications, prospective and retrospective, of the primacy of method in the present study of
politics and to do it by way of a contrast, which is deliberately
heightened, but hopefully not caricatured, between the vocation of the "methodist" [1] and the vocation of the theorist. My
discussion will be centered around the kinds of activity in-

---

1. *"Methodist.* One who is skilled in, or attaches great importance to,
method; one who follows a (specified) method." *Oxford Universal Dictionary.* Although most social scientists would contend that actual research rarely conforms to a step-by-step procedure, it remains the case
that such procedure stands as a model for what they aim at. Thus, in a
section of a textbook on research methods entitled "Major Steps in Research," the authors insert the qualification above but acknowledge that
"published research strongly suggests the existence of a prescribed sequence of procedures, each step presupposing the completion of the
preceding one." Claire Selltiz et al., *Research Methods in Social Relations,*
rev. ed. (New York, 1963), pp. 8–9.

volved in the two vocations. During the course of the discussion various questions will be raised, primarily the following: What is the idea that underlies method, and how does it compare with the older understanding of theory? What is involved in choosing one rather than the other as the way to political knowledge? What are the human or educational consequences of the choice, that is, what is demanded of the person who commits himself to one or the other? What is the typical stance towards the political world of the methodist and how does it compare to the theorist's?

The discussion that follows will seek, first, to locate the idea of method in the context of the "behavioral revolution," and, second, to examine the idea itself in terms of some historical and analytical considerations. Then, proceeding on the assumption that the idea of method, like all important intellectual choices, carries a price, the discussion will concentrate on some of the personal, educational, vocational, and political consequences of this particular choice. Finally, I shall attempt to relate the idea of the vocation of political theory to these same matters.

In compiling its recent *Biographical Directory,* the American Political Science Association distributed a questionnaire which in its own way helped raise the present question: "What is the vocation of the political theorist?" Political theorists were invited to identify themselves by choosing among "Political Theory and Philosophy (Empirical)," "Political Theory and Philosophy (Historical)," and "Political Theory and Philosophy (Normative)." Although the choices offered may signify vitality and diversity, they may also testify to considerable confusion about the nature of political theory. For their part, political theorists may think of it as an identity crisis induced by finding themselves officially assigned a classification that others have defined, a classification traceable to a set of assumptions about the nature of the theoretical life perhaps uncongenial to many theorists.

Beyond the matter of professional identity there are far more compelling reasons for raising the question of vocation. Whatever one's assessment of the "behavioral revolution," it clearly has succeeded in transforming political science. What is less clear is the precise nature of that revolution. Among leading spokesmen of the profession it has become stylish to interpret that revolution as a close facsimile of the sorts of scientific changes discussed by Thomas Kuhn in *The Structure of Scientific Revolutions.*[2] Accordingly, the behavioral revolution is described as the inauguration of a new theoretical paradigm. Such a view, I think, is mistaken. It blurs the significance of the change. A more accurate account is suggested by the following: "One of the most significant recent developments in the social sciences is the revolution in data gathering and data evaluation. This revolution depends upon the developments in techniques by which data can be collected and analyzed. . . ."[3]

Assuming that this statement reflects a widespread sentiment that guides the actual practice of the profession, it provides a clue to the nature of the changes, what they are and what they are not, and what they signify for the vocations of political scientists and theorists. Despite claims to the contrary, political science has not undergone a revolution of the type described by Kuhn in which a new and dominant theory is installed. Although an abundance of new "theories" is available to the political scientist, it should be remembered that, by Kuhn's canon, the mere existence of new theories, or even the fact that some theories have attracted a following, are not conclusive evidence of a revolution. What counts is the enforcement by the scientific community of one theory to the exclusion of its rivals.

2. I have discussed Kuhn's interpretation and its relevance to political science in "Paradigms and Political Theories," *Politics and Experience: Essays Presented to Michael Oakeshott,* ed. P. King and B. C. Parekh (Cambridge, 1968), pp. 125–52.

3. G. A. Almond and S. Verba, *The Civic Culture* (Princeton, 1963), p. 43.

Although it is sometimes contended that "systems theory" constitutes the paradigmatic theory of the revolution, it is doubtful that this claim is tenable. Not only is there confusion about which of the several versions of the theory is the preferred one, or even whether any version is useful, but, above all, the popularity of systems theory followed rather than produced the behavioral revolution.

Whatever else it may be, a revolution without an initiating theory cannot qualify as a revolution by Kuhn's criterion. It may be, rather, a typically American revolution in which theories play a minor role. American political scientists, for the most part, have not only generally supported the traditional American diffidence toward theories, but they have elevated it to scientific status. The suspicion of theories is alleged to be a powerful contributor to the political stability of America and to its genius for pragmatic rather than ideological politics. In making this assertion I am not unmindful that there is hardly to be found a journal of political science in which some contemporary has not noted that "the mere accumulation of data without a guiding theory is, etc. . . ." Nor has it escaped my attention that a wide variety of theories exists for the political scientist to choose among. To call them political theories is, in the language of philosophy, to commit something like a category mistake. Systems theories, communication theories, and structural-functional theories are unpolitical theories shaped by the desire to explain certain forms of nonpolitical phenomena. They offer no significant choice or critical analysis of the quality, direction, or fate of public life. Where they are not alien intrusions, they share the same uncritical—and therefore untheoretical—assumptions of the prevailing political ideology as that which justifies the present "authoritative allocation of values" in our society.

Nonetheless, to say that there has been no political theory which has inspired the revolution in political science is not to say either that there has been no revolution or that no intellectual patterns are being widely promoted throughout the discipline. There has in fact been a certain revolution in political science, one that reflects a tradition of politics that has prided itself on being pragmatic and concerned mainly with workable techniques. Like all technique-oriented activity, the behavioral movement presupposes that the fundamental purposes and arrangements served by its techniques have been settled and that, accordingly, it reinforces, tacitly or explicitly, those purposes and arrangements and operates according to a notion of alternatives tightly restricted by these same purposes and arrangements. The emphasis upon methods does not signify simply the acquisition of a "kit" of new "tools" but presupposes a viewpoint that has profound implications for the empirical world, the vocation and the education of political scientists, and the resources that nourish the theoretical imagination.

To contend that the idea of method is the central fact of the behavioral revolution is merely to repeat what the revolutionaries themselves have stated. "Most important, perhaps, the criteria by which one accepts or rejects statements about social life are of a special nature. The ultimate criterion is the method by which they are gathered." [4] If it should be the case that a widespread set of assumptions is commonly held among those committed to the primacy of method, it is of little consequence that the techniques are diverse and changing. What matters are the common assumptions and consequences that accompany the emphasis on technique. The extent of this transformation is such as to suggest that the study of politics is now dominated by the belief that the main objectives—acquiring scientific knowledge about politics—depends upon the adoption and refinement of specific techniques and that to be qualified or certified as a political

4. Ibid., p. 43.

scientist is tantamount to possessing prescribed techniques. Concurrent with this development there has been an effort to imbue political scientists with what is understood to be the ethic of science: objectivity, detachment, fidelity to fact, and deference to intersubjective verification by a community of practitioners. These changes add up to a vocation, a *vita methodi* that includes a specified set of skills, a mode of practice, and an informing ethic. This vocation, and the education that it requires, may mark the significance of the behavioral revolution.

At this point a protest might be made that too much is being read into the idea of method. Methods per se do not presuppose a philosophical view of things but are neutral or instrumental, analogous to the technician in being indifferent to the purposes of their master. Such an argument is not only wrong but superficial. In the first place, the elevation of techniques has important educational consequences. The requirement that students become proficient in an assortment of technical skills preempts a substantial portion of their time and energy. But more important, training in techniques has educational consequences for it affects the way in which the initiates will look upon the world and especially the political portion of it. "Methodism" is ultimately a proposal for shaping the mind. Social scientists have sensed this when they have noted that research methods are "tools" that "can become a way of looking at the world, of judging everyday experience." [5]

In the second place, the alleged neutrality of a methodist's training overlooks significant philosophical assumptions admittedly incorporated into the outlook of those who advocate scientific inquiry into politics. These assumptions are such as to reinforce an uncritical view of existing political structures and all that they imply. For the employment of method as-

5. Selltiz et al., op. cit., pp. 6–7.

sumes, even requires, that the world be of one kind rather than another if techniques are to be effective. Method is not a thing for all worlds. It presupposes a certain answer to a Kantian type of question. What must the world be like for the methodist's knowledge to be possible? This presupposition is illustrated by a recent example which listed the major assumptions alleged to underly the "movement" of political behavior. The first item was: "*Regularities*. These are discoverable uniformities in political behavior. These can be expressed in generalizations or theories with explanatory and predictive value." [6] It follows that the methodist is in trouble when the world exhibits "deformities" or emergent irregularities. As the unhappy state of theories of "development" or "modernization" suggests, similar trouble appears when the world manifests "multiformities." [7]

This is but to say that there are inherent limits to the kinds of questions which the methodist deems appropriate. The kind of world hospitable to method invites a search for those regularities that reflect the main patterns of behavior that society is seeking to promote and maintain. Predictable behavior is what societies live by; hence their structures of coercion, of rewards and penalties, of subsidies and discouragements are shaped toward producing and maintaining certain regularities in behavior and attitudes. Further, every society is a structure bent in a particular and persistent way so that it constitutes not only an arrangement of power but also of powerlessness, of poverty as well as wealth, injustice and justice, suppression and encouragement.

It is symptomatic in this connection that political scientists have increasingly taken to describing themselves as "normal

6. D. Easton, *A Framework for Political Analysis,* (Englewood Cliffs, N.J., 1965), p. 7.
7. As a recent work on political socialization (which is described as "a universal feature of political life . . .") admits: ". . . [T]he reader is forewarned that the treatment is heavily biased in favor of a model appropriate to western democracies, particularly in the United States."

scientists." [8] The phrase is Kuhn's and he used it to designate a type of scientist whose vocation is not to create theories or even to criticize them but to accept the dominant theory approved by the scientific community and to put it to work. But if we ask, what is the dominant theoretical paradigm of our normal (political) scientists, the answer is that, in Kuhn's sense, there is none. Yet, surely, although there is no paradigm derived from what Kuhn calls "an extraordinary theory," such as Galileo or Newton produced, there must still be some guiding assumptions or framework which the methodist follows. The answer, I have suggested, is that there is such a framework of assumptions. It is the ideological paradigm reflective of the same political community which the normal scientists are investigating.[9] Thus when a researcher takes "the normal flow of events in American politics" as his starting point, it is not surprising to find him concluding that "the long-run stability of the system depends on the underlying division of party loyalties." [10]

These considerations become even more compelling if we concentrate for a moment upon the "systems" theorist. If society is conceived to be a system of decision-making, and if the recurrence of unjust decisions is commonly acknowledged, it follows that the system is, to some persistent degree, a structure of systematic injustice, otherwise the idea of a system is an inadequate account. The built-in embarrassments of a particular system have sometimes been recognized, as when it is asserted that a supposedly democratic

8. See, for example, H. Eulau's language in I. de Sola Pool, ed., *Contemporary Political Science* (New York, 1967), pp. 58–59, and the more cautious remarks in A. Somit and J. Tanenhaus, *The Development of American Political Science* (Boston, 1967), pp. 174 ff.

9. This may appear contentious, but, in reality, it is only a restatement of what appears in G. A. Almond, "Political Theory and Political Science," *American Political Science Review* 60 (1966): 873–75.

10. A. Campbell, "Surge and Decline: A Study of Electoral Change," in A. Campbell et al., *Elections and the Political Order* (New York, 1966), p. 45.

system requires a certain measure of indifference or apathy, especially on the part of the poor and the uneducated. This reservation about systems that purport to be democratic, and hence participatory, is sometimes stated more bluntly when the system in question is non-Western:

> In the Congo, in Vietnam, in the Dominican Republic, it is clear that order depends on *somehow compelling* newly mobilized strata to return to a measure of passivity and defeatism from which they have recently been aroused by the process of modernization.[11]

For the most part, however, the systems theorist prefers to emphasize more formal regularities. Thus, for example, the political system is defined as a special form of "social interactions . . . that are predominantly oriented toward the authoritative allocation of values for a society." [12] What is most revealing about this definition is the location of the word "predominantly": it is placed so as to qualify the "interactions" and thereby to enable subsequent research to distinguish political from social interactions. If the same word had been used, instead, to qualify the "allocations," a substantially different view of a system would have emerged, one in which the allocations would be seen to favor some interactions rather than others. It is acknowledged in the work cited that the favored theory may "inadvertently" exclude "some elements of major importance," [13] but not that a system may require deliberate and systematic exclusion of major elements. Rather, it is agreed that "a systems approach draws us away from a discussion of the way in which the political pie is cut up and how it happens to get cut up in one way rather than another." The remedy for this "status

11. I. de Sola Pool, "The Public and the Polity," *Contemporary Political Science: Toward Empirical Theory* (New York, 1967), p. 26 (emphasis added).
12. Easton, *Framework,* p. 50.
13. Ibid., p. 48.

quo bias" is to fall back upon "partial theories" which deal with selected aspects of the *same* system, *e.g.,* theories of "decision-making, coalition strategies, game theories, power, and group analysis." [14] What is conveniently overlooked by this recipe is that it merely reaffirms in different form the same culinary assumptions about the common pie, for each partial theory claims to be a plausible account of the same whole.

That a discussion of method should naturally lead to considering some prominent theories current among political scientists is not surprising. Most contemporary theories are dependent upon the behavioral revolution, not only in the methodological sense that the theories in question look to behavioral techniques for confirmation or disconfirmation; but in the more important sense of sharing the same outlook regarding education, philosophical assumptions, and political ideology. The close linkage between contemporary ideas of theory and of methods justifies treating them as members of the same family, forming a community of common features which I have labelled "methodism." As the earlier pages have tried to suggest, the idea of method has come to mean far more than was implied by Jeremy Bentham, for example, when he called it "the order of investigation." [15] It can be better understood as constituting an alternative to the *bios theoretikos,* and, as such, is one of the major achievements of the behavioral revolution. To grasp the nature of the *vita methodi* is not only important for its own sake, but should help in distinguishing it from the activity and vocation of theory.

One way to get at the idea of method is to recognize that it has a history reaching back to ancient Greek philosophy. Like *philosophia, methodus* was often used in association

14. D. Easton, *A Systems Analysis of Political Life* (New York, 1965), p. 475.
15. *Works,* ed. J. Bowring, 11 vols. (Edinburgh, 1843), 2:493.

with the notion of a "way" (*aporie*) to truth.[16] Before long, *methodus* and *philosophia* began to diverge. Generally speaking, while *philosophia* and its sister, *theoria,* tended to stress the arduous difficulties awaiting those who sought truth, the devotees of *methodus* began to emphasize the economy of being methodical, that is, of faithfully following a prescribed sequence of mental steps, a "straight road" in Descartes's phrase.[17] The old metaphor of the "way" was subtly altered and became associated with the advantages of adhering to a beaten path rather than "blazing" a trail. A premonition of this change appeared in the Middle Ages when *methodus* tended to acquire the connotation of a "shortcut." It found popular expression in numerous attempts to compose *compendia* on various subjects.[18]

During the Middle Ages and well into the sixteenth century the idea of method remained encumbered by Aristotelian and scholastic logic. As a result, method was tightly bound by logical procedures whose main aim was to sift and order inherited knowledge and experience rather than to discover new things. Thus the two main procedures of scholastic logic were "invention" (*inventio*), or the methods by which contestable propositions could be analyzed pro and con, and "judgment" or "disposition" (*iudicium*), which comprised the methods of arranging words into propositions, then into syllogisms or inductions, and finally into whole discourses. The conservatory quality of method was illustrated in a sixteenth-century work, *The Rule of Reason,* written by

16. Heraclitus, frags. 203, 235; Parmenides, frags. 342, 344–47. G. S. Kirk and J. E. Raven, *The Presocratic Philosophers* (Cambridge, 1957). The idea reappears in Machiavelli, *Discourses,* Bk. 1, Preface; and A. de Tocqueville, *Oeuvres Complètes,* ed. J.- P. Mayer (Paris, 1961–), 1:293.

17. *Discourse on Method,* tr. J. Veitch, *The Method, Meditations, and Philosophy of Descartes* (New York, n.d.), 1:149.

18. See W. Ong, *Ramus: Method and the Decay of Dialogue* (Cambridge, Mass., 1958), p. 53 ff.; N. W. Gilbert, *Renaissance Concepts of Method* (New York, 1960), p. 3 ff.

33

Thomas Wilson and published in 1551. Declaring that "a reason [is] easier found than fashioned," he compared the logic of "invention" with the sort of traditional lore acquired by huntsmen, saying that "he that will take profite in this parte of logique, must be like a hunter, and learne by labour to knowe the boroughes. For these places [i.e., a marke whiche gieuth warnyng to our memory what we maie speake probablie] be nothyng els but couertes or boroughes, wherein if any one searche diligentlie, he maie fynd game at pleasure." In his definition of "method," Wilson clearly expressed the view of one who saw it primarily as an ordering and clarifying procedure: "the maner of handeling a single Question, and the readie waie howe to teache and sette forth any thyng plainlie, and in order, as it should be, in latine *Methodus*." [19]

Throughout the sixteenth century method continued to be thought of mainly in organizational terms. Petrus Ramus, the most influential writer of the period, reflected this tendency. "Method," according to his definition, "is of arrangement, by which among many things the first in respect to conspicuousness is put in the first place, the second in the second, the third in the third, and so on. This term refers to every discipline and every dispute. Yet it commonly is taken in the sense of a direction sign and of a shortening of the highway." [20] Despite the static nature of Ramus's conception, there was some anxiety about "the new devised aid." With his customary irony, Richard Hooker entered some reservations:

Of marvellous quick dispatch it is, and doth shew them that have it as much almost in three days, as if it dwell

19. All quotations are from W. S. Howell, *Logic and Rhetoric in England, 1500–1700* (New York, 1961), pp. 21, 23–24. The Ramist influence upon the American Puritans has been discussed by Perry Miller, *The New England Mind, The Seventeenth Century* (Boston, 1939, 1961), p. 154 ff. and Appendix A.
20. Howell, op. cit., p. 152.

threescore years with them. . . . Because the curiosity of man's wit doth many times with peril wade farther in the search of things than were convenient; the same is thereby restrained unto such generalities as every where offering themselves are apparent unto men of the weakest conceit that need be. So as following the rules and precepts thereof, we may define it to be, an Art which teacheth the way of speedy discourse, and restraineth the mind of man that it may not wax overwise.[21]

Scarcely a generation later the restraints were rejected and Descartes introduced a new "way of speedy discourse" that promised to make men "the lords and possessors of nature." [22] The crucial step between Hooker and Descartes had been taken by Bacon who developed a distinction between two kinds of *inventio,* one a technique for the discovery of things not previously known, the other for the rediscovery of something previously known but temporarily forgotten.[23] Rightly understood, method promised not only "the use of knowledge" but, above all, "the *progression* of knowledge." [24]

With the gradual development of the idea of method, its significance soon extended beyond the simple advantages of economy and efficiency of mental effort. In following a shortcut, the mind was literally "conducting" inquiry, that is, comporting itself in a special way, following a code of intellectual conduct which, while it might not automatically lead to new truths, would for the most part prevent the methodist from wandering into grievous errors. Thus method

21. *Of the Laws of Ecclesiastical Polity,* 2 vols. (Oxford, 1885), 1:6:4.
22. *Discourse on Method,* tr. Veitch, 6:192.
23. *Works of Francis Bacon,* ed. R. L. Ellis, J. Spedding, and D. D. Heath, 7 vols. (London, 1887–92), 6:268–69.
24. Ibid., 6:289. "We know that the founders [of New England] studied Francis Bacon" (Miller, op. cit., p. 12).

came to mean, among other things, a form of discipline designed to compensate for unfortunate proclivities of the mind. "I am indeed amazed," Descartes exclaimed, "when I consider how weak my mind is and how prone to error." [25]

Descartes was among the first to realize that the adoption of the methodical point of view was at least as important as the acquisition of specified techniques. To adopt a method was not equivalent to buying a new suit, to a transaction in which only the external appearance of the purchaser was altered. It was, instead, a profound personal choice, perhaps the closest functional equivalent to conversionary experience that the modern mind can achieve. At the very least, it was intended as a form of reeducation, as one of Descartes's works, *Regulae ad directionem ingenii,* implied. The educational force of the title has been partially lost in translation, *Rules for the Direction of the Mind. Ingenium* carries the meaning of "nature, character, temperament," rather than the more narrowly intellectualistic connotations of "mind." That work described the specific steps for conditioning and disciplining the *ingenium* of the novice, for "rendering [it] more apt in the discovery of yet other truths." The human tendency "to guess unmethodically, at random," not only produced error but mental flabbiness as well. "In so proceeding we are bound to weaken the mind's powers of insight" and, therefore, a strict program was required. "We ought to train ourselves first in those easier matters, but methodically. Thereby we shall accustom ourselves to proceed always by easy and familiar paths, and so, as easily as though we were at play, to penetrate ever more deeply into the truth of things." [26]

The celebrated Cartesian principle of doubt formed a vital part of the new regimen for the mind. Doubt was the means of preparing the mind for *regulae* by first depriving

25. *Meditations,* Part II in *Descartes: Philosophical Writings,* tr. N. K. Smith (New York, 1956), p. 189.
26. Rules X–XI, tr. Smith, pp. 43–44, 47.

it of the major forms of resistance. Bacon, anticipating the difficulty, had noted that "a new method must be found for quiet entry into minds so choked and overgrown" that only an *expurgatio intellectus* would suffice.[27] Radical doubt was Descartes's version of the purge. Before the mind could proceed methodically, it must be turned upon itself, stripping off acquired habits, beliefs, and values until compelled to face the primordial truth of the *cogito* whose *sum* now stood divested of its cultural heritage in an ahistorical silence. ". . . [T]hose who have learned the least of all that has hitherto been distinguished by the name of philosophy are the most fitted for the apprehension of truth." [28] What Bacon has exultingly proclaimed earlier, "I have purged and swept and levelled the floor of the mind," [29] had now been programmed by Descartes.

Descartes attached certain self-denying ordinances to his program that are not without interest in the light of the recent evolution of political science. He singled out some subjects, God among them, as privileged and, therefore, protected from the destructive effects of doubt and methodical probing. He cautioned especially against bringing the new method to bear upon questions of morality and practical action. He himself had decided to accept existing moral values as a "provisional code" before submitting all else to doubt, "lest," as he explained, "I should remain irresolute in my actions. . . ." More tellingly, since conflicting opinions often existed about what was right, he would regulate "[his] conduct in conformity with the most moderate opinions, those furthest removed from extremes. . . ." [30] On political matters he was equally cautious, but more am-

27. Cited in P. Rossi, *Francis Bacon. From Magic to Science,* tr. S. Rabinovitch (London, 1968), p. 141.

28. "Preface to the Principles of Philosophy," tr. Veitch, p. 288.

29. *Francis Bacon: Selected Writings,* ed. H. G. Dick (New York, 1955), pp. 435, 533. See also Descartes, *Discourse on Method,* tr. Smith, 4:118.

30. Descartes, *Discourse on Method,* tr. Smith, 3:111.

bivalent. On the one hand, he expressed great admiration for those political societies that exhibited the rational symmetry legislated by a single intelligence; on the other, he abstained from drawing practical conclusions from this, saying only that most societies manage to work tolerably well over the long run.[31]

Although these political remarks underscore Descartes's preference for rational method over inherited knowledge, they are mainly significant for revealing the reason for his support of the status quo: fear of disorder. He was convinced that upheaval invariably followed fundamental reform and that innovators should be warned away:

> Great public institutions, if once overthrown, are excessively difficult to re-establish, or even to maintain erect if once seriously shaken; and their fall cannot but be very violent.[32]

From a preference for the existing scheme of institutions and for "the most moderate" morals, it was easy to pass to an identification of the two so that existing arrangements were taken to be the expression of what was reasonable and "furthest removed from extremes." Such a political world snugly fits the methodist's need, not only for the security it provides for his investigations, but also for the assured regularities it gives him to investigate.

What sort of political commitment is likely from a self that has been purged of inherited notions, pledged to the support of existing political and moral schemes, yet inhibited by the belief that they are "provisional"? A self of this type is likely to treat politics and morals in a way that avoids fundamental criticism as well as fundamental commitment. This lack of commitment is connected with the special form that the fear of fundamental change takes with the political

31. Ibid., 2:103–4, 112.
32. Ibid., 2: p. 103.

methodist. He will boldly renounce any belief in a natural structure to political societies, and declare that "any set of variables selected for description and explanation may be considered a system of behavior. At the outset, whether it is a system given in nature or simply an arbitrary construct of the human mind is operationally a pointless and needless dichotomy." [33]

Once doubt has abolished all privileged beginnings, there is no compelling reason why *this* rather than *that* should constitute the point of departure or the way of conceiving the problem, just as there is no logical or scientific reason for siding with the status quo. And yet the astonishing culmination of these arbitrary choices is not a truly skeptical temper but, as Descartes frankly admitted, rigidity and single-mindedness:

> My second maxim was to be as unwavering and as resolute in my actions as possible, and having once adopted opinions to adhere to them, however in themselves open to doubt, no less steadfastly than if they had been amply confirmed.

Descartes embellished the point by a contrast between the person who clings steadfastly to a chosen belief and the confused traveller who constantly changes directions. "Even though at the start it may have been chance alone which determined . . . [the] choice of direction," and even though what the resolute person takes to be "very certain and true" may be very doubtful, he is still likely to get *somewhere,* and, at the same time, he most certainly will be relieved from "all the repentings and feelings of remorse which are wont to disturb the consciences" of those who vacillate.[34]

How does the state of contemporary political science

33. Easton, *Framework,* p. 30.
34. *Discourse on Method,* tr. Smith, 3:111–13.

compare with the Cartesian philosophy of method? Despite occasional deference paid to "the tradition of political theory," there is a widely shared belief that that tradition was largely unscientific where it was not antiscientific and that the defining characteristic of a scientific revolution is to break with the past.[35] This animus against tradition will be considered at greater length when we try to assess its significance for the study of politics. Here we are concerned with Descartes's view of politics and especially with his counsels about political change. It was easier and safer, he declared, to reconstitute the foundations of knowledge than to attempt "the slightest reformation in public affairs." [36] An echo in contemporary political science is the following:

A political system is an accident. It is an accumulation of habits, customs, prejudices, and principles that have survived a long process of trial and error and of ceaseless response to changing circumstance. If the system works well on the whole, it is a lucky accident—the luckiest, indeed, that can befall a society. . . . To meddle with the structure and operation of a successful political system is therefore the greatest foolishness that men are capable of. Because the system is intricate beyond comprehension, the chance of improving it in the ways intended is slight, whereas the danger of dis-

35. "It is the very essence of the theoretical enterprise that, if and when it seems appropriate, it should feel free to sever itself from the bonds of traditional ways of looking at political life." Easton, *Framework,* p. viii.

There is no doubt that breaking with the past has been a feature of all great theoretical innovations, including those in the history of political theory. Yet the matter is not that simple, as witness Plato's respect for tradition, Aristotle's deference to his predecessors, Augustine's retrieval of major aspects of classicism, and Machiavelli's insistence on restoring certain forms of classical political knowledge. Hobbes was probably the first writer to advocate a break in the modern sense. Some aspects of his attempt will be discussed in my forthcoming essay, *Hobbes: Political Theory as Epic.*

36. *Discourse on Method,* tr. Vietch, 2:158.

turbing its workings and setting off a succession of unwarranted effects that will extend throughout the whole society is great.[37]

It might be objected that many contemporary political scientists would disavow this formulation as extreme and would draw attention to their repeated efforts at reform. Without wishing to depreciate these efforts, the contention remains that most proposals for reform on the part of political scientists represent a narrow range of alternatives founded on the assumption that the system has no inherent defects, or if it has, that these are acceptable "costs." The result is to foreclose a genuinely theoretical discussion which would seriously question and reflect upon the qualities of the system as a whole. Accordingly, the political scientist tends to follow the Cartesian path of extolling the existing as "the most moderate" or "further removed from extremes," and then defending it as though it were "very certain and true." This has taken the by now familiar form of identifying the American political system with "normal politics" and then seeking to establish by empirical methods the factors which produce it. There then follows the general explanation that the system has functioned normally, i.e., in a stable way, because it has avoided immoderation, i.e., "extremism" or "intensity." America has been spared these evils, it is alleged, not because of the excellence of her institutions or the virtue of her citizenry, but because of such factors as: the absence of ideological conflicts and political passions, a healthy amount of voter apathy, a measure of voter ignorance, political parties whose genius is to abstain from presenting clearly defined alternatives, the influence of cross-pressures which fragment the citizen's loyalties and reduce his commitments to the

37. Edward C. Banfield, "In Defense of the American Party System," *Voting, Interest Groups, and Parties,* ed. B. Seasholes (Glenview, Ill., 1966), p. 130.

consistency of Jello, a strategy of decision-making which favors "small or incremental change" because it is not disruptive,[38] and a system where the access to power succeeds in keeping at bay the poor, ignorant, deviant, and deprived.

It would be easy, especially at the present time when attacks upon liberal pluralism are increasing, to dismiss as an unfortunate lapse the way in which contemporary political science has come to such good terms with American politics. To accuse political science of an ideological bias is not to explain why it succumbed to the bias, or whether the nature of political science in America is or has always been such that identification with the going scheme of things is a recurrent temptation. Only a superficial view would hold that the condition of American political science can be remedied merely by substituting an opposing ideology. Perhaps the problem is far more deeply rooted in the past of American political science and American political society itself. If this should be the case, it would be mere antebellum nostalgia to attempt to return to the state of political science before the behavioral revolution. If such an attempt were made, it is likely that both political science and political theory would be found similarly tainted.

To expose the common root of a problem as vast as this is patently beyond our present scope, but a suggestion as to its nature is perhaps possible. Two assertions by Tocqueville supply the starting point. The first is: "Hardly anyone in the United States devotes himself to the essentially theoretical and abstract portion of human knowledge." The second is: "Among democratic nations . . . the woof of time is every instant broken and the track of generations effaced." [39] These may be characterized as a diffidence toward theory and

38. Braybrooke and E. Lindblom, *A Strategy of Decision* (Glencoe, Ill., 1963), p. 73.
39. *Democracy in America,* ed. P. Bradley, 2 vols. (New York, 1945), 2:42, 99.

history. Rather than attempt to trace the course of this diffidence, let us try to suggest how it is manifested in contemporary political science, but remembering that today's political science is remarkable for its Cartesian methodism and for its protestations about the importance of theory as a guide for empirical research. The possibility to be explored is whether the age-old problem of America, its suspicion of theory and of the human past, has not been worsened by the behavioral revolution, especially in the domain of education.

The first methodistic act for the Cartesian was to purge the self of the opinions acquired by upbringing, education, and common experience. The contemporary methodist performs the same act of divestment, except that he will use the language of social science in order to explain that he must, as far as possible, rid the mind of biases and preconceptions, such as those produced by class, status, occupation, family, religious upbringing, or political attachments. In so doing, he is performing a true ritual, the reenactment of the archetypal American experience of breaking with the past. Or, if this seems too esoteric, perhaps the purged methodist is merely a footnote to Tocqueville's remark that "America is one of the countries where the precepts of Descartes are least studied and are best applied." [40]

This antitraditionalist bias, cultivated in the name of the elimination of bias, has manifested itself on numerous occasions during the past decades as the effort to diminish the significance of "traditional political theory," as it has revealingly been called. Some have wished to have it eliminated entirely from the education of political scientists, while others have been mainly concerned to substitute a more scientific version of theory, and still others have wished to rescue individual "propositions" from the corpus of the ancient literature and submit them to operational testing.

40. Ibid., 2:3.

Leaving aside the criticisms which are antitheoretical in principle, the other responses are interesting because what they are objecting to is not "theory" but to a tradition of theory. Stated differently, what is bothersome about the history of theory is that it displays the working out of an inherited form, which is what a tradition is all about. Political theory has been perhaps the only field of study in all of American political science to exhibit this peculiar feature. Moreover, since the vast bulk of the literature which composes the tradition is European, as well as ancient, it is not difficult to see why it should be an object of suspicion.

This same bias is also manifested against the traditional forms of knowledge to which the methodist falls heir when he chooses to become a student of politics. As an ancient field of study, political science has acquired considerable knowledge about laws, constitutions, institutions, and unwritten practices. This inherited knowledge evokes a typically Cartesian and American response:

> . . . [T]raditional methods [of political science]— i.e., history writing, the description of institutions, and legal analysis—have been thoroughly exploited in the last two generations and now it seems to many (including myself) that they can produce only wisdom and neither science nor knowledge. And while wisdom is certainly useful in the affairs of men, such a result is a failure to live up to the promise in the name of political *science*.[41]

Although one might be troubled by the kind of human concern which would provoke a confrontation between "political wisdom" and "political *science*," the antithesis has the merit of opening the question: What is political wisdom? Put in this vague form, the question is unanswer-

41. W. Riker, *The Theory of Political Coalitions* (New Haven, 1962), p. viii.

able, but it may be reformulated so as to be fruitful. The antithesis between political wisdom and political science basically concerns two different forms of knowledge. The scientific form represents the search for rigorous formulations which are logically consistent and empirically testable. As a form, it has the qualities of compactness, manipulability, and relative independence of context. Political wisdom is an unfortunate phrase, for as the quotation suggested, the question is not *what* it is but *in what* does it inhere. History, knowledge of institutions, and legal analysis were mentioned. Without violating the spirit of the quotation, knowledge of past political theories might also be added. Taken as a whole, this composite type of knowledge presents a contrast with the scientific type. Its mode of activity is not so much the style of the search as of reflection. It is mindful of logic, but more so of the incoherence and contradictoriness of experience. And for the same reason, it is distrustful of rigor. Political life does not yield its significance to terse hypotheses but is elusive, and hence meaningful statements about it often have to be allusive and intimative. Context becomes supremely important, for actions and events occur in no other setting. Knowledge of this type tends, therefore, to be suggestive and illuminative rather than explicit and determinate. Borrowing from M. Polanyi, we shall call it "tacit political knowledge." [42]

The acquisition of tacit political knowledge is preeminently a matter of education of a particular kind and it is on this ground that the issue needs to be joined with the political methodist. The mentality that is impatient of the past and of traditional political theory is equally curt with the requirements of tacit political knowledge, which is rooted in knowledge of the past and of the tradition of theory. The knowledge that the methodist seeks is fairly characterized

42. M. Polanyi, *Personal Knowledge* (New York, 1964), passim.

in his own language as composing a "kit of tools" or a "bag of tricks." To acquire knowledge of techniques is no small matter, for they are often difficult and require considerable "retooling," which is to say that they imply a particular kind of program of instruction in specific methods.

Tacit political knowledge, on the other hand, accrues over time and never by means of a specified program in which particular subjects are chosen in order to produce specific results. Whatever may be the truth of the adage that he who travels lightest travels farthest, diverse, even ill-assorted baggage is needed because the life of inquiry preeminently demands reflectiveness, that is, an indwelling or rumination in which the mind draws on the complex framework of sensibilities built up unpremeditatedly and calls upon the diverse resources of civilized knowledge. But if the life of inquiry is narrowly conceived as the methodical "pursuit" of knowledge, it is likely to become not a pursuit but an escape from the spare and shabby dwelling that Descartes literally and symbolically occupied when he composed his *Meditations.* Even those who would wish to address their minds to "data" are aware that data are constituted by abstractions, and that usually what has been culled from the phenomena are the subtle traces of past practices and meanings that form the connotative context of actions and events.

To recognize the connotative context of a subject matter is to know its supporting lore; and to know the supporting lore is to know how to make one's way about the subject field. Such knowledge is not propositional, much less formulary. It stands for the knowledge which tells us what is appropriate to a subject and when a subject matter is being violated or respected by a particular theory of hypothesis. Although appropriateness takes many forms, and we shall be returning to some of them, it is impossible to reduce its contents to a checklist of items. For example, can we say with exactness what is the precise knowledge that makes us uneasy with statements like the following?

> The interesting issues in normative political theory are in the end generally empirical ones. . . . There does exist, however, *one interesting problem in political theory* which is strictly normative. That is the problem of evaluating mixes of desiderata. . . . It may be called the 'utility problem' or in still more modern terminology, the 'dynamic-programming problem.' . . . On this strictly normative problem of program packages more progress has been made in the past half century than in all the previous 2,000 years of political theory put together.[43]

Although these assertions may appear absurd, it is not easy to say why, except that some important political and theoretical questions are being rendered unrecognizable. Behind the assertions, however, lie some important attitudes towards knowledge. These bear upon the contrast between methodistic knowledge and the forms of theory congenial to it and, on the other hand, the kind of knowledge characteristic of tacit political knowledge and the forms of theory built upon it. The methodistic assumption holds that the truth of statements yielded by scientific methods has certain features, such as rigor, precision, and quantifiability. The connection between the statements and their features is intimate so that one is encouraged to believe that when he is offered statements rigorous, precise, and quantifiable, he is in the presence of truth. On the other hand, an approach to the "facts" consisting of statements which palpably lack precision, quantifiability, or operational value is said to be false, vague, unreliable, or even "mystical." In actuality, the contrast is not between the true and the false, the re-

43. Pool, ed., op. cit., pp. 23–24 (emphasis added).

liable and the unreliable, but between truth that is economical, replicable, and easily packaged, and truth that is not. Methodistic truth can be all these things because it is relatively indifferent to context; theoretical truth cannot, because its foundation in tacit political knowledge shapes it towards what is politically appropriate rather than towards what is scientifically operational.

Questions concerning appropriateness, context, and respect for a subject do not concern effete matters, but very practical ones. They involve the resources, or the lack thereof, that we draw upon when the decision concerns matters for which there can be no certitude. What "belongs" to a given inquiry is one such matter, and how to decide between one theory rather than another, or between rival methods, are others. Yet the kind of knowledge necessary to these decisions, tacit political knowledge, is being jeopardized by the education increasingly being instituted among political scientists. To illustrate the problem, we might consider the implications for tacit political knowledge of a typical proposal for increasing the student's mastery of methods. Our example is a recent volume on survey research methods for undergraduates and graduates in political science. In the spirit of Descartes's *regulae,* the authors describe it as a "handbook" or "manual," "a checklist" or inventory of "do's and don'ts" whose aim is to encourage the "empirical emphasis" in political science. Not content with offering a manual of technical instruction, the authors claim that advantages of an educational and vocational kind will be promoted if survey research is made part of the curriculum. Thus the instructor, impaled by the twin demands of teaching and research, is reassured that the two can be reconciled if students are put to work learning survey methods while conducting his research. Further, the method is extolled as a way of overcoming the shortcomings of "the lone scholar" whose skills are inadequate for dealing with the size and range of problems confronting empirical political science. The imperative, "resources must be increased," decrees that the lone scholar be replaced by "group activity and team-work." In the same vein, it is claimed that "the educational advantages for students are impressive" and among the putative advantages are the acquisition of an *ingenium* with traits congenial to the new emphasis:

> . . . students gain the opportunity to learn more about themselves. . . . Too few students get the experience of fighting to remain neutral while carefully probing attitudes hostile to their own. Such instruction in self-control is valuable for the headstrong and overprotected.

Despite the tenor and direction of this conception of education, it is insisted that the new generation of students will be able to do "what was not expected of the previous generation of college students—i.e., to discover new knowledge as well as to acquire old." [44]

But will they? As for acquiring "the old," the authors bemoan the fact that political science departments have been hampered by the "lack of knowledge of research skills" and that the conventional academic calendar does not afford sufficient time for students to learn "sampling, interviewing, coding, analysis, etc." Exactly how the student will "acquire the old," when the demands of the "new" are so great, is not discussed. In this connection it is relevant to recall Kuhn's description of the way scientific education has been affected by this determination to consolidate scientific advances and insure cumulative knowledge. He characterized scientific education as "narrow and rigid . . . probably more so than any other except perhaps orthodox theology." Current scientific training is not well designed "to produce the man who will easily discover a fresh approach," but it

44. C. H. Backstron and G. D. Hursh, *Survey Research,* ed. J. Robinson (Evanston, Ill., 1963), pp. xi–xv, 4, 13.

is admirably suited for preparing "normal scientists" and for enabling the community to readapt itself when a fundamental change occurs in theoretical orientations. "Individual rigidity is compatible with a community that can switch from paradigm to paradigm when the occasion demands." [45] To the best of my knowledge, political scientists who otherwise approvingly cite Kuhn have consistently declined to take up the implications of his analysis of scientific education.

Although the invention of methods, like the invention of theories, demands a high order of creativity and is entitled to the highest praise, something important, perhaps ironical, occurs when that discovery is institutionalized in a training program. The requirements for those who are to use the theory or method are very different from the talent that discovered them, although, paradoxically, the technical skills may be the same. Descartes noted that a child might become as proficient as the genius in following the rules of arithmetic, but he never argued that the child could discover the rules. This is so, not simply because of the chance element in discovery, but because of the more baffling questions of the personal and intellectual qualities of the discoverer and of the cultural conditions of discovery.[46]

In this context the contemporary methodist's notion of training becomes significant. The idea of training presupposes several premeditated decisions: about the specific techniques needed and how they will be used; about what is peripheral or irrelevant to a particular form of training; and about the desired behavior of the trainee after he has been released from his apprenticeship. The idea of theorizing, on the other hand, while it presupposes skills, cannot specify briefly and simply the skills needed, their degree, or combinations.

45. T. Kuhn, *The Structure of Scientific Revolutions* (Chicago, 1962), p. 165.
46. R. Taton, *Reason and Chance in Scientific Discovery*, tr. A. J. Pomerans (New York, 1962), p. 64 ff.

Kepler's followers could be contemptuous of their master's Platonism and astrology, as Newton's admirers were of his religious fascinations; but it would be risky to discount the influence of these extrascientific considerations upon the formation of the respective theories.

The impoverishment of education by the demands of methodism pose a threat not only to so-called normative or traditional political theory, but to the scientific imagination as well. It threatens the meditative culture which nourishes all creativity. That culture is the source of the qualities crucial to theorizing: playfulness, concern, the juxtaposition of contraries, and astonishment at the variety and subtle interconnection of things. These same qualities are not confined to the creation of theories, but are at work when the mind is playing over the factual world as well. An impoverished mind, no matter how resolutely empirical in spirit, sees an impoverished world. Such a mind is not disabled from theorizing, but it is tempted into remote abstractions which, when applied to the factual world, end by torturing it. Think of what must be ignored in, or done to, the factual world before an assertion like the following can be made: "Theoretical models should be tested primarily by the accuracy of their prediction rather than the reality of their assumptions." [47] No doubt one might object by pointing out that all theorizing does some violence to the empirical world—to which one might reply that while amputations are necessary it is still better to have surgeons rather than butchers.

It is not enough, therefore, to repeat commonplaces, viz., that facts are senseless without theoretical concepts, or that the meaning which facts acquire from a theory is purchased at the price of shaping the facts by the theoretical perspective employed. It is not enough because so much depends upon

47. A. Downs, *An Economic Theory of Democracy* (New York, 1957), p. 21.

the kind of theory being used and the personal and cultural resources of the user. Perhaps it is some debilitating legacy of Puritanism that causes us to admire "parsimony" in our theories when we should be concerned that the constitution of the factual world depends upon the richness of our theories which, in turn, depends upon the richness of the inquiring mind. This concern may well be what fundamentally unites the scientific theorist and the so-called traditional theorist.

When a scientist observes a fact, he "sees" it through concepts which are usually derived from a theory. Facts are, as one philosopher has neatly put it, "theory-laden." Kepler, for example, observed many of the same facts as his predecessors, but because he viewed them differently a new era of science was ushered in.[48] The same might be said of Machiavelli, as well as of every major theorist from Plato to Marx. Some theorists, as Tocqueville suggested, see differently, others see farther. All would probably have agreed with Tocqueville that, for the theorist, nothing is more difficult to appreciate than a fact,[49] and nothing, it might be added, is more necessary as a condition for theorizing than that facts not be univocal. If they were, creativity and imagination would play a small role and it would be appropriate to speak of theorizing as a banausic activity, as "theory-construction." If facts were simply "there" to be collected, classified, and then matched with a theory (or with the observation-statements derived from it), the political scientist might well declare: "Whether [a] proposition is true or false depends on the degree to which the proposition and the real world correspond." [50] But although

48. N. R. Hanson, *Patterns of Discovery* (Cambridge, 1965), p. 5 ff.
49. The remarks from Tocqueville are to be found in *Oeuvres complètes*, 1:12, 14, 222.
50. R. Dahl, *Modern Political Analysis* (Englewood Cliffs, N.J., Prentice-Hall, 1963), p. 8.

everyone is ready to acknowledge that facts depend upon some criteria of selection or of significance, what is less frequently acknowledged is that such criteria usually turn out to be fragments of some almost forgotten "normative" or "traditional" theory.

Because facts are multifaceted—more so than a rigid conception of empirical theory would allow—they are more likely to yield to the observer whose mental capacities enable him to appreciate a known fact in an unconventional way. As one philosopher has said; "Given the *same* world it might have been construed differently. We might have spoken of it, thought of it, perceived it differently. Perhaps facts are somehow moulded by the logical forms of the fact-stating language. Perhaps these provide a 'mould' in terms of which the world coagulates for us in definite ways." [51] Once again we are confronted by the warning that the richness of the factual world depends upon the richness of our theories: "The paradigm observer is not the man who sees and reports what all normal observers see and report, but the man who sees in familiar objects what no one else has seen before." [52] Thus the world must be supplemented before it can be understood and reflected upon.

Vision, as I have tried to emphasize, depends for its richness on the resources from which it can draw. These extra-scientific considerations may be identified more explicitly as the stock of ideas which an intellectually curious and broadly educated person accumulates and which come to govern his institutions, feelings, and perceptions. They constitute the sources of his creativity, yet rarely find explicit expression in formal theory. Lying beyond the boundaries circumscribed by method, technique, and the official definition of a discipline, they can be summarized as cultural resources and itemized as metaphysics, faith, historical sensibility, or, more

51. Hanson, op. cit., p. 36.
52. Ibid., p. 30.

broadly, as tacit knowledge. Because these matters bear a family resemblance to "bias," they become sacrificial victims to the quest for objectivity in the social sciences. If scientists have freely acknowledged the importance of many of these items,[53] how much more significant are these human creations for the form of knowledge, political science, which centers on the perplexities of collective life, on objects which are all too animate in expressing their needs, hopes, and fears.

Doubtless the objection will be raised that if a discipline is to be empirical its practitioners must be equipped to "handle" data in ways approximative of the sciences which have been more successful, and that to suggest otherwise is to consort with the heresy of saying that philosophical and moral knowledge may lead to a better empiricism. Yet we might consider the following:

Throughout the history of political theory a student will find a preoccupation with the phenomenon of "corruption." Today, however, we scarcely know how to talk about it,[54] except when it flourishes in non-Western societies. Yet it is a common and documented fact that "organized crime" exerts significant power and influence, controls enormous wealth, and exhibits many of the same features which ordinarily arouse the interest of political scientists, e.g., organization, authority, power, kinship ties, rules, and strong consensus. Despite the promising research possibilities, no

53. E.g., K. Popper, *The Logic of Scientific Discovery* (New York, 1961), pp. 19, 38.

54. An exception would be S. Huntington, "Political Development and Political Decay," *World Politics* 17 (April, 1965), 386–430. As an illustration of a contemporary way of dealing with the problems the reader is referred to A. A. Rogow and H. D. Lasswell, *Power, Corruption, and Rectitude* (Englewood Cliffs, N.J., 1963). This work criticizes Acton's epigram, points out how a like animus against power led to the separation of powers doctrine, how the latter frustrates the majority, and how the problem can be handled by organizational and bureaucratic sanctions.

textbook on American government provides a place for organized crime in "the system," no study of "polyarchy" or community power has taken cognizance of it. It is not farfetched to suggest that this empirical oversight is connected with the belief that moral knowledge is empirically irrelevant.

Or, to take another example, one can think of many fine empirical studies which have never been conducted because contemporary political science has substituted the bland, status-quo-oriented concept of "political socialization" for the ancient idea of "political education." Instead of blinkering the inquiring eye with a postulate that "conduct is *politicized* in the degree that it is determined by considerations of power indulgence or deprivation of the self by others," [55] we should take seriously an old-fashioned hypothesis, such as that advanced by J. S. Mill, that "the first element of good government . . . being the virtue and intelligence of the human beings composing the community, the most important point of excellence which any form of government can possess is to promote the virtue and intelligence of the people themselves." [56] Then we might be better sensitized to the importance of genuinely empirical studies of truly fundamental political concern. For example, think of the empirical richness of an inquiry into the current structure of income taxes, especially in terms of the moral and political implications it holds for civic education. The structure of income taxes is a registry of the power and powerlessness of our social, economic, and ethnic groups, of the official way we rate the value of various social activities by the one

55. H. D. Lasswell and A. Kaplan, *Power and Society: A Framework for Political Inquiry* (New Haven, 1950), p. 145.
56. *Representative Government,* Ch. II (Everyman edition, p. 193). My point would not be affected if political socialization were defined in some other contemporary mode, e.g., learning "roles," or as "a readiness to tolerate outputs that are perceived to run contrary to one's wants and demands. . . ." (Easton, *Systems Analysis,* p. 272).

standard generally accepted. It is also a system of incentives for behavior that define what is virtuous, unvirtuous, and morally indifferent; and, by tacitly encouraging behavior otherwise deemed blameworthy, encourages the gradual legitimation of that behavior, and thereby shapes what used to be called "the virtue of the citizenry." It would be difficult to imagine a richer field for behavioral inquiry or one more likely to yield important knowledge about the quality of life in this republic. Yet it remains unharvested because our impoverished understanding of civic virtue and education has caused us to neglect the field.

Finally, one cannot help wondering whether political science, having jettisoned "metaphysical" and "normative" preoccupations about justice in favor of research into "judicial behavior" and the "judicial process," are not reaping the results: an inability to address a major phenomenon like the dangerous rash of *political* trials in America today and to reflect upon what these trials signify for the future of the authority and legitimacy of the state.

If the presence or absence of the moral and philosophical element affects the process by which theories constitute the empirical world, the choice among theories would seem to be a serious matter. But, again, the contemporary mood trivializes what is involved in a theory's formulation and thereby obfuscates the importance of the choice among rival ways of constituting the world. The following quotation may be extreme but it does disclose the fantasies of the behavioral scientist about theories:

> In a report entitled *Communication Systems and Resources in the Behavioral Sciences,* the Committee on Information in the Behavioral Sciences outlines an ideal system that would in effect provide researchers with a computer analogue of the intelligent, all-informed colleague. Such a colleague would read widely, have

total recall, synthesize new ideas, always be accessible, and be sensitive to each researcher's needs. . . . The computer based system could respond to an individual's direct request for facts, data, and documentation; it could take the initiative and stimulate the researcher by suggesting new ideas, facts, or literature of interest; it could react intelligently to a scientist's work (analyze its logic, trace implications, suggest tests); and it could help disseminate ideas and provide feedback from the scientific community.[57]

If we can safely assume that choosing a theory or a method is not quite the same as choosing a helpful friend who, as Nietzsche taught, must be worthy of being your enemy, we might want to press the question further. When we choose a theory or a method, are we choosing something momentous, like a self, or something innocuous, like an "intellectual construct" or "conceptual scheme"? or something depersonalized, like "a series of logically consistent, interconnected, and empirically verifiable propositions," or like "a generalized statement of the interrelationships of a set of variables"?

Undoubtedly these characterizations tell us something about the formal features of a theory, but they are deceptive in their parsimony. If the question is slightly reformulated to read, What is the human significance of choosing a theory?, then it becomes evident that much more is involved. Choosing a theory is significant for two conflicting reasons: it initiates new ways of thinking, evaluating, intuiting, and feeling; and it demands a substantial sacrifice in the existing forms of these same human processes. The first point is obvious, the second less so. This is because, like the law of treason, history books tend to be written by the victors and

57. *Political Science*, Newsletter of the American Political Science Association, Vol. I, No. 1 (Winter, 1968), 25 (col. 1).

hence the sacrifices which accompany the triumph of a new theory are apt to be overlooked or bathed in a kind of Jacobite nostalgia.

The history of political theory is instructive on this score, for many of the great innovative theorists were highly self-conscious about choosing among theoretical alternatives. They knew that the true drama of theorizing involved offering a theory which could not be accommodated within prevailing values and perceptions of the world. When Hobbes allowed that his readers would be "staggered" by his theory,[58] he was not merely stating the obvious fact that his views concerning religion, authority, rights, and human nature were incompatible with traditional religious and political notions, but was making the more profound point that unless his readers were prepared to revise or discard those notions, they would not be able to grasp the full meaning of the theory and the theory itself could not become an effective force in the world. The same general assumptions had been made by Plato in his challenge to traditional Greek values and to the democratic ethos of Athens, and by St. Augustine in his effort to demolish classical notions of history, politics, virtue, and religion. Among more recent writers, none has been as sensitive as Max Weber to the emotional and cultural losses attendant upon the commitment of scientific rationalism.

Where our contemporary way of talking has not obscured the drama and demands of theorizing, it has trivialized them. Theories are likened to appliances which are "plugged into" political life and, since it is the nature of appliances to be under sentence of built-in obsolescence, "theories are for burning," leaving only a brief funereal glow which lights the way to "more scientific theories and more efficient research procedures." [59] If adopting a theory were equivalent

58. *De Cive,* ed. S. P. Lamprecht (New York, 1949), Pref. ad finem.
59. D. Apter, *The Politics of Modernization* (Chicago, 1965), p. x.

to "trying out an idea," testing an hypothesis, or selecting a technique, there would be little reason to object to treating it casually.

At the very least, a theory makes demands upon our time, attention, energy, and skills. More fundamentally, the adoption of a theory signifies a form of submission with serious consequences both for the adopter and for those who imitate him, as well as for the corner of the world which the theory seeks to change our mind about. A certain sensibility is needed, a quality of thinking and feeling that is not readily formulable but pertains to a capacity for discriminative judgment. Why is this so? To compress the answer severely, in political and social matters we tend to think in one of two ways: in trying to explain, understand, or appraise we may ask, What is it like?, or What is appropriate? The first way invites us to think metaphorically, e.g., Hobbes's argument that a representative is like an agent, or the contemporary notion of a political society as a system of communications. Ever since Plato, theorists have recognized the fruitfulness of metaphorical thinking, but they have also come to realize that at certain crucial points a metaphor may become misleading, primarily because the metaphor has a thrust of its own which leads to grotesque implications for the object or events which it is supposed to illuminate. A recent example of this pitfall is provided by Karl Deutsch's *Nerves of Government,* which argues for the concept of a communications system as a useful and proper model for political theory. The argument rests on a combination of metaphors and the success of the argument depends upon a confusion of the two. The first metaphor consists in likening the nature of human thinking and purposive action to the operation of a communications system, e.g., the "problem of value" is like a "switchboard problem" or "consciousness" is "analogous" to the process of feedback.[60] The second

60. *The Nerves of Government* (Glencoe, Ill., 1963), pp. 94, 98.

metaphor involves the reverse procedure: a communications system may be treated like a person. Human qualities, such as "spontaneity," "freedom of the will," and "creativity" can be "built into" a machine, and then it becomes possible to propose empirical propositions about society derived from the operations of the machine. But the whole argument depends upon, first, mechanizing human behavior and, second, humanizing mechanical processes. Once this is accomplished, grotesque results follow, e.g., internal rearrangements in a system, or in a person, which reduce goal-seeking effectiveness are described as "pathological" and are said to resemble "what some moralists call 'sin.' "[61]

A second way of judging asks, what is appropriate? Appropriateness of judgment cannot be encapsulated in a formula. This is because it depends upon varied forms of knowledge for which there is no natural limit. This dependence is rooted in the basic quest of political and social theory for theoretical knowledge about "wholes" made up of interrelated and interpenetrating provinces of human activity. Whether the primary theoretical task be one of explanation or of critical appraisal, the theorist will want to locate "divisions" in the human world and embody them in theoretical form. For example, what aspects of the division that we call "religion" have a significant bearing on the activity called "economic"? Perforce, a political theory is, among many other things, a sum of judgments, shaped by the theorist's notion of what matters, and embodying a series of discriminations about where one province begins and another leaves off. The discriminations may have to do with what is private and what is public, or they may be about what will be endangered or encouraged if affairs move one way rather than another, or about what practices, occurrences, and conditions are likely to produce what states of affairs. The

61. Ibid., pp. 91–92.

difficulty is the same regardless of whether the theoretical intention is to provide a descriptive explanation, a critical appraisal, or a prescriptive solution. By virtue of their location in a whole, one province shades off from and merges into others: where, for example, does the cure of souls end and the authority of the political order over religion begin? where do the effects of technical education merge into questions about ethics and character? where does the autonomy of administrative and judicial practices start and the "mysteries of state" stop? how much of the impetus for the Crusades is to be assigned to religious motives and how much to political or economic considerations?

If, as Plato suggested long ago, the task of theory is to locate "the real cleavages" in things and to "avoid chopping reality up into small parts" or drawing false boundaries,[62] then the sense of what is appropriate is critical. Given the theorist's preoccupation with wholes, the interconnectedness of human provinces, the values and expectations with which men have invested each of their provinces, and the ultimate bewildering fact that man is single but his provinces are multiple, a theoretical judgment which, by definition, must discriminate can only be restrained from rendering inappropriate determinations if it is civilized by a meditative culture. To be civilized is not only the quality of being sensitive to the claims and characters of many provinces, but, according to an older definition, rendering what is proper to a civil community.

If the preceding analysis has any merit it will have suggested that the triumph of methodism constitutes a crisis in political education and that the main victim is the tacit political knowledge which is so vital to making judgments, not only judgments about the adequacy and value of theories and methods, but also about the nature and perplexities of

62. *Politicus,* 262 b–c.

politics as well. Here lies the vocation of these who preserve our understanding of past theories, who sharpen our sense of the subtle, complex interplay between political experience and thought, and who preserve our memory of the agonizing efforts of intellect to restate the possibilities and threats posed by political dilemmas of the past. In teaching about past theories, the historically minded theorist is engaged in the task of political initiation; that is, of introducing new generations of students to the complexities of politics and to the efforts of theorists to confront its predicaments; of developing the capacity for discriminating judgments discussed earlier; of cultivating that sense of "significance" which, as Weber understood so well, is vital to scientific inquiry but cannot be furnished by scientific methods; and of exploring the ways in which new theoretical vistas are opened.

For those who are concerned with the history of political theories, the vocation has become a demanding one at the present time. How demanding it is can be seen by glancing at Kuhn's account of the manner in which scientific invention treats its own past.[63] In the formative period of their education students are required to master textbooks rather than to familiarize themselves with the creative writings of the great scientists of the past. The characteristic teaching of scientific textbooks, according to Kuhn, is to show how the great achievements of the past have prepared the way for the present stage of knowledge and theory. As a result, discontinuities are smoothed over or discarded, or unsuccessful theories are assumed to have been inferior, and the idea of methodical progress dominates the entire account.

How easy it is to impoverish the past by making it appear like the present is suggested by the way in which social scientists have lapsed into the same idiom as Kuhn's scientific textbooks. "As Aristotle, the first great behavioral scientist,

63. Op. cit., pp. 162–68.

pointed out a long time ago . . ." [64] or, again, "the behavioral persuasion in politics represents an attempt, by modern modes of analysis, to fulfill the quest for political knowledge begun by the classical political theorists," although it is admitted that classical theory is "predominantly prescriptive rather than descriptive." [65] What seems to have been forgotten is that one reads past theories, not because they are familiar and therefore confirmative, but because they are strange and therefore provocative. If Aristotle is read as the first behaviorist, what he has to say is only of antiquarian interest and it would be far more profitable to read our contemporaries.

What we should expect from a reading of Aristotle is an increase in political understanding. What we should expect from the study of the history of political theories is an appreciation of the historical dimension of politics. The cultivation of political understanding means that one becomes sensitized to the enormous complexities and drama of saying that the political order is the most comprehensive association and is ultimately responsible, like no other grouping, for sustaining the physical, material, cultural, and moral life of its members. Political understanding also teaches that the political order is articulated through its history; the past weighs on the present, shaping alternatives and pressing with a force of its own. At the present time the historical mode is largely ignored in favor of modes of understanding which are inherently incapable of building upon historical knowledge. One of the most striking features of game theory, communications models, and mechanical systems is that in each case the organizing notion is essentially historyless.

The threat to political understanding is not to be denied

64. Berelson and G. Steiner, *Human Behavior* (New York, 1964), p. 13.
65. Eulau, op. cit., p. 7. See also G. A. Almond and B. Powell, *Comparative Politics: A Developmental Approach* (Boston, 1966), p. 214; H. Alker, *Mathematics and Politics* (New York, 1965), pp. 6–8.

by arguing that we can substitute more precise functional equivalents for older language or that we can translate older notions into more empirical terms. From time immemorial writers have talked of the "burdens" of ruling, the "anguish" of choosing, and the "guilt" of actors who must employ coercion. To assimilate these actions to the calculations of gamesters or to describe them as "decision-making" or "outputs" is to distort both sides of the analogy. If in game-playing, for example, anguish, burdens, and guilt were recurrent features, the whole connotative context surrounding the idea of a game would be lost and nobody would "play." The ancient writer Philostratus once remarked of painting that no one could understand the imitative techniques of the painter without prior knowledge of the objects being represented. But when the attempt is being made to convey knowledge, not by imitative techniques, but by abstract signs and symbols which stand for objects commonly understood, everything depends on whether one truly understands what the symbol means. Does he understand, for example, the kinds of discriminative judgments which have been suspended when the symbol of an "input" is made to stand equally for a civil rights protest, a deputation from the National Rifle Association, and a strike by the U.A.W.? Does he understand that what allows him to discriminate between these "inputs" is a tacit knowledge derived from sources other than systems theory? Again, will he be able to compensate for the fact that systems theory makes it possible to talk about an entire political society without ever mentioning the idea of justice, except in the distorting form of its contribution to "system maintenance"? Is he aware that if one can focus on the American political order as a *system,* he does not have to confront the unpleasant possibility of it as an *imperium* of unsurpassed power. If, in rebuttal, the political scientist claims that the sort of studies referred to above really do presuppose the knowledge which would

64

make political sense out of formal methods, then it is necessary to reply that the contemporary political scientist threatens to chalk around himself a vicious circle: his methods of study presuppose a depth of political culture that his methods of education destroy.

But what of the vocation by which political theories are created rather than transmitted? Testimony that such a vocation has existed is to be found in the ancient notion of the *bios theoretikos* as well as in the actual achievements of the long line of writers extending from Plato to Marx. How shall we understand this tradition as containing an idea of vocation which is relevant both to the challenge raised by the prestige of science and to the contemporary state of political life?

In what follows I shall develop the thesis that the traditional idea of political theory displays some features which resemble forms of scientific theory, but which, by virtue of their political bearing, are uniquely the properties of political theory. As a way of bringing out the distinctive nature of this vocation, I shall call it the vocation of "epic theorist," a characterization which probably seems pretentious or precious, but which has been selected in order to call attention both to the unusual "magnitudes" of this form of theorizing, and to its distinguishing purpose and style.

Perhaps the pretentiousness of the phrase may be lessened by briefly recalling a comparable conception of theory in Kuhn's work. He employs the phrase "extraordinary" science to describe the contributions of the great scientific innovators. Kuhn's main point is that these theories mark a break with previous ones; that is, they inaugurate a new way of looking at the world, which includes a new set of concepts, as well as new cognitive *and* normative standards. Taking this as a suggestion of how to think about great theories, the first feature shared by epic theorists has to do with magnitudes. By an act of thought, the theorist seeks to reassemble the whole political world. He aims to grasp present structures and interrelationships, and to re-present them in a new way. Like the extraordinary scientific theory, such efforts involve a new way of looking at the familiar world, a new way with its own cognitive and normative standards.[66]

The second aspect of epic theory can be brought out if we look upon a theory not only as a structure of formal features, but also as a *structure of intentions.* The structure of intentions refers to the controlling purposes of the theorist, the considerations which determine how the formal features of concept, fact, logic, and interconnection are to be deployed so as to heighten the effect of the whole. In using the word "purposes" I mean to acknowledge that the structures exhibit considerable variety, and yet I also mean to maintain that there has been a persistent feature in all of them, one which may perhaps seem naïve to our age of unmasking where all emperors are naked. All of the major theories of the past were informed by "public concern," a quality which was not incidental to the activity, but fundamental to the very notion of being engaged in *political* theory. The cynical "realist," Machiavelli, professed; "I love my country more than my soul." [67] In his dialogue *Utopia* Thomas More wrote emphatically about the theorist's commitment: "If you cannot pluck up wrongheaded opinions by the root, if you cannot cure according to your heart's desire vices of long standing," he declares to the pure political philosopher, represented by Hythloday, "yet you must not on that account desert the commonwealth." [68] Hobbes, who was never one to romanticize men's motives, represented himself as "one whose just grief for the present calamities of his country" had driven him to theorize.[69] Similar sentiments abound in the

66. Here it is only necessary to recall Plato's long discussion of cognition or Hobbes's effort to place political philosophy upon a new and more scientific basis.

67. Letter to Vettori, April 16, 1527.

68. *Utopia,* tr. E. Surtz (New Haven, 1964), Bk. I, p. 49.

69. *De Cive,* op. cit., p. 18.

writings of Plato, Augustine, Locke, Rousseau, Bentham, Tocqueville, and Marx, among others. This unanimity suggests that if a Plato or a Marx had said what the modern scientist says repeatedly, and what some social scientists come perilously close to saying, namely, that they are not responsible for the political and social consequences of their inquiries, it would appear more foolish than blameworthy. Concern for *res publicae* and *res gestae* are as irreducible and natural to the vocation of theorist as a concern for health is to the physician. This quality of caring for public things contrasts sharply with the mental set that believes "the formulation of the topic into a research problem is the first step in scientific inquiry and, as such, should be influenced primarily by the requirements of scientific procedure." [70]

Because history suggests that all political societies have both endured and employed violence, cruelty, and injustice, and have known the defeat of human aspirations, it is not surprising that the theorist's concern for *res publicae* and the commonweal has issued in theories which, for the most part, have been critical and, in the literal sense, radical. Why this is the case and the import of it for the contemporary vocation of theorist can be shown by recurring once more to Kuhn. He has argued that scientific revolutions tend to occur when research begins to turn up persistent "anomalies," i.e., when phenomena are encountered that cannot be squared with the theory. To qualify as an anomaly the phenomena, should, in principle, be explicable by the theory; or, stated differently, the anomaly must be relevant to the kinds of problems for which the theory purports to furnish and explanation. It does not count as an anomaly if it raises a question which the theory cannot be said to recognize as important and hence be expected to answer.

The concept of anomaly suggests that a scientific crisis occurs because something is wrong "in" the theory. When

70. Selltiz, op. cit., p. 31.

nature does not conform to the scientist's expectations, he reacts by reexamining his techniques and theories. He assumes that the "mistake" lies with one or the other, not with nature. The bearing of this upon political science becomes clearer when we consider some frequent criticisms directed at traditional political theories by contemporary political scientists. It is charged that such theories are useless in explaining voting behavior, political apathy, the formation of politically relevant attitudes, and the precise degree of actual control exercised by the electorate. "If someone were to ask, 'How can I learn about what sorts of people participate most in politics, and why?' I would urge him to start with the most recent studies and work backwards. I seriously doubt whether he would get much help from Aristotle, Rousseau, or the *Federalist Papers*." [71] From such criticisms one would conclude that traditional political theories are valueless because they cannot explain why the political world is as it is. There is, in other words, something "wrong" in the theories. Whether this type of criticism will stand depends upon a prior understanding of the intentions of epical theorists: to what were their theories a response? As we have noted earlier, when it is believed that something is "wrong," scientists look for the error in the theory, not in the world. The same assumption is echoed by a contemporary behaviorist when he writes; "If there is a crisis, then, it is a crisis in the theory of representation and not in the institution of representation." [72] The assumption of the epic theorist has been of a different and contrasting kind. He has been preoccupied with a particular magnitude of problems created by actual events or states of affairs in the world rather than with problems related to deficiencies in theoretical knowledge. To be sure, problems-in-the-world and problems-in-a-theory are often interconnected, but the former has taken

71. Dahl, op. cit., p. viii.
72. Eulau, in Pool, ed., op. cit., p. 55.

precedence among epic theorists and has been determinative of the latter. The shaping experience has been the recurrently problematic state of the political world, not the problematic state of theories about that world. What is problematic emerges when political life is experienced either as a threat or as a promise. Most of the important theories were a response to crisis; they have reflected a conviction either that political action might destroy certain civilized values and practices, or that it might be the means for deliverance from evils, such as injustice or oppression. These polarities can be illustrated by the contrasting responses of Burke and Paine to the French Revolution, or of Tocqueville and Marx to the events of 1848. The point is not that theories come in pairs, or that the "same" events can be viewed very differently and equally persuasively; but rather that epic theories issue not from crises in techniques of inquiry, but from crises in the world.

In the language of theory, crisis denotes derangement. One form of derangement is the result of forces or conditions beyond control, e.g., the plague that hit Athens during its struggle against Sparta and, according to Thucydides, weakened the vital conventions governing Athenian political life. Other kinds of derangement are closer to what Aristotle called contingent matters, that is, matters about which men can meaningfully deliberate and choose. These kinds of derangements are the result of certain types of "errors" or "mistakes": errors in *arrangements,* in *decisions,* and in *beliefs.* Obviously the three types are often interrelated and combined: mistaken beliefs may produce faulty arrangements and foolish decisions; an unwise decision, e.g., one which overextends the resources of a society, may encourage mistaken beliefs, such as the illusion of omnipotence. Despite their obviousness, these three types may help in clarifying the defining, specific problems of traditional political theory. It is too vague to leave it that theorists are stimulated by problems-in-the-world, and it is misleading to say simply that they are drawn to a class of problems about which something can and should be done. What is all-important is that a problem be a truly theoretical one. A problem such as that presented by the inefficiency of postal services or the ineffectuality of legislative committees may be traceable to errors in arrangement (such as faulty delegations of administrative authority), or to mistaken beliefs (such as that seniority is the most expedient principle for determining committee chairmanships), or to a combination of erroneous arrangements and mistaken beliefs. Without denying the practical importance of these problems, they are not theoretical but technical in nature: they concern the most expeditious means of achieving goals which are, for the most part, agreed on beforehand. Likewise, the question of what decision is proper under particular circumstances is a matter for practical reason or judgment, not for theory.

There is one setting, however, in which specific arrangements, decisions, and beliefs become theoretically interesting. That is when they are "systematically mistaken": when arrangements or decisions appear not as random consequences of a system that otherwise works tolerably well or as the result of the personal foibles of a particular officeholder; but as the necessary result of a more extensive set of evils which can confidently be expected to continue producing similar results. Such a system would be systematically deranged. An illustration of what is being argued here is provided by Plato's criticism of Athenian democracy. The main thrust of his criticism was not directed against certain policies which he opposed, or even against the democracy's condemnation of Socrates.[73] Rather, the main thrust was towards arguing that bad policies and actions were bound to occur

73. If the Seventh Letter is to be believed, Plato also condemned the government of the Thirty, which included some of his kinsmen, for their threats against Socrates (324 d–e).

in one form or another, because the entire polity was systematically ordered in a mistaken way. Another example is provided by Marx. His case against capitalism did not rest on the charges that it chained the workers to a subsistence level, produced wastefully, and unfairly enriched those who owned the instruments of production. It was aimed, instead, at exposing the logic of capitalism which made injustice, alienation, and exploitation inevitabilities rather than contingencies.

This concept of the *systematically* mistaken explains why most political theories contain radical critiques. Their authors have tried to get at the basic principles (in the sense of starting-points) which produce mistaken arrangements and wrong actions. This same impulse determines why a political theory takes the form of a symbolic picture of an ordered whole. That it is a whole is dictated by its function, which is to be complementary to, or a substitute for, the systematically disordered whole which the theory seeks to displace. The possibility that the factual world is the outcome of a systematically disordered whole produces still another major difference between the epic political theorist and the scientific theorist. Although each attempts to change men's views of the world, only the former attempts to change the world itself. Although the scientist surely may claim for his theories the daring, beauty, and imaginativeness that are claimed for other forms of endeavor, he will concede that at some point his theory must submit to confirmation by the world. T. H. Huxley spoke sadly of "beautiful" theories tragically murdered by "an ugly little fact." Plato, in contrast, had asked defiantly; "Is our theory any the worse, if we cannot prove it possible that a state so organized should be actually founded?" Epic theory, if it has not strictly attempted to use theory to murder the ugly facts of the world, has taken a very different view of them, refusing to yield to facts the role of arbiter. Facts could never prove the validity of a true theory, because facts, in the form of practices or actions, were "less close to truth than (is) thought." [74] Thus for Plato the political facts of Athenian democracy were perfectly consistent with the theory of democracy, but the theory itself was systematically mistaken in its organizing principles, that is, deranged.

When we turn our attention to political life in the modern states, its appearance seems more suitable to methodical inquiry and mechanical models or theories. Our political and social landscape is dominated by large structures whose premeditated design embodies many of the presuppositions and principles of methodism. They are deliberately fabricated, their processes are composed of defined "steps," and their work is accomplished by a division of specialized labor whose aggregate effect seems marvelously disproportionate to the modest talents which are combined. Not only do these organizations impart regularity and predictability to the major realms of our existence thereby furnishing the conditions whereby methodical inquiry can pursue its goal of scientifically verifiable knowledge with reasonable hopes of success—for what could be more hopeful than to know that the political and social world is deliberately fashioned to produce regular and predictable behavior?—but also, since these organizations are uniquely the product of mind, rather than of mysterious historical forces, we are able to say with far greater confidence than Hobbes and Vico, who first announced the principle; "We can know it, because we made it."

Yet this is the state of affairs which the greatest modern philosopher of method, Max Weber, foresaw and despaired of, a world of bleak, forbidding, almost sterile reality, dominated by large and impersonal bureaucratic structures which nullified the strivings of those political heroes evoked in

74. *Republic*, tr. Cornford, p. 473.

"Politics as a Vocation." "A polar night of icy darkness and hardness" was his description of the world to come.[75] In a fundamental sense, our world has become as perhaps no previous world has done, the product of design, the product of theories about human structures deliberately created rather than historically articulated. But in another sense, the embodiment of theory in the world has resulted in a world impervious to theory. The giant, routinized structures defy fundamental alteration and, at the same time, display an un-challengeable legitimacy, for the rational, scientific, and technological principles on which they are based seem to be in perfect accord with an age committed to science, rationalism, and technology. Above all, it is a world which appears to have rendered epic theory superfluous. Theory, as Hegel foresaw, must take the form of "explanation." Truly it seems to be the age where Minerva's owl has taken flight.

It would seem, then, that the world affirms what the leaders of the behavioral revolution claim, the irrelevance of epic theory. The only trouble is that the world shows increasing signs of coming apart; our political systems are sputtering, our communication networks invaded by cacophony. American society has reached a point where its cities are uninhabitable, its youth disaffected, its races at war with each other, and its hope, its treasure, and the lives of its young men dribbled away in interminable foreign ventures. Our whole world threatens to become anomalous.

Yet amidst this chaos official political science exudes a complacency that almost beggars description. It is excusable that a decade ago a political scientist could contend that only a "fanatic" would want to "maximize" political equality and popular sovereignty at the expense of other values, such as leisure, privacy, consensus, stability, and status. But it is less excusable to find the following in a recent collection of

75. H. Gerth and C. W. Mills, *From Max Weber: Essays in Sociology* (New York, 1946), p. 128.

papers delivered before the American Political Science Association and subsequently published under its imprimatur: "Our discipline is enjoying a new coherence, a pleasant sense of unity, and self-confident identity that fits its rapid growth and healthy mien." [76] Polanyi has remarked that "it is the normal practice of scientists to ignore evidence which appears incompatible with the accepted system of scientific knowledge, in the hope that it will prove false or irrelevant." [77] In this spirit American political scientists continue to devote great energy to explaining how various agencies ingeniously work at the political socialization of our citizens and future citizens while mobs burn parts of our cities, students defy campus rules and authorities, and a new generation questions the whole range of civic obligations. And while American political scientists have laboriously erected "incrementalism" into a dogma and extolled its merits as a style of decision-making that is "realistic," it is apparent to all that the society suffers from maladies—the decay of the cities, the increasing cultural and economic gap between our minorities and our majority, the crisis in the educational system, the destruction of our natural environment—which call for the most precedent-shattering and radical measures.

Amidst all this, a political scientist approvingly quotes the following from a social scientist: "To argue that an existing order is 'imperfect' in comparison with an alternative order of affairs that turns out upon careful inspection, to be unobtainable may not be different from saying that the existing order is 'perfect.' " [78]

This assertion poses squarely the issue between political theory on the one side and the alliance between the methodist

76. Pool, ed., op. cit., p. vii. The essays by Eckstine and Dahl are excepted.
77. Op. cit., p. 138.
78. A. Wildavsky, *Politics of the Budget Process* (Boston, 1964), p. 178.

and the empirical theorist on the other. The issue is not between theories that are normative and those that are not; nor is it between those political scientists who are theoretical and those who are not. Rather it is between those who would restrict the "reach" of theory by dwelling on facts which are selected by what are assumed to be the functional requisites of the existing paradigm, and those who believe that because facts are richer than theories it is the task of the theoretical imagination to restate new possibilities. In terms of theory, the basic thrust of contemporary political science is not antitheoretical so much as it is deflationary of theory. This is most frequently expressed in the anxiety of the behaviorist who discovers that the philosophy of democracy places excessive demands on the "real world" and hence it is the task of political science to suggest a more realistic version of democratic theory. Thus the authors of *The Civic Culture* admit that it would be possible to "explain" the low degree of political involvement on the part of citizens by "the malfunctioning of democracy." But, they caution, this kind of explanation rests on a belief "that the realities of political life should be molded to fit one's theories of politics." A "somewhat easier and probably more useful task," they contend, is suggested by "the view that theories of politics should be drawn from the realities of political life." Because "the standards have been set unreasonably high," the theory should be changed.[79]

Is it possible that in this genial, Panglossian twilight Minerva's owl is beginning to falter as it speeds over a real world that is increasingly discordant and is beginning to voice demands and hopes that are "unreasonably high"? Perhaps it is possible, especially if we remember that in Greek statuary Minerva's pet was a screech-owl, for a screech is the noise both of warning and of pain.

79. Op. cit., p. 475.

Two Concepts of Politics &
Democracy: James &
John Stuart Mill

ALAN RYAN

As AN INTRODUCTORY NOTE TO THE substance of this paper, I should like to start by not apologizing for begging in my own favor the major problems involved in interpreting historical texts in political theory. It will be obvious from the body of the paper that James Mill and his son appear here to illustrate a wide thesis concerning two contrasting images of the nature of politics, images that are important in their own right, and especially so in the context of recent Anglo-American political science. It might be complained that thus to use them involves riding roughshod over historical accuracy, or—to change the metaphor—that I have thrust my protagonists into a Procrustean bed of my own devising, ignoring the eccentricities, the quirks of doctrine that any biographer has to stress. A real defense against such a charge can only lie in the insights hopefully provided by the paper itself; but I should at once state that if I must plead guilty, I remain unrepentant. For my purpose is not to recreate exactly what James Mill or J. S. Mill thought he was saying, but rather to elucidate with all the assistance that hindsight can give us what kind of case each of them was making.

It is possible—it is certainly often asserted—that nothing useful can be said about *the kind of case* that is made, that the exceptions and qualifications are always so numerous and so important that respectable work can only come from considering the particular case in its particularity.[1] I do not believe this to be true, and for that reason I am not persuaded that there is any reason of principle why the kind of enterprise here attempted should prove fruitless. But it is obvious enough that taking liberties with history in this manner cannot extend to faking the evidence nor yet to overlooking evidence that might either strengthen the case here made or less fortunately demolish it outright. In this sense what is argued here is vulnerable to the historian's expertise. And to the extent that this paper concentrates rather narrowly on only two essays by prolific writers, both of whom wrote a good deal about closely related issues to those discussed here, and both of whom spent their professional lives in political administration, it obviously runs rather large risks in this direction. It is no part of one's duty to regret taking risks; but it is perhaps part of that duty to admit that they are taken.

I

The wider thesis, in the light of which I want to look at the two Mills, is this: there is visible in the political thought

1. I take it that this is one of the tenets of Michael Oakeshott and his supporters.

of the past century and a half a division of opinion over the point or the goals of political and social life in general. This division lies between the adherents of what one might call an 'economic' or 'market' account of social life on the one hand and the partisans of a 'participant' or 'self-developmental' account on the other.[2] These are not self-explanatory terms; indeed at this point they are only gestures towards explanations that will appear in due course. The distinction is very closely allied to that which Hegel noted in the *Philosophy of Right,* where it forms the basis of the distinction between Civil Society on the one hand and the State on the other. Civil Society forms that area of social life which adequately satisfies the capacities of human nature so far as it is a subject for political economy; the State, on the other hand, satisfies the noneconomic need to belong to a community of rational beings, the need to be absorbed into a life of loyalties that cannot be traded in or bargained over. There is a version of the distinction in much of what Marx says about bourgeois society and again in much of what the English Idealists had to say in criticism of their utilitarian predecessors. It is, however, a dichotomy which cannot in the nature of things succeed in ranging all political thinkers unequivocally on one or other side of the divide. Thus to represent J. S. Mill as concerned only with the quality of citizen participation in a common life, as if he had nothing whatever to say about the accommodation of interests, the eliciting of bargains, and the like would plainly be pre-posterous. It is of course a general truth that any picture of what is involved in political participation must make some assumptions about the nature of the political system within which the citizen is called on to participate; and it is equally

2. Anthony Downs, *An Economic Theory of Democracy* (New York, 1957), yields me this label; but the account is, as he notes, provided in e.g., Joseph Scumpeter, *Capitalism, Socialism and Democracy* (London, 1943), ch. 22 and 23.

true that a concern for the stability and efficiency of the political system as a quasi-economic order must make some assumptions about the participation or nonparticipation of those who come to market.

A potentially more damaging objection to the dichotomy as drawn is the claim that anything said in the 'economic' vocabulary can be said equally well in the 'self-developmental' vocabulary and vice versa, so that the distinction between them is merely verbal. A proper reply to this objection would involve a careful account of the relationship between fact and theory in political science. Here we can do little more than illustrate what the objection amounts to. Let us take an issue central to this paper, the difference between 'market' and 'self-developmental' accounts of political participation. On a market theory of politics, participation appears to the citizen as a cost that he incurs in gaining for himself some part of those private goods in the enjoyment of which his happiness consists. Participant accounts, on the other hand, regard such participation as a gain to the individual in that it hopefully increases his self-awareness, strengthens his sense of belonging to a community of moral equals, and increases his sense of rational mastery over the environment. Now it is undeniable that a concern with these latter qualities is a central preoccupation with a distinctive political tradition of which Rousseau, Hegel, Marx, and the English Idealists are typical spokesmen. Such concepts lie at the heart of their account of the social world, a world that is praised by Hegel for its supposed adequacy in making such goods available to us, but is damned by both Rousseau and Marx for the obstacles it offers to their wider diffusion or more perfect possession.

It seems equally obvious that these concerns are alien to 'classical' utilitarianism, as preached by Bentham or James Mill. But, must we conclude that this is a matter of the theory? May it not be a matter of the theorist only? Can we not—as we see J. S. Mill asking himself after his exposure to Coleridge—accommodate within the economic categories of the empiricists the insights of the Idealist theorists of self-development? Thus, over participation, can we not simply add into our account such previously unthought of benefits as increased self-awareness, perhaps so many of them as to make it no longer a net expense but a net benefit, independently, that is, of its instrumental efficacy? My own view is that in the end such an attempt runs into so many difficulties as to render the revised account incoherent, but there is no simple proof of this point; the tautological results of such attempts in the literature of politics and sociology amount at best to weak inductive arguments on my side.

And doubts about the efficacy of the translation in one direction presumably apply with as much or as little force to translations in the other direction. Thus, suppose we attempt to translate the conclusions of a cost-benefit account of political participation into the language of self-development —a translation that we might ascribe to Hegel in his account of Civil Society. The individual in Civil Society alienates one aspect of his character to the business dealings of commercial life; indeed in bourgeois society he may find great fulfillment in leading the life of the good bourgeois. It looks initially, of course, as if a Rousseauist concern with constant involvement in the life of the community is a necessary consequence of any 'self-developmental' view; yet Hegel takes some pains to escape this consequence. It is not that he drops the typically Hegelian mode of analysis to argue suddenly for the merits of apathy on a cost-benefit basis; what he does instead is to claim that rationality and self-realization do not require that we spend much, perhaps any, of our time actively engaged in political or any other form of public life. He does not on the face of it renounce the goal of self-development; rather he argues that for most of us the way to self-realization is to do just those things that our station in our society calls upon us to do. We may, thus, express ourselves completely in leading just the life which a utilitarian, nonparticipant, market theorist of politics would have commended to us as the way to minimize costs and maximize benefits. Here, too, I think the idea that we can simply translate the conclusions of the one theorist into the words of another is eventually incoherent. At the very least, we have on our hands the historical problem of explaining how it is that Hegel's views were regarded as a very real betrayal by the Young Hegelians; the obvious answer is that the conclusions he came to *did* betray the moral concerns that the theory is centrally engaged with. At best, the translator is faced with awkward overtones which seem inevitably to attach to one way of speaking; at worst he is faced with two radically different images of human nature.

One thing, however, must be conceded. The dichotomy with which we are working does not readily categorize thinkers as more democratic and less democratic. It is a matter of brute historical fact that not all the thinkers who make so much of self-development are wholehearted democrats. Hegel, plainly, was concerned to argue *against* democracy, and it was scarcely an enthusiasm for industrial democracy that Mill picked up from Coleridge. In part, this is only to concede an old point, that there is no very direct connection between the social and political *Weltanschauung* of a thinker and the detailed social and political prescriptions he may issue. Indeed, it is only to admit that a central problem for political thought is to try to elicit the connection between the far-ranging theory and the substance of political action. And what this seems to mean at this point in the debate about the condition of contemporary democratic theory is that we need to find a way to utilize the insights of both the utilitarians and the Idealists—that we need to make Rousseau talk *to* Hume rather than at him or past him, that we need to make Mill and T. H. Green speak a common language, or for that matter Robert Dahl and the Students for a Democratic Society. Still, this is to be too concerned with wider goals and deeper anxieties; it is time to move on to the dramatis personae of the paper.

II

The first thing I want to do is to elucidate through the *Essay on Government* what I mean by saying that James Mill's essay is a classical economic model of democracy, a complement to classical economics and to utilitarian ethics. In general, commentators have made rather too little of this aspect of the essay; Elie Halévy's distinction between the natural and the artificial identification of interests tends rather to differentiate between politics and economics.[3] Most critics of the essay have relied heavily on Macaulay's devastating attack on it; and it is true that this demonstrated very clearly the ambiguity inherent in the axiom that everyone pursues his own self-interest, the dubiousness of the concept of human nature as there utilized, and the apparent absence of any sort of common sense.[4] Where they have not used Macaulay's arguments, they have pointed to Mill's hope that political power would fall into the hands of the new industrial and professional middle class, to his intention of denying the vote to women and to men under forty, as if such departures from the institutional and ideological pieties of twentieth-century Britain and America render all argument superfluous. I do not precisely set out to 'defend' James Mill's *Essay;* indeed, it seems to me an eminently dislikable document. But it has virtues that ought not to be neglected. Its most important claim to intellectual stature is that it provides a classical economic model of democratic government,

3. E. Halevy, *The Growth of Philosophic Radicalism* (Boston, 1967), pp. 486–90.
4. *Macaulay's Complete Works* (London, 1906), 7:327–71.

and thus stands at the head of a line of thought extending down to Joseph Schumpeter or Anthony Downs, a line of thought that provides many of the explicit or implicit assumptions with the aid of which we still practice political science. In other words, Mill displays in a very clear shape the intellectual model underlying much that is presently written about the operations and the difficulties of American and British government. Of course much of what he says has been improved upon, and much has been rendered obsolete since, in particular, the growth of mass parties. For all that, many of the premises and not a few of the conclusions of recent writers are there. Although this paper concentrates on the issue of political participation, it by no means exhausts the possible issues.

Mill assumes, in the fashion of all economists (and of Thomas Hobbes, their greater grandfather), that the natural goal of each man is to maximize his own well-being.[5] He says, rightly enough, that political truths ought to be culled from the widest possible examination of human nature; but he concludes after a strikingly cursory inspection of the evidence that human happiness or well-being consists in maximizing one's pleasures and minimizing one's pains, that we are happy in proportion as our pleasures are many and our pains are few.[6] To belabor the obvious, this account of happiness closely resembles the picture of economic motivation assumed in classical economics; we suffer work in order to gain an income, and in this process we obviously want to maximize the difference between the gratification we can purchase through the money we earn and the pain it causes us to expend our efforts in securing that money. Similarly, in *any* walk of life, we want to maximize the surplus of pleasure over the pain incurred in securing it or (to

5. *Essay on Government,* ed. C. V. Shields (Library of Liberal Arts, n.d.), p. 48.
6. Ibid., p. 48.

cater to the gloomy side of Mill's character) at any rate to minimize the deficit.

But Mill's theory is not economic only in this sense. It is an economic theory in a more explicit sense too. An important fact about the world we live in is that it is a world of scarce resources; and this means that we have to work for our pleasures. But work by definition is a pain and we cannot therefore wish to work more than we have to. What this must entail is that each person wants to receive as large a proportion of the product of his efforts as he can.[7] Now, to belabor the point again, it is a theorem of classical economics that in a perfect market all factors are rewarded precisely according to what they are worth to the market at large— leaving aside such complications as rent. Even without the refinements of marginalist analysis, the broad outlines of this conclusion were available to Mill. Now, if it is a free market that allows men to receive as much as possible of the product of their own labor, we have already reached the point in the argument where we can say that the overwhelmingly important task for a government is to ensure that a free market operate. In the light of this consideration, it is no wonder that one very great difference between Mill and his successors like Schumpeter is in their attitude to groups; Mill rejected the proposals for corporate representation current at his time with complete contempt.[8] In his eyes these proposals were merely ways of handing a political monopoly position to groups that already enjoyed a monopoly position in the economy. Thus, of course, Mill invoked a politics founded on the principles of perfect competition to defend a market founded on the same principles; but Schumpeter's defence is of a politics founded on the principles of oligopolistic competition, whose main task is the regulation of an economy based on the principles of oligopoly not perfect

7. Ibid., p. 49.
8. Ibid., pp. 77–82.

competition. This is plainly an important difference; none-theless, the important identity is the extent to which they are both economic theorists of politics in this double sense.[9]

Men, then, are bent on maximizing their individual happi-ness, on piling up a surplus in the psychic bank. The major means to this goal is the market. But the market can only function if contracts are observed and enforced, if there is proper control over the currency if fraud is suppressed. If men could get what they wanted without having to accept the restraints put on their actions by the market, they would presumably do so; thus the major aim of government is to stop them. But both the establishment and the exercise of governmental authority are threatened by another fact about human nature, which again is Hobbesian in origin. Put simply, it is that men are insatiable and will want to acquire goods ad infinitum; but crucially it is not of all goods that this is true, but especially of power.[10] Power is the one thing that enables men to be sure of the future in a world filled with competitors, a world in which outcomes are otherwise unstable. It seems to be Mill's view, as it is certainly Hobbes's, that the reason lies not in any viciousness inherent in human nature but simply in the exigencies of a competitive situation. Unlike Hobbes, Mill wastes no time on the intellectual fantasy of the state of nature; indeed, unlike Hobbes, he is not so much concerned to show that all men everywhere are insatiable as to argue that there is no guarantee that our rulers will be less insatiable than their subjects. Thus is created the problem which Hobbes presumed to be out of the way; if we can locate in any pair of hands power suffi-cient to protect us from each other, will this power not be

9. I hedge at once by agreeing that the analogies between economic and political life can at best be partial; for a useful argument about one point of breakdown in the analogy see D. Stokes "Spatial Models of Party Competition," *American Political Science Review* (1963):368–77.

10. *Essay on Government,* pp. 58–59.

used to plunder us instead, for the benefit of him who holds the power? In essence, most of Mill's essay is devoted to solving this puzzle.

One way of explaining Mill's solution would simply be to summarize what he has to say about the traditional types of government and their weaknesses. It can, however, be more adequately elucidated in terms of the market model. It is plain enough that Mill's assumptions rule out any form of monarchy or aristocracy; such governments amount to handing ourselves over to what are by definition 'sinister interests.' If a firm could charge whatever prices it liked on the market, it would charge monopoly prices; similarly a monarchy amounts to a monopoly in politics and will take monopoly gains out of the political system. And the same thing applies to any aristocracy that contrives to avoid quarrelling about how to divide the spoils among its members. These governments will be such as to maximize only their own good and not that of the people as a whole.[11] Mill dismisses almost as rapidly the traditional arguments for checks and balances and for a system of separation of powers;[12] any such separation is illusory, since a coalition will instantly form to take over a monopoly of power—if power is divided among three groups, any two will combine against the third, supposing that all three do not rather combine against the public.[13] It is usually, and in general rightly, urged against Mill that if all governments were as careless of constitutional forms as he supposes, then no form of government whatever could secure us against the oppression of our rulers. Against this, it does not seem unfair to suggest that the Anglo-American enthusiasm for the separation of powers and for the doctrine of checks and balances may well have blinded

11. For a recent discussion of the activities of 'interests' in something like Mill's sense, see Mancur Olson, *The Logic of Collective Action* (New York, 1968), cch. 5 and 6.

12. *Essay on Government*, pp. 63–66.

13. Ibid., p. 63.

us to the extent to which coalitions between interests have formed and flourished, and not always for the general good. Mill's conclusion, at any rate, is simple enough; what we require is some method of ensuring that power is placed only in the hands of persons who are unable to use it for any purposes contrary of the interests of the people at large. Were the whole nation able to take decisions on its own behalf, there could be no question of the dominance of sinister interests; but this is plainly impracticable. The problem thus amounts to securing the same result by other means; and the means according to Mill is through the device of representation.[14] We the people, who would act rightly—who could not under processes of free bargaining act otherwise—but who are disqualified by our numbers from actually gathering together, delegate persons to act on our behalf. We are too many to take decisions, but our delegates are few enough to decide and act; if they are appropriately selected and properly controlled, they cannot but act in the public interest. Of course, there are some extremely awkward questions raised by a bald assertion of this sort. On the premises of any one so empiricist as Mill, who are 'the people,' and how can this entity or nonentity take decisions, control anyone, or fail to control anyone? There is surely an ambiguity here created by Mill's basic premise of the natural proclivity of each man to pursue his own individual interest; what can the 'public' interest be, and how could anyone be led to pursue it? Without answers to these questions, how can we give a plausible account of how the public interest is served by the device of representation? [15]

14. Ibid., p. 67.
15. Mill's case for the belief that simple representative democracy will maximally serve the 'common' (or the 'general' or the 'public,' for there seems no clear distinction here) interest is never stated. It is therefore not clear what it is, in spite of the hostile attention it has received from the time of Macaulay onwards. In *Political Argument* (London, 1965), p. 241 n, Brian Barry suggests that Mill thought that everyone except the sinister interests shared a 'common net interest'; this he says,

The answer is to account for the processes of representation in quasi-economic terms, by representing the political system as a market, and the behavior of voters and those for whom they vote in a manner analogous to that in which we represent the behavior of buyers and sellers of goods. The individual voter is in the market for a policy that will be in his own interest, i.e., that which maximize his utility, just as he shops about in the economic market for goods that will yield him a maximum of utility.[16] Representatives in a democracy thus turn out to be delegates in the search for utility maximization, a view that entirely coheres with the radical view of representation in the early nineteenth century. Their platforms are, so to speak, the shopping lists according to which they seek at the level of national policy-making to maximize the welfare of their electors. There is a natural connection between such an account of representation and the view that politics exists in order to harmonize the activities of rational egoists; and it is important to see that representation as a device does not look anything like so centrally important once we conceive of politics in other terms. For Rousseau, to take an obvious example, representation can solve nothing, since the object of social and political activity is in large part to integrate the individual in communal ac-

and quite correctly, is untenable since it is all too likely that a certain stable majority will have an interest in policies detrimental to a certain stable minority. Obviously, the examples of American Negroes and Ulster Catholics support Barry here. A possible alternative reading is that Mill thought of governments as only concerned to hold the ring between competing interests, so that in effect it would only be a very limited class of policy that was ever under discussion. Of course, it is just possible that Mill was simply muddled and that he equivocated between aggregative and distributive senses of *all,* thus believing that if the people pursued each his own interest, this would somehow mean that each pursued the interest of all. The only thing to be said unequivocally in Mill's defence here is that he is at least engaged in a serious attempt to protect the public interest against private interests, which is more than can be said for such books as D. B. Truman, *The Governmental Process.* See, e.g., Olson. op. cit., pp. 122–25.

16. cf. Downs, op. cit., ch. 3, especially pp. 36–45.

tion, a thing that simply cannot be done at second hand.[17]
That we can delegate a man to go and vote as I and others
decide he should is an important fact when we think of
political activity as essentially self-interested in the utilitarian
manner—or in the way in which most pressure-group theorists think of it now. But if social and political life is concerned with such goals as self-expression and self-realization, it is on the face of it hard to see how anyone else can
express *my* self on my behalf or can through his activities
realise *my* capacities. If politics cannot be reduced to a form
of quasi-economic bargaining, then the fact that I can get
someone else to bargain on my behalf ceases to be the central
fact about the possibility of mass democracy. For James Mill
there seems to have been no problem, but only because he
chose not to face it. Although a good deal of his talk about
the people and the visibility of a 'public interest" looks more
Rousseauist than reductionist or Benthamite, the logic of his
position is surely that he would have to give an account of
the people's choice and the public's interest that was in-
dividualist and reductionist. The general interest must be
derivable by way of some process of summing the gains and
losses of individuals under alternative policies.[18] To work out
what kind of policies would be in the general interest we
must presumably make the kind of calculations that John
Rawls has investigated concerning the kinds of bargains that
could be struck by rational egoists.[19] Long-run considerations
about uncertainty, vulnerability, and the like might well lead
us to accept all the major institutions of the free market and
the policing arrangements that attend it; in the absence of

17. *Social Contract* (Everyman Library, 1910), Bk. 3, ch. 15, pp.
82–85.
18. But, of course, the objections to any such procedure have been
devastatingly put in Kenneth Arrow, *Social Choice and Individual
Values* (New York, 1951).
19. See, e.g., "Distributive Justice" in P. Laslett and W. G. Runci-
man, eds., *Philosophy, Politics and Society*, series 3 (Oxford, 1965),
pp. 58–82.

89

clear information about our prospects under given procedures, we should all have to accept policies in the general interest rather than our own. In the short run, we can expect to see much more clearly how we could make gains; but since everyone else can see this and move to cut the gain off from us, we should once again be forced to espouse the general rather than our sectional good. And it goes without saying that the real world will yield less of this desirable state of affairs to the extent that the real world departs from the assumptions embodied in the model, in respect of differential access to information, inequalities of power, and the like.

For this account of Mill, I do not want to claim any great novelty; it may push Mill rather fiercely into the market mould, but at the level of doctrine rather than biography it is no injustice. There are all manner of things about Newton that a biographer would tell one about, which do not concern the physicist; and what is here being claimed is that about Mill's doctrines we can crystallize many of the commonplaces—and some of the more startling recent assertions —about the way in which liberal democracy can and should work. A good example here is the issue of political participation, on which a lot of recent attention has been focussed. On the market theory, participation is a cost to the individual since it requires much the same activities to vote rationally as to shop sensibly—we need to expend time and energy in gaining information, i.e., we have to work. To expend energy on work is itself a pain and is costly in terms of diverting energy from other activities with a higher direct yield in pleasure.[20] From this it follows that a person would not desire the suffrage, let alone desire actually to use it, unless he thought that his vital interests would suffer if he did not—or, but very implausibly, that direct political action would yield him a high utility compared with other activities. It might be

20. Downs, op. cit., cch. 11–13.

argued that a *utility maximizer* (i.e., an optimist), as distinct from a *disutility minimizer* (i.e., a pessimist), would find this less convincing; the ambitious and the optimistic will want to be active just as they will cheerfully take risks and work harder in order to pile up fortunes over and above what they can reasonably think they need to avoid hardship. There is no simple answer to this point; for the purposes of this paper it is enough to point out how little of an optimist James Mill was and how unlikely he thought it that any rational man would be an optimist; again, his conception of what politics could achieve may very well have been such to leave little room for ambition.

For more general theoretical purposes, it is of course very important to remember that any cost-benefit analysis of behavior is very vulnerable to speculation about temperament. For Mill anyway, the way ahead is simple; we work to avoid the evil of starvation; if we could eat without working we should do so, and similarly if we could have the benefits of the suffrage without voting, we should do so. Thus Macaulay's attack on Mill's refusal of the suffrage to women is not entirely well taken. It is not, as he so contemptuously asserts, a case of dogmatizing away the interests of half the human race.[21] For Mill's defence, if it could hardly be word for word, is at any rate thought for thought that of a writer like Downs,[22] and to some extent much like that of Bernard Berelson and indeed any of dozens of consensus theorists in the nineteen fifties.[23] If someone will look after your interests

21. Macaulay, *Works,* 7:354.
22. Downs. op. cit., ch. 14: "The Causes and Effects of Rational Abstention."
23. Berelson et al., *Voting* (Chicago, 1958), pp. 305–13. But of course there can be perfectly good utilitarian arguments for *increased* participation as well; thus, S. Verba has recently argued that the acceptance of low levels of participation that he and his coauthor shared in *The Civic Culture* was a mistake, in the context of the U.S. at any rate, since there is an irreducible minimum of accurate information about the needs of the poor, the aged, the unemployed, and the racially op-

for you, then there is no earthly reason why you need engage in political activity at all—not even to the extent of trying to find out who are the candidates for office nor what their policies are. The effort you do not expend on this sphere, you can expend to better effect elsewhere. After all, political activity is only one of those activities which may increase your utility-flow, and possibly not the most effective by a long way. This argument is not a defence of 'functional apathy,' be it noted; our argument here is only concerned with the gains and losses to the individual, not with the needs of the political system as a whole. The arguments for functional apathy only consider the utility to society at large of the abstention of a class of persons whose entry onto the political scene might cause chaos. So far as those individuals are concerned, their own interests might indicate something else altogether, for if they are sufficiently ill-provided for under the present arrangements, it is likely that any degree of social disruption will affect them only marginally for the worse and possibly much for the better. The case made by Mill is different; it is much more akin to the defences of 'privatization' or 'depolitization'—other forms of satisfaction are so readily available, and the satisfaction they yield is so great that politics can safely be ignored. On Mill's analysis, then, we can say that anyone who can safely do without the vote will not want it, or will not use it; and this is individually and socially rational, since elections are expensive and Mill envisages their being frequent, which would be very costly indeed if there were universal suffrage and universal use of the suffrage.

But, what Mill has become known for as much as anything is the defence of concentrating power in the hands of the

---

pressed which no authority, however benevolent, can dispense with if it is to relieve their distress. Verba, however, rejects in explicit terms the New Left argument for 'participatory democracy' as in itself conferring a good upon the participant (*Annals,* September 1967).

middle classes; this may resemble, but is certainly not quite the same as the defence of the political entrepreneur by Robert Dahl and others. Mill's argument is that the interests of the middle class are identical with the interests of society as a whole. It is not clear what sort of an argument he thinks he has to back up this assertion. The usual commentator's ploy is attractively easy and is even employed by J. S. Mill in discussing his father's politics; we are to see the *Essay on Government* as primarily a piece of propaganda against such long standing bugbears of the radicals as civil-list pensions, duties on food and raw materials, and the like, and thus we do not have to look for arguments at all. A certain amount of philosophical paint is often applied to political programmes; that is what is happening here. J. S. Mill says rather plaintively that his father was a practical man who would have dealt with the facts as he found them, as he did in the course of his experience at India House.[24] But to my mind this defence yields too much. James Mill knew perfectly well that he could not state as an empirical truth that all good governments had been those managed by the middle classes —it could not be true, if for no better reason than that the middle class that Mill defended was a historical novelty. But the way out of the apparent concession is obvious. All good governments can be accounted for as the result of checks of a noninstitutionalised sort upon the power of the ruling group to rule in its own selfish interest; wherever the general good was promoted we would expect to find a process like that of bargaining taking place in however covert a way. A society may manage to work some sort of market economy in the absence of a conventional currency because people adjust their behavior accordingly—the case imagined by Locke of a pre-monetary state of nature where barter flourished shows that the case is anyway conceivable. So, equally,

24. J. S. Mill, *A System of Logic* (London, 1906), Bk. VI, ch. 8, sec. 3.

a political system other than representative government may achieve many of the utility-maximizing objectives we set ourselves. The advantages of a formally constituted representative system are those that always attach to institutions with specific purposes, advantages mostly of a division of labor. Still, does even this guarantee the truth of Mill's assertion about the harmony of middle class interests and the general interest? Surely not; but we can go further. It may not be a general truth that representative government only works well with middle class control; but the general argument rests on the qualities which Mill ascribed to the middle class of his day. These qualities are of course those of economically rational man—and they can be summarized as industry and knowledge.[25] Mill's belief that education and the wider dispersion of knowledge would be forces for stability rather than for chaos seems to be explained on this view. We have no need of spectacular personal qualities in a world that is managed by rational well-informed people, since the calculations of such people should always yield identical results in terms of public policy. Mill believed that, as things stood when he wrote, the middle class had more or less a monopoly of these desirable virtues, so that it was from the middle class that the rational bargainers that democracy needs would mostly be drawn. As rational men, they could see that it was in their long term interest to create a working class in their own image—diligent, provident, and intelligent; and this of course was what was in the interest of the working class also. Thus, on Mill's premises, the most rational political policy for the working class as a whole was to accept the leadership of the middle class, while for individual members of the working class, it was rational to follow the direction set by middle class 'opinion leaders.'

Putting the argument as briefly as this makes it look hair-

25. Cf. Robert Dahl. *Who Governs?* (New Haven, 1961) and J. Schumpeter, loc. cit., for what is in essence a similar defence of the entrepreneurial role in political life.

raisingly simplistic. This is not entirely a vice, since many good theories have this kind of simplicity about them at first sight. What is important is what can be done with them, and what can be done, as we have seen is that we can show how Mill's argument underlies much of the recent acceptance of such phenomena as deference voting, voter ignorance, low involvement, and the like as not regrettable but desirable phenomena. Another current debate on which the utilitarian theory is illuminating is the validity of taking stability as in some sense a measure of political democracy. The demonstration of this point shows interestingly how political and economic theory can come together to reinforce what must have partly been a nontheoretical response to Cold War alarms about subversion and civil war. Like any piece of classical economics, Mill's picture of politics rests on an ambiguity in its basic premises which leads to some doubt about how to evaluate his conclusions. The proposition that all men try to maximize their own welfare hovers uncertainly between the status of logical truth and empirical falsity.[26] In consequence, there is a good deal of difficulty in applying the notion of optimality to the performance of an entire economy—we simply cannot tell whether an economy is maximizing welfare or not. As is well known, there are two ways out of this problem: one is to set up what look like rational standards for overall performance and to assess the actual performance of an economy by these; the other is to work with the notion of Pareto-optimality and say that any situation is optimal where there are no desired trades left to be made. In other words, a situation is optimal where no one can better his position after he has compensated anyone made worse off by his move.[27] The attractions of Pareto-optimality are obvious in that it enables us to dispense with making our

26. Mill, *A System of Logic,* Bk. VI, ch. 8, sec. 3; Macaulay, *Works,* 7:365.
27. See J. M. Buchanan and G. Tullock, *The Calculus of Consent* (Ann Arbor, 1965), for the incessant employment of this device.

own judgments about what would be a desirable social mix of products and to leave the arbitration to the people involved. But to call any situation optimal, we must make two assumptions—firstly that people are free to make any trades they wish to make, and secondly that people have adequate information, since otherwise there will be possible moves not taken up. There are many complications over and above these, and many more in the field of analysing moves between one Pareto-optimum and another; but these can be ignored here. The basic point is that it is very plausible to equate stability under conditions of freedom as being the same thing as democracy; for what can stability indicate except that the trades possible in the circumstances have been made? This is not to say that democracy entails stagnation, since it is obvious that new goods will appear, tastes will change, and there will be a good deal of bustle in the market-place. Nonetheless political stability indicates that the public interest is served.[28] It is true that James Mill was so conservative; he was willing to use the threat of mob terror to get concessions from the political incumbents of his day.[29] Nonetheless, his theory is nondynamic in the same sense as most of classical economics—normality is the situation where equilibrium is achieved and the market is cleared of unwanted policies and unsatisfied demands. And such an equilibrium situation is for Mill market democracy, even if large numbers of people take very little part in the processes by which this equilibrium is achieved and maintained. To make the picture fully coherent and convincing, we should have to explore at greater length the various qualifications here left implicit; for instance, we have said nothing about the re-

28. This tendency of argument is particularly marked in Robert Dahl, *A Preface to Democratic Theory* (Chicago, 1956), ch. 5, where it is argued that the persistence of stable 'polyarchy' is to be accounted for by its success in attending to all legitimate interests.

29. See J. Hamburger, *James Mill and the Art of Revolution* (New Haven, 1963), for the elaboration of this point.

quirements of free access to the market, nor about the analogues to the requirements of perfect information. It is, however, notable that many of Mill's occasional writings were precisely about those topics that such qualifications involve—popular education and the freedom of the press among them.

James Mill has generally had a bad press from the critics, and it is not hard to see why. If there were no other reason, we should probably dislike him for the education which he inflicted on his son. Most of us—Alexander Bain is a notable exception in this—take an uncritical attitude to J. S. Mill's account of his education and a correspondingly critical attitude to the father who devised it. For those who dislike utilitarian politics he is a cherished bête noire—and the class of those who dislike utilitarian politics is a very large one, including almost all forms of nineteenth and twentieth century conservatives, almost all forms of revolutionaries, and many forms of reformist socialists. He seems tailor-made for abuse —to be accused of advocating "steam engine government," "anachronistic syllogising," "heartlessness," "doctrinaire narrowness," and so forth. To redress the balance a little, it is worth saying a few words in defence of at any rate the *kind* of case he was making. The various forms of classical economic theory have been in many ways the most dazzling achievement of the social sciences; to see how true this is, one has only to think of the longevity and vigor of this one branch of the social sciences. Classical economics brought large numbers of hitherto unexplained phenomena under intellectual and to some extent social control and set up standards for other social sciences to aim at. The use of notions akin to homeostasis in economics long antedates their use by cyberneticists and then by political scientists. What is even more to the point is that classical economics was tied in very closely to a scientific theory of individual psychology and to a moral philosophy that were themselves attractive for quite independent reasons. It seemed, therefore, that a social science was in the making that would allow important questions both of explanation and policy to be answered, no matter in what society they were asked. Even where the answers that were found were not those expected, progress was made; for the theory enabled social scientists to make mistakes they could explain. And that is a neglected but very vital function of all theory. The fruitfulness of the approach would take a lot of documenting, but in the context of democratic politics, surely the evidence is simple enough—and it is sufficient to cite the work of Schumpeter or Downs. An obvious weakness of Mill's initial model is that he has nothing to say about parties, or about groups, save to mistrust them as sinister interests. If the market theory of democracy were to survive, it had to be brought to face the reality of less than perfect competition. In essence, Schumpeter's revision of the theory of democracy is applying the democratic model to the situation of oliogopoly. And the new model as much as the old leaves us with the same questions. We no longer have to justify a curtailed suffrage, but we do need to explain a limited use of the vote; we no longer bother about the power of landlords nor about civil-list pensions; but we still worry about the rake-offs of well-entrenched chairmen of Congressional committees; in other words we still perceive democracy as an instrument for utility-maximization, and thus we still have to concentrate on what look like exorbitant prices being asked for political action, and we still try to remove obstacles to the making of reasonable bargains. Naturally, we employ much the same intellectual categories as the Mills for this purpose and make much the same assumptions about the goals of the citizenry and their rulers. James Mill remains no less dislikable for his place in such a tradition, but it would be folly to deny the intellectual appeal of so long-lived and flourishing a tradition.

III

Nonetheless, our next task is to turn precisely to the dissatisfaction with this tradition which agitated the younger Mill. In other words, in terms of the categories we initially began with, we must turn from economic to self-developmental democracy; away from utility as a central notion and onto the idea of progress, self-realization and growth. But before we do so, it is necessary to say a preliminary word about whether J. S. Mill was a democrat at all. A number of writers have questioned whether Mill would have thought of himself as a democrat; perhaps the longest and most careful statement of these doubts was offered by J. H. Burns some twelve years ago in two articles on the history of Mill's changing views on the subject.[30] It seems to me, however, that all such doubts are fairly futile; Mill's last word on the subject in his *Autobiography* certainly describes him as a democrat[31]—we may choose to refuse the title to him in the light of his defence of plural voting and the like inegalitarian provisions of *Representative Government,* but if the question is one of his self-ascription, there is no good reason to ignore the evidence. If, however, the question is one of whether he *ought* to have thus described himself, the matter is wide open to dispute over the essential and nonessential tenets of democracy. The trouble with an account such as Burns's is that it hides the fact that beneath a remarkable willingness on Mill's part to experiment with practical devices of one sort and another, there was an almost equally remarkable consistency in basic aim. The point that I wish to establish is that J. S. Mill was at once more ambitious for democratic politics than his father had been and at the same time more pessimistic about those areas where his father had

30. *Political Studies* (1957), pp. 158–75 and 281–94; see in particular the final sentences on p. 294.
31. J. S. Mill, *Autobiography* (New York, 1956), p. 199.

been most cheerful—notably in his estimate of the harmony of interests between the middle class and the laboring poor, and again in his estimate of the willingness of the laboring class to submit indefinitely to the leadership of the middle class. This means that more is at issue than any simple maximization of utility, while the dangers of mass tyranny are constantly present to him—dangers that are all but ruled out of his father's account by definition. Save to the extent that it reminds us that liberalism and democracy are by no means inevitably allies, arguing that J. S. Mill was not a democrat serves little or no purpose. What obviously does matter is that we should see clearly in what way the goals he defends in *Representative Government* and elsewhere differ quite radically from those that his father valued, and how right his Idealist successors and critics were to think these goals more than a little at odds with traditional utilitarianism.

Where James Mill's *Essay on Government* is very brief and apparently very simple, *Representative Government* is a great deal longer and more complex. Moreover its length and complexity do not mean that it is a completely adequate guide to Mill's reflections on the essay's premises. Many of these have to be culled from his long wrestling with Saint-Simon and Comte, from his attempts to do justice both to Bentham and to Coleridge, from his efforts in the *Principles of Political Economy* to separate out the area of free choice from that of economic necessity. Mill's famed inconsistency derives from a less famed but more consistent belief in the importance of doing justice to a great variety of goods, rather than to one at the expense of all others. The consistency of his interests means that the high and sometimes rather absurd faith he places in technical devices—the defence of 'fancy franchises' in *Representative Government* and in his occasional writings—is part and parcel with the grave fears he expresses in *Liberty*. The importance of *Liberty* in the light of *Representative Government* is plain from the outset; for both works illustrate the extent to which progress replaces utility as the key conception. In the essay *On Liberty,* Mill insists that he appeals only to utility; but he immediately moves away from any simple utilitarian defence of individual freedom by qualifying the claim: the utility in question is that which is founded on man's permanent interests as a progressive being.[32] But this, manifestly, is to make the principle of maximizing utility logically dependent on the principle of maximizing progress. So, equally with *Representative Government,* the goal is no longer that of maintaining a stable and efficient administration in the service of maximum general utility; now it essentially involves notions of change and progress.[33] So emphatic is Mill upon this point that he makes it the text for a criticism of the doctrine common to Coleridge and to Comte that societies involve principles of change and principles of rest, and thus that there ought to be parties of order and parties of progress. For him, order is desirable only in the limited sense that if there is to be progress, then certainly we must not slip backwards; but the value of order is solely its value as a condition of progress. The criteria of progress, too, are not very obviously utilitarian, for the progress Mill defends is scarcely related at all to economic goods, nor to the aim of piling up an ever larger supply of things to be consumed by the members of a society. Primarily the progress desired is improvement in the quality of the human beings composing the society. It can be fairly objected that James Mill also was concerned to improve the quality of the human character, and that an emphasis on what is now called socialization—a concern for the educative effects of the political system—was common to both the Mills and to most utilitarians. But what this objection misses is the difference in the aspects of character that J. S. Mill

32. *On Liberty,* in *Essential Writings of John Stuart Mill* (New York, 1961), p. 264.
33. *Representative Government* (New York, 1965), pp. 32–39.

cared about. So far as he was concerned, his father and Bentham had systematically neglected the most important aspects of human nature—the list of their shortcomings is given in the famous essay on Bentham and is fairly extensive.[34] We might in James Mill's world take pains to socialize men into industry and probity and into a calculating kind of intelligence; we should not care to make them bold, imaginative, individual, and sensitive. Yet it is these qualities that J. S. Mill most wants to preserve and encourage; a flock of honest and businesslike sheep would be total failures as a society of developed human beings.[35]

To say that by comparison with his son James Mill worked with a static and timeless picture of human nature and of social and political life is no way to contradict what was earlier said about his radical politics. What is at issue is somewhat similar to what is said to be at issue when equilibrium theorists in sociology are accused of building conservatism into their explanations of social life; they reasonably retort that the sort of equilibrium involved can change radically—the stability required is at a fairly high level of abstraction.[36] Similarly, when James Mill is said to have a static view of human nature, there is no suggestion that he would have denied that men can come to develop new tastes or to change their minds about what they want. His emphasis on the insatiability of one desire—that for power—shows that there is dynamism in the picture. Nonetheless, the differences between father and son remain untouched. For the father, power is a special case, in that the desire for power is parasitic upon the desire for goods in the usual sense; and even com-

34. *Essays on Politics and Culture,* ed. G. Himmelfarb (New York, 1963), pp. 97–99.
35. Thus the final words of *On Liberty, Essential Writings,* p. 360.
36. Thus see for hostility to equilibrium notions, D. Easton, ed., *Varieties of Political Theory* (New York, 1966), pp. 145–47, and for a defence, G. C. Homans, *The Human Group* (New York, 1950), pp. 304–5.

pared with Hobbes he is imperceptive about humanity's apparent tendency to accept 'fancy' values—as for example the desire to win for the sake of winning and not for the sake of the prize. But for the son, we simply fail to understand human nature if we ignore the fact that men use the satisfaction of one desire as a mere stepping-stone to the acquisition of new desires, quite often incomparable with the old. James Mill tends to lump men's choices together; but the younger Mill's account concentrates much more steadily on the personal and the idiosyncratic. For him, the choices a man makes are what go to make up his self; and the ability to choose one's own character is for him practically an obsession.[37] Since our choices both reflect and create our characters, the need to have the widest possible range of choices available becomes paramount. The point is illustrated most clearly by a negative consideration—what the fears were that agitated them. James Mill, in essence, desires to keep the hands of the rulers out of the national till; democracy is as much as anything a means of ensuring that our rulers do not misconduct themselves with the funds they take out of our pockets. But J. S. Mill's great fear is of mass despotism. It is not a fear of what has recently obsessed theorists of 'mass society'; in spite of the spectacle of Louis Napoleon, he does not fear the aroused mass that blindly follows the charismatic leader. It is not the frenzy of the masses but their lethargy which chiefly frightens him. We could say, however, that he shares a fear of totalitarian democracy, for he certainly fears the overwhelming pressures of a united public opinion, an opinion whose answer to all social and political problems is summed up in the imperative to be like everyone else. But as *Liberty* makes clear, it is not that such a despotism will be brutal or violent—its effectiveness may well be the greater for the gentleness with which the pressure is ap-

37. E.g., *A System of Logic,* Bk. VI, ch. 2, sec. 3, where Owen's fatalism is the target.

plied. The ills to guard against are passivity, inertia, timidity, and intellectual stagnation. *Liberty* and *Representative Government* are of a piece in their concerns, with the difference that the former essay is concerned with the total social and psychological problem, the latter with its more directly political implications. Thus, if we must sum up the basic political goals of the younger Mill in contrast with the elder, it is that social and individual existence must be kept open-ended, that the potentialities for growth, change, and development must receive the first priority. It is the view of the educator in an extended sense, that of the defender of an education that is received not as a preparation for some further goal, but for its own sake.

An illustration will serve to flesh out so summary a statement. Among the views that are defended in *Representative Government,* perhaps the most mocked is the defence of open voting and a nonsecret ballot.[38] Its interest is that though the conclusion may seem merely quaint by now, the argument underlying it is disquieting still. For Mill, voting is an act with two aspects: aggressive and defensive we might call them, or other-regarding and self-regarding. The vote is an instrument with which to defend our rights and with which to make our claims felt. But it is also an instrument of control over the lives of others; when we vote we necessarily help to bring about the implementation of policies that bind others as much as ourselves. If we are willing to accept the task of controlling other people to any extent, we must in reason be willing to account to them for how we propose to exercise that control. To vote is to commit oneself to courses of action for the whole community; if the choice is not merely frivolous or merely selfish, it can be defended on principle in front of other people; if it has to be thus defended, the knowledge of this fact will very likely make

38. *Representative Government,* ch. 10, especially pp. 202–5.

voters think more carefully about what it is that they are doing. It hardly needs emphasising how different a demand upon voter's motivation this makes from that made by James Mill. Plainly there are lots of practical objections to be raised against the idea of open voting. On the available evidence of what voters *do* know, *do* feel, and—given their education, employment, and general life-style—could plausibly be expected to know and feel, Mill is asking much too much. He overestimates the extent to which most of us are able or willing to defend our views—if we have any—in front of a potentially hostile audience, even if that audience is armed with nothing more than words. Again, it may be said that no audience would long confine itself to words once it was invited to have strong feelings about matters. Any government as predicated on dispute as this one, would move from democracy to anarchy in very short order. On the other side it can be replied that our evidence all comes from a form of democracy not much like that desired by Mill; we do not know, and we are forced to speculate on rather little evidence, how much more controlled and reasonable people would be if they were brought up to argue about public matters. But whatever the evidence will reveal, Mill makes a point of some importance in these days of 'other-directed' man. Is there not something slightly peculiar when people equate the secrecy of the ballot with the belief that political opinions are a private matter? On any possible view of the distinction between private and public life, voting is an element in one's public life—so is Mill right in seeing secrecy as at best a concession to human frailty and to the inadequacy of legal safeguards? Certainly the argument clarifies the differences between the two Mills. For the elder Mill voting involves trying to get what you can in the political competition; for J. S. Mill it involves defending your own perception of society and its needs, and thus it involves exposing yourself to new influences, competitive views of the world, new demands on your capacities. It thus seems to be quite un-like shopping for policies in your interest; it is a—on the face of it gruelling—piece of social and political education.

Given that much of the recent literature on political participation has in fact been a literature on the voting—and nonvoting—habits of the English and American public, we ought now to explore further the view of political participation which characterises J. S. Mill's politics. We have already seen that a utilitarian may well decide that a rational man would fare excellently were he to ignore politics altogether. The so-called 'apathetic' individual may very well be promoting his own interests, even where there is no question of his having reasoned his way through to such a conclusion. The conclusion will still be true, so long as the increased costs of participation are larger than benefits got from it. James Mill's argument about the costs and benefits to women may be thought to have received support from the facts so far known about feminine political behavior, even though few of them have heard of James Mill.[39] The arguments offered by J. S. Mill on this score amount to a repudiation of the view that participation is a cost to the individual, and it is this argument we must clarify. On the market view, participation bears costs because it involves an allocation of time and effort away from other sources of pleasure; like all activities, it bears an opportunity cost by definition—all activities involve not doing those things that are strictly ruled out by doing them; it also bears a cost above its opportunity cost, namely the pains of work. To reject the applicability of the notion of opportunity costs here is to reject the applicability of cost-benefit analysis to human behavior; to reject the added costs of 'work' in this instance is to part company to some extent with the axioms of political economy. Thus, in arguing for the view that participation is a good to

39. *Essay on Government*, p. 74.

the individual, J. S. Mill has at least to part company with the usual utilitarian views on work. And indeed it comes as no surprise to find that he does just this. The defence of participation as a good is paralleled by the emphasis placed by Mill on the moral value of public-spirited work. An important instance of this occurs in Mill's discussion of the industrial and military life—a point on which he had learned from Comte.[40] An army is a body of men devoted to an intrinsically evil end—namely destruction and killing; by contrast industrial life is devoted to the praiseworthy goals of creating more goods for people to enjoy. And yet the effects of these ways of life on those who take part in them are very different from what we should expect. The army can call upon intense loyalty, devotion, individual courage, and a sense of common purpose among all its members; the factory can call on nothing of the sort, and Mill in fact was very disenchanted with the grabbing, meanness, and selfishness of industrial and commercial life. Mill's advocacy of cooperatives was part of the hope that communal ventures other than military ones could call out the same sort of loyalties as only armies had done in the past. To introduce considerations such as these was to alter drastically the inherited political stance.

Political participation thus becomes important because political life is part of an irreplaceable public life and because the life of common action is different in kind from our private pursuits. An aspect of the essay on *Liberty* that is usually overlooked in this context is the extent to which Mill's defence of individual freedom against social constraint rests on the firm belief that an unconstrained involvement in the affairs of the community could thereby be liberated. Mill believed quite as firmly as did antithetical figures like Hegel that a man can only have an adequate concern for

40. J. S. Mill, *Auguste Comte and Positivism* (Ann Arbor, 1962), p. 149.

himself by having an adequate concern for others, and that isolation from the common life of the society was stunting even to individuality. Of course *Liberty* would not be what it is if this were its main point, and Mill's emphasis on *free* involvement, *uncoerced* interest is not in question. But to infer from Mill's libertarian views that he cared little for cooperation is quite as foolish as to infer from the fact that he was dedicated to many of the goods that Comte was concerned for that he shared an equal enthusiasm for Comte's follies. It would be equally a mistake to turn Mill into a hack liberal-conservative as to turn him into a disguised Comte or Marx.

The stress on the educative aspect of political life recurs very clearly in Mill's treatment of local government.[41] Mill had very mixed feelings about the growth of centralized government; on the one hand he valued expertise and saw quite plainly that 'big government' had come for good; moreover he accepted the need for a permanent civil service with whose work the political authorities ought not to interfere once clear instructions had been issued. With the desire for efficiency there blended the natural pride of the Examiner of the East India Company who knew that its administration was the most efficient in Britain and the Coleridgean concern for the maintenance of a clerisy of enlightened intellectual leaders. This was an alarmingly elitist combination, even if it was only one side of Mill's politics. It was, however, much modified by an enthusiasm for local loyalties, gained from sources as diverse as de Tocqueville and Adam Ferguson. The saving virtue of de Tocqueville's America was the initiative and the vigor displayed in local self-government; and it was this that Mill hoped to retain for democracy in England. He was quick to argue that at a local level men could govern themselves in the most literal sense of the words; they could not only vote other people in, they stood a good

41. *Representative Government*, ch. 15, especially p. 286.

chance of holding office themselves.[42] In other words, the old Aristotelian criteria for citizenship could genuinely be fulfilled. And where they could be, they should be, since self-government was its own best preparation. The educative effects of this kind of citizenship were much emphasized by Mill; and his arguments are increasingly repeated by people working in exactly this sphere. Welfare workers, poverty programme leaders, community project advisers tend to accept increasingly that only where the poor and unorganized take an active part in the management of their own rehabilitation is the programme really effective. And equally true to Mill's anxieties are the accountants and the administrators who fear they will have no books to balance and no account to give. But at the very worst Mill's argument is no worse than the belief that a child who is taught to play a musical instrument will almost certainly not be a musical prodigy but may still grow up with a greater appreciation and enjoyment of music. Equally, the average voter may be quite unlikely ever to become a national figure; but he will be better able than at present to make rational and considered judgments about what the national figures do. There is nothing peculiar to Mill about the claim that local politics and local concerns can most readily offer the chance of sustained popular participation; as a long-standing pluralist position it is to be found in Jefferson as well as Montesquieu; and as the example of Rousseau indicates, it is not a prerogative of the pluralists to hold the belief. Yet it is in the end an argument resting on beliefs about what will satisfy people that can only with some difficulty be made to look remotely utilitarian.

Along these dimensions, then, *Representative Government* emerges as a critique of the older Mill's essay. Where the political search leads James Mill to a political order

42. Ibid., pp. 286–87.

which will maximize utility by harmonizing the strivings of rational egoists without any great call on their political virtue, it leads his son to the advocacy of measures that will keep society on the move both intellectually and emotionally, that will strengthen society as a community of evolving individuals. For James Mill the dispensability of political life— for example the establishment in its place of a permanent but honest bureaucracy—is both logically and morally a possible undertaking; in his view satisfaction is essentially something inner and private, a sensation of pleasure that is causally linked with the events in the outside world. There is no hint that the source of pleasure matters for any other than causal reasons, that is, for reasons connected with how much pleasure it will give, and how certain it is to give it. All that the theory allows room for is questions of efficiency—the goal is that our pleasures be many and our pains be few. There is here no room for those criteria which J. S. Mill was later to call the aesthetic criteria of appraisal, which he regarded as being ultimately the most important.[43] The politics of James Mill is the politics of the consumer, not the politics of the agent, no matter how activist he himself was. Politics is dispensable, because politics is a means to an end, in principle replaceable by a more efficient means if one should be found. For the younger Mill, things could hardly be more different. He was always desperately hampered by the atomistic psychology inherited from Bentham and before him Locke; but he was so sure of the facts to be explained that he was ready to allow confusion to overtake the theory rather than to deny the undeniable. And the crucial fact was that pleasures differed in kind as well as in quantity; the kind of pleasure is determined by the source from which it comes, so that more pleasure taken in a less worthy object cannot begin to count against less pleasure taken in a more worthy ob-

43. *Essays on Politics and Culture*, p. 116, cf. *System of Logic*, **Bk. VI**, ch. 12, sec. 6.

ject.[44] The highest pleasures, therefore, are those that are taken by the best kind of person; and such a person takes pleasure in the worthiest objects. And for Mill, the best kind of man is one who is rational, active, open-minded, socially engaged. It is a commonplace how uneasily Mill's moral views repose upon their psychological base; more interesting than that commonplace is to elucidate what it is that he incorporates so uneasily. And in essence, the things he brings in are elements in a political life whose merits are more at home in the universe of a mid-nineteenth century Aristotle than a middle-class philosophical radical. And even where the two Mills agree in their views, this agreement is often illusory. Thus, they seem almost equally inegalitarian in their view of the working class; but where the older Mill thinks that the working class will be indefinitely willing to take its cue from the middle class, much as he thought that India would indefinitely be content to be administered by an English company, the younger Mill does not agree. Moreover, although he was alarmed about the effects of class-dominated government and anticipated all sorts of foolishness from an uneducated democracy. John Stuart Mill did not in the end want to see middle class tutelage continue for ever, just as he was willing to see India outgrow English government. For in the last resort, the desire to make one's own decisions, to be one's own master, is constitutive of a peculiarly human excellence, and in its absence life would be flat and worthless. There are, of course, many other areas into which such a comparison eventually leads us; among those most urgently in need of some exploration are those which cluster round J. S. Mill's slow but steady evolution towards an individual kind of liberal socialism.

IV

Finally, there is a last word to be said about the importance of the contrast which this paper has been concerned

44. Cf. the agonised discussion in *Utilitarianism*, ch. 2.

with. It is not only a question of trying to become clearer about where the two Mills stand in the history of democratic thought—interesting though this would be at the level of intellectual history alone. It is rather that behind our more down-to-earth thoughts about politics there stand larger preoccupations, which are both historically more stable than many of our factual beliefs and less amenable to ready factual testing. It is thus that elucidating the ideas of James Mill and J. S. Mill can contribute to our present need to be self-conscious about the ideological preconceptions that we bring to the study of politics. And what, hesitantly, I want to suggest is that democratic theory in the past century and a half has operated, not within *an* ideological framework, but within two rather ill-fitting conceptual schemes. And this perhaps goes some way to explain why it is that political science hardly ever yields the conclusive answers that its practitioners hope for. If two conceptual schemes depict man as on the one hand a private being, a consumer who comes into the market for goods, whose behavior is to be understood in contractual and bargaining terms, and on the other hand as an agent, a being whose need is to make the world conform to plans he shares as a member of a community, then it is no wonder that we are still in difficulties about simple questions, such as whether we live in a democracy. Of course, we may dismiss such considerations as many political scientists do and take refuge in institutional definitions of one sort and another, stipulating that such things as the presence of more than one political party, the bloodless transfer of power, the unforced turnout of a certain number of voters, and the like cumulatively entitle us to call a state a democratic one. But this 'definitional stop' will only work for one move; it simply serves to raise the question of why we should choose these criteria as the important ones, what sort of relation they bear to the goal of self-government or whatever it may be. And at this point the problem appears all over again, for we shall surely have to explain why the existence of these institutions enables people—or impedes them—to have what they want more successfully. And this entails having something for which the shortest title is 'a view of political human nature.' And what this brief account of James and John Stuart Mill's ideas indicates is that we seem to have not *a* view of human nature, but two not obviously compatible views.[45]

45. Steven Lukes, to whom I am much indebted for comments on this paper, complains that this conclusion is disappointingly equivocal. He is quite right; it is equivocal; but it faithfully reflects the doubts I feel about the status and validity of the distinctions I have tried to draw. I must also thank Melvin Richter, Julian Franklin, Quentin Skinner, and Michael Freeman for their advice, their questions, and their encouragement.

A Passion for Politics: The Vital Core of the World of Machiavelli

MARTIN FLEISHER

IT APPEARS TO HAVE BEEN MACHIA-
velli's fate that he, even more than most other political
thinkers, has come in for an embarrassingly large number of
disparate interpretations. Statesmen, scholars, and plain propa-
gandists alike have more frequently made him a subject of
bitter contention than of sweet consensus. And yet in this year
in which we celebrate the five hundredth anniversary of his
birth, there is one observation about Machiavelli we may make
that seems indisputable—Machiavelli lives.[1] He lives today

1. As noted in the Introduction, this paper was originally delivered
at a conference celebrating the five hundredth anniversary of Machiavelli's birth. It is worth observing that for Machiavelli and his contemporaries, as for the ancients, a eulogy or panegyric delivered at some
public occasion took its most important purpose to be to inspire its

with a vitality that few other political thinkers can boast. More remarkably, he has enjoyed this vitality uninterruptedly since the sixteenth century. In contrast to Aristotle or Hobbes, Spinoza or Montesquieu, there has never been a need to revive him because he has never died. What more fitting tribute could there be to the greatness of the man for whom a crucial criterion of the greatness of states is their longevity? If he is not exactly immortal, Machiavelli can claim a continuous life approaching that of his beloved Roman Republic—what greater glory can one ask for?

Any attempt to come to grips with Machiavelli's thought would do well to give proper weight to the phenomenon of his vitality. Clearly it would be simplistic to argue that this vitality is due solely to our hero's *virtù*. We know better in part because Machiavelli knew better. His concern with the problem of the relation between individual ability and the politico-historical situation has passed into the mainstream of Western thought to become a perennial topic of inquiry and speculation. If he did not believe that the combination of will and ingenuity could carry all before them, nevertheless he carefully distinguished himself from his friend and fellow Florentine Guicciardini, for whom, in the face of the infinite variety and weight of circumstances, it was impossible for human intelligence and human energy to make any consistent headway. In the last analysis, Guicciardini sees man as a helpless hostage of fortune overwhelmed by times and events. Machiavelli will have no part of his compatriot's historical fatalism: there is no question but that human action can be efficacious. He becomes preoccupied with the study of modes of action and their relation to different situations precisely in order to clarify further the role of *virtù* in human destiny.

---

hearers to emulation and imitation of worthy forebears. If we honor the dead, not in the letter but in the spirit and deed, our lives are quickened as theirs were.

If we were to take our clue from Machiavelli and seek the explanation for his longevity in the nature of his *virtù* and its relation to changing times, the result, in barest outline, might appear as follows. In the seventeenth century Machiavelli enjoyed his greatest influence among thinkers of republican persuasion like Harrington, Spinoza, Neville, and Sidney. They prized him for his insights into the dynamics of political life and for his celebration of civic culture; and, since they were generally men who advocated change, perhaps they prized him above all for his political activism— for his idea, that is, that a people who have not been corrupted beyond the point of no return can revitalize their political existence and regain control of their fate through acts of political intelligence and energy inspired by bold leadership. In eighteeth-century France the antimonarchical and anticourt proponents of a life of vigorous participation in civic life, like Montesquieu and Rousseau, turned to Machiavelli as much for the congeniality of his spirit in this regard as for the usefulness of many of his specific ideas. Italy caught up with this Machiavelli in the nineteenth century when the fathers of modern Italian culture and of the modern Italian nation, men of the Risorgimento like De Sanctis, embraced him as the incarnation of the will to political unity and national greatness. And Italy has chosen to follow him into the twentieth century. Gramsci, *The New Prince,* explains why today it is the revolutionary party that possesses the political capacities of *virtù* and prudence in Machiavelli's sense and that embodies his mission of transforming the character of Italian life. What more imposing evidence do we need that Machiavelli lives and gives life to others, and is not simply embalmed in academia, than Gramsci's desire to assimilate Leninism to the great Florentine?

If we pause here, fully acknowledging that this is not even a bare outline, we may observe that the situations in which these political theorists have looked to Machiavelli inevitably involve a felt need for the formation and expression of the political will of the community. Despite the fact that he lived in and worked for one city-state while spending his leisure time pondering the fate of other city-states, Machiavelli has proven to be vitally relevant to those living in the era of the emergence and spread of the national-state system and the rich and tumultuous development of the internal political life of Western peoples, at least in part because of his insistence upon viewing the political life of a people as the highest expression of its culture.

I feel, however, that the causes of his longevity are also to be found at other levels. For example, as important as the fact that Machiavelli elevates political life to such heights—here he is far from being the first or the most important influence, Plato, Aristotle, and Cicero, among others, having gone before him—is the way in which he conceives of political life and, more generally, of man's life in the world. For, to put it plainly, in the world of Machiavelli politics is primary because, in essence, life is inescapably and excitingly political. Machiavelli's passion for life and his passion for politics are one. His longevity owes at least as much to his particular *virtù,* to the dramatic expression of vital insights into this life, including his idea of *virtù* itself, as to his fortune, the situations in which his writings were encountered by others. This paper is concerned with some aspects of Machiavelli's *virtù,* namely, his idea of the source and nature of human activity as well as the nature of his own vitality. Let this be emphasized. There is no pretense of a rounded treatment. The relation of Machiavelli's psychology to his ideas on the structure of history and political entities is certainly a fit and impotant subject for inquiry but it is only of peripheral interest here.

The focus, then, is on but one phase of the thought of Machiavelli—his psychology. And the aim is to elucidate that psychology by the simple method of a detailed study and analysis of Machiavelli's actual usage of certain key terms and the order of their relation to each other.

1. ANIMO

The word Machiavelli employs most frequently to denote the center of man from whence emanates his actions is *animo*. There is no reason why we cannot loosely translate this as "soul," taking care not to read into it classical or Christian meanings and metaphysical concerns when these are not present. Thus it is obvious that speculation on being and related problems is not one of Machiavelli's burning interests. In his general disdain for speculative knowledge and his skepticism as to the existence of a speculative faculty of mind Machiavelli reflects a fairly widespread sixteenth-century attitude. When he served the city of Florence he was occupied with the intimate affairs of state and when he went into involuntary retirement he did not seek repose in a retreat to arcadian nature or elevated literary or philosophical culture. Instead, he chose to remain close to these same political concerns. If he now contemplated other times and other places, he did so not in order to rise above politics in an act of philosophical or religious levitation or to locate human culture elsewhere than in political life and turn his back on it all as vanity of vanities. Instead, he turned to the past for the practical political purposes of working out the guidelines to action and inspiring his contemporaries to undertake the necessary political acts. He also wrote in the hope that his writings would catapult him back onto the political stage he dearly loved and poignantly missed. How different from Cicero who, in those periods of forced retreat from Roman politics, ostentatiously sought consolation in the cultivation of philosophy and other artifacts of Hellenic culture. How immensely different from Plato whose gaze could never rest for long on restless mundane matters but irresistibly rose to contemplate a harmonious cosmos beyond earthly polity and visible stars. Even among Machiavelli's compatriots, Florentines of civic humanist persuasion like Salutati and Bruni, one gets the impression that political life does not provide the altogether proper and fully adequate environment for the soul. What a striking contrast Machiavelli affords to all this: for him politics is the very life of the soul. It is the grand love that rules him sometimes to the very point of tyranny but that, nevertheless, he does not seek to escape. In truth it is not merely a question of a personal predilection. Machiavelli may himself not desire an exit from politics, but what is crucial is that his notion of the world of man provides no exit for anyone.

It should come as no surprise, therefore, to find that the soul, Machiavelli's *animo,* as it emerges from his writings is through and through political in nature. What exactly this means calls for explanation.

If we relieve the soul of much of its interiority and of some of its acquired Hellenic features, particularly the aspiration to harmony, we begin to approximate to Machiavelli's usage. As the source of motion, the spring of life, *animo* lacks the architectonic structure and balance of the Platonic or classical psyche. It is not so clearly distinguished into parts, nor are these so easily recognized as elements of a harmonious and unified whole. Its characteristic qualities are not balance and harmony, autonomy and peace. As the mover it is certainly not itself in unmoved repose. It is, rather, in continual motion. And this motion is not uniform; it does not partake of the divine. Instead, like all earthly motion, it is irregular and variable. In such a soul reason does not reign. The proper functioning and fulfillment of the soul are not dependent on the highest faculty of the soul, reason, properly arranging the other faculties (Plato), or totally dominating them (Stoics—more accurately, the rational soul dominating the body), or the faculties having their natural place and limit which they are capable of recognizing (Epicureans).

Machiavelli characterizes the motion of the soul in many ways that reveal its (anticlassical) nature to us. For instance, a prince should win friendship with "grandezza e nobiltà d'animo" (p. 70) and inspire "li animi de' sua cittadini" (p. 50).[2] Machiavelli calls on the Medici to redeem Italy from the barbarians "con quello animo" (p. 105), which is appropriate to such just causes. Savonarola is praised for "la dottrina, la prudenza e la virtú dello animo suo" (p. 233). And his *animo* is also described as "ambizioso e partigiano" (p. 234). In addition to being ambitious and partisan, *animo* can be strong (p. 397), inflamed (p. 359) or cooled off (p. 261), disposed to rebellion (p. 389) or obstinately bent on revenge (p. 392). It can be restless (p. 257), malignant (p. 135) and false (p. 230) but also free (p. 203) and possessed of greatness (p. 102) and *virtù* (p. 31, 41, and passim —the relation of *virtù* to *animo* will be discussed below).

When Machiavelli uses the term *animo* as an adjective it conveys the notions of vitality and boldness, action and force, even more strongly. One man is "feroce et animoso" in contrast to another who is "effeminato e pusillanime" (p. 65). A particularly active and vigorous pope, Sixtus IV, becomes "uno papa animoso" (p. 51) and a capable prince is described as "potente et animoso" (p. 50). As one would expect the full force of *animo* as a source of vitality emerges in its use as a verb. Thus a most important effect of the Roman religion for Machiavelli, one that mightily helped to make Rome great, was its ability to "animire la Plebe" (p. 161).

2. All references to Machiavelli's works are to the Feltrinelli edition, Niccolò Machiavelli, *Opere* (Milan, 1960–65). Unless otherwise indicated, they refer to Volume 1, 1960. Translations (occasionally altered) are from L. J. Walker, tr., *The Discourses of Niccolò Machiavelli* (London, 1950), Machiavelli, *The Prince,* tr. George Bull (Baltimore, 1961), and Allan Gilbert, tr., *The Letters of Machiavelli* (New York, 1961). Page references are given only for the Italian.

The soul, then, is the source of animation, of movement
and action. But, as we have observed, unlike the classical
soul it neither moves and determines itself according to fixed
principles nor is it moved and determined by some unmoved
mover or world order. Platonic *eros* and Stoic *logos* as inspiring, animating, or ordering principles are gone.

In one of its basic meanings, the term denotes sheer spiritedness. Thus soldiers long for leaders of martial spirit ("d'
animo militare," p. 79—see, too, pp. 309 and 318). Agathocles the Sicilian behaved like a criminal and for his inhu-
manity Machiavelli denies him general *virtù* but to explain
his successes he refers to "tanta virtù d'animo e di corpo" (p.
41).

Now, what is this virtue of the soul? It would appear to
be the same as that of any other faculty or power: its own
particular excellence. Thus as *animo* or spirit it has *virtù*
when it is fully itself and it is most fully itself performing
politico-military deeds. This interpretation is further supported by Machiavelli when he speaks of wasting the "virtù
dello animo" (p. 31). We shall see that *animo* most fully
realizes itself in political greatness, but for now let us note
several things about *animo* as spiritedness. A horse or a man
may be *animoso* and have "tanta virtù d'animo" and yet kill
for no cause or in other ways behave badly. On the other
hand the implication is that a horse with little spirit is not
much good as a horse, and, similarly, a man without *virtù
d'animo* is not much good as a man.

The question thus becomes: if someone is not much good
as a man, can he be a good man? While Machiavelli may not
be prepared to abandon certain criteria of what is good, virtuous, or human [3] even if these cannot be completely derived

3. There is, I believe, a tendency by H. Baron, F. Gilbert, R. Ridolfi,
and others so to stress the "humanist" in Machiavelli as to turn him into
more and more of a "moralist" by overplaying just these elements at
the expense of the role of *animo, appetito, ambizione,* and similar
notions.

from his root concepts of *animo, virtù, grandezza, gloria,* etc., it is equally true that the measure of *umanità* can never be less than these. This is crucial to the understanding of the concept of *animo:* the soul is properly dominated by the qualities of spiritedness, courage, action. These are its virtues, the virtues of man. A cowardly soul is no soul. When Machiavelli wants to talk of resolve or courage he uses the term *animo* itself (pp. 195, 316, 403, 404, etc.). And if *vile* is used to mean "timid," *animoso* is employed to indicate resoluteness and spirit (p. 329). To strengthen the courage of an army is to "fermare gli animi" (p. 490). When cowardice enters the soul it is not merely corrupted but entirely lost (p. 472). Thus, men who are men act the man in good and bad fortune ("tengono sempre lo animo fermo," p. 469). And there is nothing like military discipline for developing the guts and stamina to stand up to the vicissitudes of life. Significantly, when Machiavelli does take up the topics of equanimity and dignity, those favorites of classical psychology, it is not primarily to hold them up as ideals but mainly to stress the virtue of military training in achieving them (*Discourses,* III.31).

Now, while there may have been differences as to exactly what were the proper relations and proportions needed to attain equanimity, as well as the discipline by which it was actually to be realized, the classical world (Platonic, Stoic, Epicurean) agreed with surprising unanimity to the existence of the soul as the center of man's being, to the integrity or unity of human faculties, and to the ideal of the properly balanced and poised soul sustaining and guiding itself under the tutelage of reason. The West took over this group of propositions as dominant ideals of its culture. From it came the ideals of the dignity of man and the supreme value of self-determination. It conditioned and helped determine the Western canon of human virtues. For reasons that are already obvious and for others that will be elaborated below, the soul of Machiavellian man cannot be a center of peace, harmony, or self-control. Without considering whether they are desirable or not, equanimity and integrity are beyond man's grasp. Thus the *virtù* of *animo* that Machiavelli celebrates is magnanimity, not equanimity—greatness (with its reference to an external standard), not balance (with its reference to some inner criterion). And on those rare occasions when Machiavelli invokes equanimity its meaning is shifted from a moral to a politico-military virtue. In this connection we may note in the reference above that the equanimity to be maintained is the equanimity of the soldier —persistent courage and no braggadocio. Such discipline and not stoic self-control is a major bulwark against luxury, idleness, softness and the pusillanimity that lie in wait to rob the *animo* of its fibre and manhood and turn it into an *animo effeminato,* than which there is no lower hell into which the *animo* can sink for Machiavelli.

This discussion should add another dimension to the importance Machiavelli attaches to military training and a militia. His hostility to mercenaries lies deeper than the fact that they are unreliable; contrariwise his championing of a militia rests on more than their dependability. Involved is a concept of the best education for the man and the citizen—for a republican the two cannot be separated. Such an education must have military training as its basis since it is the discipline that properly conditions the *animo.* In passing it is worth noting that for Machiavelli the quarrels between scholastics and humanists, dialecticians and rhetoricians, and questions of quadrivium and trivium—the major educational disputes and problems as formulated by his contemporaries—are mostly beside the point. Military training, the masculine life par excellence, is the only adequate preparation for life.

The multiplication of examples should serve to demonstrate this central feature of *animo* and its relation to the evaluation of men. *Animo* as courage or manliness is a value for Machiavelli, but, as suggested, it is not the sole criterion of good actions. Indeed, one criterion cannot be found in the soul. The measure of man in part lies outside man, but not, as we have already observed, in the rational cosmos of the Stoic or in some supernatural realm. The break with dominant Greco-Roman and Christian ethical systems is epitomized in the importance and particular role assigned to *i tempi, l'occasione,* etc. Circumstances and consequences of actions play a part in their evaluation. Effectiveness is of overriding concern, hence, the actions of men are to be judged by their results (p. 74). It follows that a prince, or for that matter a republic, should possess "a flexible *animo,* varying as fortune and circumstances dictate" ("uno animo disposto a volgersi secondo ch' e' venti e le variazioni della fortuna li comandono," pp. 73–74).

It can now be seen that Machiavelli's significance for the history of the problem of value consists not in the substitution of one set of values for another but rather in the introduction of different criteria of value. The *animo* continually and changeably desires or values things. It is truly vital— the genuine source of human values. And what it desires or values most is the ability to command any desire or bestow any value it wishes. Viewed from this perspective value is entirely a subjective matter. But the actual ability to command value is a function of social circumstances as well as of desire. This is the objective moment in the realization of value: the command of objects of desire that constitutes the supreme value—*the power to designate and appropriate values*—is a function of the social, more particularly the political order. (For Machiavelli, political power, not money, is the primary source of such command.) And the successes and failures of such orders can be observed and judged. Of course, in the last analysis, what the *animo* craves is the recognition of this greatness. Once again, the only fit arena for it to display itself is politics, for all other forms of greatness (artistic, philosophical, etc.) are ultimately determined by political greatness.

2. AMBIZIONE

The other feature of the *animo* which is of interest is its content—its relation to motives, desires, passions. The terms most often used by Machiavelli to describe or account for human action, be it in the context of the family or the city, are *desiderio, voglia, appetito, ambizione, umore, passione.* At first glance the realization that these terms are not used at all times in a strictly fixed and constant manner would seem to make it difficult to establish their meaning and relation to each other and to *animo* with any degree of precision. And when it is discovered that Machiavelli occasionally uses some of these terms interchangeably, the situation would appear to be totally out of hand. But on closer scrutiny it turns out that the barriers to understanding are not that great. If the meanings are not fixed they do cluster around common centers and the interchanging of words emphasizes the need to focus on and get at the root phenomena: a shift in words does not always signal the designation of different phenomena.

The use of *ambizione* as a word to describe the conduct of individuals and groups is a favorite with Machiavelli.[4] To judge by the frequency of its appearance in some of the most important of Machiavelli's general observations, it is not merely a question of a verbal mannerism but of something that is fundamental to his thought. Thus Machiavelli envisages ambition, by its very nature overreaching and overweening, to be a major threat to the order of a republic (p. 236, repeated on pp. 246–47). Men go from one ambition to another (p. 236), from wanting to protect their liberty to the desire to dominate others. Machiavelli devotes

4. I have counted over one hundred occurrences of the word in *The Prince* and the *Discourses.*

an entire discourse (*Discourse,* I. 46) to the need for external limits to men's ambitions. It is in the very nature of *ambizione* not to be self-delimiting, and it is in the nature of man to be ambitious ("la natura degli uomini è ambiziosa e sospettosa," p. 198). Its very universality makes the denial of ambition incredible. Machiavelli frequently appeals to ambition to explain the main danger to the order and longevity of republics (see, e.g., pp. 148, 151–52, 153). It is also held to be a chief cause of wars, domestic and foreign (wars result "per ambizione de' principi o delle republiche che cercano di propagare lo imperio," p. 297). Jealousy is related to ambition. And hatred, the hatred of one state for another, is engendered by the ambition to dominate (p. 426).

From what has preceded it is apparent that Machiavelli uses *ambizione* to describe the actions of states and classes as well as individuals. In analyzing the Roman Republic to discern the sources of its longevity and greatness Machiavelli discovers these to lie in the laws that constrain, among other things, ambition and the ambitious. Every republic has its *grandi* and its *popolari* (p. 139—at other places Machiavelli talks of *potenti* or *nobili* instead of *grandi*) and the distinguishing mark of the former is its *ambizione* (pp. 207, 218, etc.). The *animo* of the nobility is *ambizioso* whereas the souls of the populace are described as *animi inquieti* (p. 139). This is not to be taken to mean that the people are not ambitious; ambition is simply more intensely characteristic of the *grandi.* Moreover, the ambition of the nobility tends to be a greater threat to the liberty of a republic than that of the people. The desire of the *grandi,* who seek glory, is to dominate, while the desire of the people who are concerned with security is to avoid being dominated (p. 139).

It is not desirable, even if it were possible, to suppress the ambitions and appetites of either class because without the *animo* of the *grandi,* which in its full ambition thirsts for

126

glory, there would be no chance of achieving greatness for the republic in its encounters with other states, while, in the absence of the vitality of the populace, there would be an inadequate supply of the vigorous arms equally necessary for such long-lived greatness. Besides, since the ambitions of each class are necessary to sustain a people both internally and externally and since these ambitions are by nature infinitely expandable, the only check on the appetites of one class are the appetites of the other. Machiavelli does not entertain the possibility of a tertium quid, a permanent third order which can mediate between the other two or stand above them and impose itself upon them. In this sense order is immanent and not transcendent—it is delimited by the interplay and conflict of forces and may be thought of as a tension rather than a stasis or harmony. Machiavelli, as we well know, directly attributes the achievement and preservation of Roman order and liberty to the clash of popular *inquieti* and noble *ambizione*.

Because of the dynamic nature of ambition no order or tension can be permanent. Besides, matter is never informed once and for all; there is recurrent need for reformation and revitalization. The lawgiver's role does not necessarily vanish with the founding of a political order. New provisions must be made to meet new situations. For example, to curb further the ambitions of the Roman *grandi* Machiavelli sees a need for and justifies the institution of the tribunes. Such tribunes must be given power to do an effective job. But this sets up the further problem of means to curb the ambitions of the tribunes, and so on, and so on (pp. 423, 425). There will always be a need for politics, for different ways and means.

Ambition, then is ubiquitous; it is also very powerful. The principal cause of war, it dominates the individual or republic under its sway. It can have a blinding effect on a person, depriving him of judgment and prudence: "Yet so great is man's ambition that, in striving to slake his present desire, he gives no thought to the evils that in a short time will follow in its wake" (p. 339). Character (*ingegno*), nature (*natura*), and upbringing notwithstanding, men change and it is *ambizione* and *appetito* that bring about these changes (pp. 230–31).

It is hoped that the above instances convey a concrete sense of Machiavelli's usage of the term *ambizione*. It is now time to draw together all this material prior to moving on to a consideration of other terms crucial to an understanding of Machiavelli's description of the human condition. It should be clear that for Machiavelli ambition is a motive which cannot be limited by reason but only by some other force. The limits are all external to the individual. Once this fact is recognized the fictitious nature of the classical soul stands exposed for all to see. The classical sage never existed either, because it is not in man's nature to achieve that kind of tranquillity, inner repose, and indifference to outer events and social circumstances. It would have been incomprehensible to the Stoic or Epicurean to describe one and the same man as wise *and* restless. For them, and for most of us, the terms are mutually exclusive, yet the description flows easily from Machiavelli's pen (p. 224).[5]

The importance of ambition and its role in Machiavelli's thought can be gathered in summary fashion from the following paragraph with which he opens one of his discourses:

> Ancient writers were of opinion that men are wont to get annoyed with adversity and fed up with prosperity, both of which passions give rise to the same effects. For, whenever there is no need for men to fight, they fight for ambition's sake; and so powerful is the sway that

5. Machiavelli's translators have more difficulty with it than does Machiavelli. The Italian is "sagace ed inquieto," yet despite the "ed" Walker cannot bring himself to translate it as "and"; he uses "but" instead.

ambition exercises over the human heart that they never relinquish it, no matter how high they have risen. The reason is that nature has so constituted men that, though all things are objects of desire, not all things are attainable; so that desire always exceeds the power of attainment, with the result that men are ill content with what they possess and their present state brings them little satisfaction. Hence arise the vicissitudes of their fortune (*il variare della fortuna*). For, since some desire to have more and others are afraid to lose what they have already acquired, enmities and wars are begotten, and this brings about the ruin of one province and the exaltation of its rival. (Pp. 215–16.)

Ambition is clearly related to desire. If one wants, it is the desire for the means to satisfy all desires, but more importantly, it is the desire for others to acknowledge one's superiority. We have seen that both Stoic and Epicurean conceive of natural desires as limited: they can be satisfied. Therefore, there is no objective source of conflict in the world. Concord is rooted in the true nature of things. Machiavelli holds that desire is ultimately insatiable. The fact that man cannot acquire everything he desires, especially glory, is the source of both human discontent and ambition. The human condition, then, is one of: 1) discontent; 2) desire for the means to satisfy desires; 3) domination of *animo* by these powerful desires and not by reason; 4) competition or conflict with others for these means; 5) scarcity and not abundance by virtue of the nature of human desire.

The rejection of the classical notion of scarcity as being due simply to subjective error and hence corrigible by proper education and discipline marks another of Machiavelli's sharp breaks with ancient traditions (Platonic, Aristotelian, Stoic, and Epicurean) actively being revived in his own day. Scarcity is now accorded ontological status—it is a constitutive element of Machiavelli's world. Man's relation to the world of objects of his desires is never simply a matter of his own capacities delimiting and appropriating their proper objects. First, indeed, because he does lack the internal measure of good and adequate objects, or, to put it another way, such objects delimited by mind or common senses in which one can find true and permanent satisfaction do not exist for Machiavelli. Second, and more crucially because man's relation to the objects of his desire is always mediated by other men and their desires. Since these others are not necessarily the willing or docile means to the realization of our own desires there is no basis for the classical idea of social order as natural and/or harmonious. Hence, Machiavelli's preoccupation with the problem of how order is established, secured, maintained, and perpetuated—hence, that is, Machiavelli's preoccupation with politics.

The point is worth making twice. Let us look at it from a slightly altered perspective. Since the scarcity of objects is the result of the nature of appetite and passion, and not the other way around, competition or conflict between men is natural and inevitable. And it is precisely in this sense that men are political animals; men find themselves in a situation where they must concern themselves with each other as *means* to their satisfaction and, therefore, they are concerned with controlling these means or, what is the same thing, with politics and the domination of others.

They are concerned with others for yet another political reason. Since they desire glory—the definitive political ambition—and this requires public recognition of their *magnoanimo*, politics is their natural realm. Finally, politics is implied in still another way: the public recognition of greatness is itself a source of political power.

For the relation of ambition to appetite, desire, humor, passion, etc., it is necessary to return to the texts. In the

Discourses the Roman generals Manlius Torquatus and Valerius are praised for their services to the republic. Using different methods (*diversi modi*—p. 449), they were equal in *virtù* and *gloria* and equal in effectiveness. Machiavelli wants to know what accounts for the differences in method. He invites us to consider *la natura* of Manlius: his is "l'animo . . . forte" (p. 447). This "fortezza d'animo" accounts for his mode of conduct. Thus his orders are explained by the fact that "he was constrained first by his nature and then by his desire (*desiderio*) to see those orders carried out which his natural appetites (*il suo naturale appetito*) had prompted him to issue," (p. 450). Here *natura, animo,* and *appetito* are linked. Their relation to ambition can be seen in the following passage: "How easily men are corrupted and in nature become transformed, however good they may be and however well brought up" is illustrated by the case of Quintus Fabius who, "though an excellent fellow, was after a while blinded by a little ambition and . . . changed his good habits for bad," (p. 230). This recalls the similar transformation of Nicomaco in Machiavelli's *Clizia.* The lesson Machiavelli draws from this propensity is for legislators "to be all the more ready to restrain human appetites," (p. 231).

Here ambition and appetite are used synonymously, and if we look elsewhere in Machiavelli's writings we discover that this is not accidental: he attributes the same qualities to appetite as to ambition and says that both give rise to the same problems. For example, at one point Machiavelli speaks of the need to "frenare gli appetiti" (p. 231), to restrain the appetites, and at another he uses the phrase "freno all'ambizione" (p. 423). Recalling that he has described ambition as insatiable, changeable, basic to man, and capable of blinding judgment (p. 339), here is what he says of appetites: the world would look the same to man if his judgments and appetites were the same "but, as man's appetites change, even though their circumstances (*i tempi*) remain the same, it is impossible that things should look the same to them seeing that they have other appetites, other interests, other standpoints" (p. 273). Not only do appetites change like ambitions but they are also insatiable and similarly affect judgment, again for the same reasons (p. 273). If Machiavelli recognizes a fundamental class cleavage in every city along the line of different ambitions, he also talks of "due appetiti diversi" and "due umori diversi" (p. 45). And under Machiavelli's fine Italian hand appetite like ambition is politicized. The most relevant appetites for Machiavelli are not the hunger for food, the lust for women, nor the desire for wealth, but the longing for political security and the passion for political glory.

The relation and characteristics of desire are very close to ambition, appetite, and humor (see, e.g., pp. 140, 215, 274, 503), as is avarice, which Machiavelli frequently couples with or uses in place of ambition (p. 132). And from avarice or distrust Machiavelli derives ingratitude (p. 197). Again ingratitude is treated in terms of its public-political significance and consequences in contrast, for example, to the tendency in Roman Stoicism (from Cicero to Epictetus) to internalize it gradually so that it becomes a question of a private-moral vice and/or to drop it down in the list of vices. Machiavelli actually devotes four discourses to the topic of ingratitude, the burden of these being that ingratitude represents a real danger to the order of a republic or principate which can be effectively minimized if steps are taken to insure a more equitable distribution of the honors and goods of the society. Moral exhortation and demands for self-control are eschewed in favor of altering external arrangements to overcome what is now viewed as a political and not a moral problem.

Stopping short of offering a complete catalogue of human motives as found in the writings of Machiavelli, we may briefly note that envy frequently occurs in the company of ambition (pp. 342, 467) and that envy or fear are made the progenitors of still another powerful emotion, hatred (men hate "o per timore o per invidia," p. 271), which, in turn, can constitute a grave threat to the political order when it takes possession of the *animo* of a people.

3. INGEGNO, PRUDENZA, INGANNO

To round out this survey of human powers and motives it is necessary to turn to the nature and role of reason and intellect. As indicated above, Machiavelli has dethroned reason in the polity of the soul—it neither rules nor reigns, its function now is that of counsellor or advisor to ambition and appetite. Solely concerned with ways and means, it does not determine the ends of action. Machiavelli does not have a concept of moral reason; there is no room in his world for natural law. What he does recognize is the human power to discern and devise the most effective means for accomplishing one's ends. The terms he most frequently uses to designate this power are *ingegno, prudenza, inganno.*[6] These connote natural wit, ingenuity, intelligence, cunning, and similar notions.

Before proceeding to investigate these terms it may be well to dispose of a possible source of misunderstanding in connection with another term Machiavelli uses whose English cognate is reason, i.e., *ragione.* It is generally employed by him in the course of explaining something and refers to discursive reasoning. Used in this sense it is interchangeable with *cagione* (cause or motive) and is not relevant to our present discussion.

If, as Machiavelli firmly believes, we realize our ends in the world either through deception (*fraude*) or force

6. It may be useful to recall that *ingegno* and *inganno* are not etymologically related.

(*forza*), and the former usually counts for more than the latter, we can appreciate the role and importance of *inganno* in life. The power to plot and deceive is the power to obtain and secure the objects of one's desires. This ability is certainly an important weapon in the wars of desires competing for satisfactions. Scheming and planning, arranging matters so that the outcome will be satisfactory, are both necessary and natural to such a world. In addition to this idea of plot or scheme, Machiavelli's *inganno* contains the idea of deception. The two ideas are obviously not identical. In a world in which the means and modes of being successful are often in conflict with the official ethic, deception, as the masking of one's true intent and motive, becomes a necessary part of an effective and successful tactic. For every deceiver there must be the deceived, and Machiavelli finds there is no shortage of the latter (p. 73). Political power is a function of what people believe, whether true or not.[7] Belief, then, not knowledge is central to political behavior and hence the world of politics does not recognize the classical distinction between appearance and reality.

From Machiavelli's usage it can be seen that to be deceived is the same as to err in judgment. Judgment may be mistaken when it bases itself on superficial acquaintance. "Men in general judge by their eyes rather than by their hands; because everyone is in a position to watch, few are in a position to come in close touch with you. Everyone sees what you appear to be, few experience what you really are" (p. 74).[8] The voice of the diplomat and political insider is clearly detectable in this passage. Familiarity to the point of tactile acquaintance with the actors in the political sphere does not necessarily breed contempt, but it does allow you to feel if

7. See, e.g., Ch. 18 of *The Prince*. The same treatment of *inganno* is to be found in the *Discourses*.

8. This theme is not restricted to *The Prince*. It is taken up in the *Discourses*, D.I.47 being devoted to it.

they are clothed or naked. The aura that majesty casts vanishes at such close range and along with it vanish all other political arcana. But since so few, if any, can get that close, in politics appearances are all important while what you really are counts for little. Appearances, then, constitute the reality of politics.

Now, the very fact that judgment can be in error, unless determined after close scrutiny and familiarity, provides one basis for the use of deception: it is the conscious exploitation of this particular fallibility of judgment. It is not easy to distinguish a person's true motives from his professed motives. Moreover our own desires and the prevailing ethic are further potential sources of erring judgment. But Machiavelli lets drop a hint that judgment may not be all that faulty. Over and above the fact that in matters close to home people are not deceived, people base their judgment upon results (p. 74). There is the implication that this standard, basing judgment on real consequences rather than apparent intentions, is not only widespread in practice but may be a more fitting way to conduct judgment than the accepted standard.

Judgment is also misled by the application of those general principles or ideals, which comprise the dominant ethic, to individual cases because they set up presuppositions about human behavior which do not necessarily conform to actual conduct. Machiavelli cites the case of a people deceived by acts seemingly done out of goodwill, honesty, and generosity, but, in fact, completely motivated by ambition (p. 236). People are deceived because they are trusting and not suspicious. They take professed motives and intents at their face value. The disparity between the ideals of the civilization and the practices necessary to survive is a principal source of self-deception and deception of others. Machiavelli indicts ideality in the name of a reality he discovers and exposes in the actual world. The discovery necessarily involves working with an ethic and a psychology that depart from official doctrine.

An example of one such transvaluation of Western values is given in Machiavelli's questioning the bona fides of good faith to which the defense of *inganno* is related. If the human world is so constituted that you cannot put your faith in faith, but you do so anyway, you have erred in your judgment, and the root of the error is not the world but the ideals. Rid yourself of these illusions. For it is they, Machiavelli would seem to be saying, and not the passions and appetites, that belong to that world to which the ancients, with Plato in the lead, attributed the ontological status of mere "appearance." Thus, certain values and institutions are weakening Italy. If Italy is to be revived and renewed and Italian civilization saved from the French, Spanish, and German barbarians, the Italian *animo* must be purged of these debilitating elements. Italians can learn from the despised enemy Ferdinand of Aragon, who "never preaches anything except peace and good faith" but "is an enemy of both one and the other, and if he had ever honoured either of them he would have lost either his standing or his state many times" (p. 74). Here, then, is an example of the rejection of good faith as a basis for political relations in favor of the skillful use of *inganno*. So much for *fraude*. Parenthetically, we may observe that with respect to *forza* Machiavelli too wants the Italians to learn from the barbarian enemy; the example of the Germans and Swiss who take military training and discipline seriously, and, more particularly, the example of the latter who rely on their own militia are recommended for Italian emulation.

For ancient examples of the absolute need for the use of *fraude* and *inganno*—here and elsewhere, the two are used interchangeably (e.g., on p. 181 "o fraude o forze" becomes "ingannato o sforzato")—Machiavelli turns to the actions of the Persians and the Romans:

Xenophon, in his life of Cyrus, calls attention to the need for deceit (*ingannare*). For in view of the amount of fraud (*fraude*) used in the first expedition Cyrus made against the King of Armenia, and of the fact that it was by means of deceit (*inganno*), not by means of force (*forza*), that he acquired his kingdom, one cannot but conclude from such actions that a prince who wishes to do great things must learn to practice deceit (*è necessario imparare a ingannare*, pp. 311–12).

And this holds for republics as well as for princes:

Since in all her decisions, whether by chance or by choice, Rome took all steps necessary to make herself great, she did not overlook fraud (p. 312).[9]

Rome, of course, prided herself on her *fede*, Machiavelli to the contrary notwithstanding. Her historians, including Livy, praised her for civic faith while contending that it was not only morally laudable but also politically expedient. In their eyes it was a principal contributor to Rome's rise to greatness. In the light of Livy's verdict Machiavelli's decision to emphasize the role of *fraude* in Roman greatness is all the more significant.

It may not be possible always to make one's way by wits alone, but the witless like Messer Nicia in Machiavelli's *Mandragola* are lost from the beginning.

The term *ingegno* is employed by Machiavelli to designate wit of a high order. While it is not to be confused with *inganno*, *ingegno* sometimes occurs in contexts where it is obviously very close in meaning to *inganno*. To cite one example: in *The Prince*, Machiavelli offers the career of Oliverotto da Fermo as an instance of a man rising to power

9. For other instances of Machiavelli's position see D.II.13. The entire discourse is given over to the discussion of whether the rise to great heights of fortune is promoted more by *fraude* or *forza*.

through wit rather than through force (*per essere ingegnoso,* p. 42). In the *Discourses* (II. 13) Machiavelli takes up the same topic in a more general context. Its message is that "men rise from a low to a great position by means rather of fraud than of force." Here the terms used are *fraude* and *inganno* (pp. 311–12), but the conclusion is the same. There is one place in *The Prince* where the familiar construction "o fraude o forza," "o inganno o forza" actually gives way to "o . . . industria o . . . forza" (p. 25). This startling employment of the good old sober Roman moral virtue of *industria* as a synonym for *fraude, inganno,* and *ingegno* may stand as a measure of Machiavelli's departure from the moralizing propensities of Cicero and of the Roman Stoicism of Seneca and Epictetus.

Whether it be called *ingegno* or *inganno,* the quality of guile counts for more than *forza* in achieving the political heights. However, Machiavelli does seem to reserve *ingegno* for situations which stress the need for outstanding ability. In talking of the difficulty of maintaining one's political power Machiavelli makes the point that under particularly trying circumstances a prince must be a "uomo di grande ingegno e virtù" (p. 34). And in the famous exhortation to liberate Italy with which Machiavelli ends *The Prince* he calls attention to the superiority of the Italians, saying that all they lack is a capable leader: "li Italiani sieno superiori con le forze, con la destrezza, con lo ingegno" ("The Italians are superior in strength, in skill, in inventiveness" p. 103).

Render *ingegno* as wits, ingenuity, or cunning, Machiavelli does not use the term in a pejorative sense. It refers to the ability to devise, contrive, or arrange things so that the desired goal is reached. It has some of the meaning which makes it the etymological relative of "engineer." It focuses on technical ability as sheer technical ability, free of moral overtones. And this ability is not disdained. Thus, if Machiavelli's own work is found wanting, he confesses, with rhetorical modesty, in his introductory remarks to the *Discourses,* that it is due to his own "ingegno povero" (p. 123). In the dedicatory introduction on the previous page Machiavelli talked of "povertà dello ingegno." Clearly, *ingegno* is an important human capacity. Its value is not to be underestimated in a human world whose stuff and material are passions and appetites that depend upon human skills to order things so as to realize their aims if man is not to be the mere plaything of fortune or of others.

Prudence, *prudenza,* the last of the three terms relative to reason, retains, in Machiavelli's writings, its traditional meaning of practical reason, the guide of everyday conduct and action. Since Machiavelli does not recognize a faculty of theoretical reason, there is no power of reason superior to *prudenza.* Even if prudence means for Machiavelli what it means for Cicero, we should expect a change in its content and measure, or what amounts to the same thing, the demoralization of the term. "A prudent ruler cannot, and should not, honor his word when it places him at a disadvantage and when the reasons for which he made his promise no longer exist" (pp. 72–73). The contrast with Giovanni Botero's definition of political prudence underlines the same point. As to the policy of the ruler, Botero tells us: "First he must make a reputation for prudence rather than astuteness, prudence being a virtue whose function is to seek and to find convenient means to bring about a given end. Astuteness has the same object, but differs from prudence in this: in the choice of means, prudence follows what is honest rather than what is useful, astuteness takes nothing into account but interest." [10]

In common with *inganno* and *ingegno,* Machiavelli's *prudenza* is rooted in his conception of the human world. Prudence is not to be measured principally by the existing

10. Giovanni Botero, *The Reason of State,* tr. P. J. and D. P. Waley (New Haven, 1956), p. 49.

standards of right and wrong but by the requirements of the situation, by necessity, and by the assessment of the best means to achieve one's ends. Prudence is not synonymous with caution, nor is it the dominance of reason over the appetites and passions. It is, instead, the cool calculation of what must be done in a given situation to accomplish one's purposes without judgment of the situation being unduly affected by passions or the contemporary conventions and ideals of right and wrong. This must not be taken to imply that prudence controls the passions; rather, it serves them, but the better to serve them, it must be free properly to gauge the situation.

One of the best explications of this meaning of prudence is to be found in Machiavelli's correspondence. Interestingly, the definition is not Machiavelli's own; he is reporting what he heard Savonarola preach after being forced by papal and secular authorities to slow his attack upon the city of Florence. Savonarola explains and justifies this retreat under pressure as prudent. What is prudence? "Prudentia est recta cognitio agibilium." And what is the measure of straight thinking in practical matters? Machiavelli reports Savonarola as saying that men have always had and have a goal in life, though these goals may differ. For the Christian the goal is Christ. Therefore, the Christian should serve God "con somma prudenzia e osservanzia de' tempi" (*Opere,* vol. 6, p. 31). And Savonarola goes on to explain that this means we are to vary our tactics according to the times—when it is time to risk one's life for God one does it, when it is time to conceal oneself one serves God by concealment (*Opere,* vol. 6, p. 31). Machiavelli observes that Savonarola himself has this valuable ability to change his tactics with the times. At another place, this time in the *Discourses,* Machiavelli refers to the fiery reformer as a man of prudence (p. 233).

Prudence, then, is the ability to adopt the course of action best suited to realize one's purpose. It is, before all else, a political talent. The reason prudence is not as common as might be supposed is to be found in the obstacles to the selection of right means. These would seem to include: 1) passions and appetites that can blind one to the actual situation; 2) conventional morality preventing one from discerning proper motives and tactics; 3) being set in one's ways or methods of acting. This last obstacle is a favorite of Machiavelli's—he comes back to it again and again. What it involves is simply the reluctance and extreme difficulty people have in changing their ways or *modi di procedere* especially when these have brought success in the past. It takes the highest prudence and *virtù* to be able to change one's ways to fit them to the requirements of new situations. There is no question that for Machiavelli this represents the consummation of the art of the statesman.

How highly Machiavelli prizes prudence and *virtù* can be seen from the role he allots to them in accomplishing what for him, in contrast to Savonarola, are the most important goals or ends of life: the proper ordering of a republic and the salvation of Italy. Book 1 of the *Discourses,* which is preoccupied with the problem of the best way to order and reorder public life, is full of admiration for those men who have succeeded in this work. One of the qualities most frequently attributed to them is prudence. Moses, Lycurgus, Solon, Romulus—they all knew what had to be done to order properly the *res publica,* and they boldly and vigorously did what was necessary to these ends.

> The prudent organizer of a state whose intention it is to govern not in his own interest but for the common good . . . should contrive to be alone in his authority. Nor will any reasonable man blame him for taking any action, however extraordinary, which may be of service in the organizing of a kingdom or the constituting of a republic. It is a sound maxim that reprehensible

actions may be justified by their effect, and that when the effect is good, as it was in the case of Romulus, it always justifies the action. For it is the man who uses violence to spoil things, not the man who uses it to mend them, that is blameworthy.

The organizer of a state ought further to have sufficient prudence and virtue not to bequeath the authority he has assumed to any other person . . . (pp. 153–54).

In the last chapter of *The Prince* where Machiavelli issues a passionate call for someone to save Italy, he specifies that the savior must be *prudente e virtuoso* (p. 101). In this context the meaning of both *prudenza* and *virtù* stand out: the prudent man will know what needs to be done to order public life properly and how to acquire the power to do the great work. He will have the *virtù* and the energy, resolution, manliness, and daring to carry it through. This is a man of *grandezza d'animo.*

In a letter to Piero Soderini, Machiavelli uses *prudenza* in the more conventional sense. He tells Soderini: "I see not in your mirror, which reflects nothing but prudence, but in the one used by most men—that one must look to the ends of things and not the means by which the ends are reached," (*Opere,* vol. 6, p. 229). We know from Machiavelli's writings, including the epitaph he composed for Soderini, that, in fact, Machiavelli was very critical of Soderini's "*prudenza,*" prudence in the more conventional sense, which Machiavelli held to be responsible for Soderini's downfall and the simultaneous collapse of the Florentine republic Machiavelli was so closely identified with. Machiavelli's prudence, "the one used by most men—that one must look to the ends of things and not the means by which the ends are reached"—might have saved the republic. This is the concept of prudence that is to be found in Machiavelli's letters, plays, discourses, and historical writings. Let one more instance of it suffice: when Servius Tullius became King of

Rome and began to make war plans, he discovered no trained
soldiers in Rome since the state had not been at war for
forty years. Instead of using Samnites or Tuscans, he decided,
being the supremely prudent man he was ("come uomo
prudentissimo," p. 186), to train the Romans. The lesson for
the Florentine republic is clear. And so great was his *virtù*
("e fu tanta la sua virtù," p. 186), that in a short time he
turned out first-rate Roman soldiers. Machiavelli praises
Tullius's virtù and prudence again in *The Art of War* (*Opere,*
vol. 2, p. 515). He was truly a great leader: possessed of
intelligence to see the need to rely on one's own arms and
not those of auxiliaries and mercenaries; and also possessed
of the ability and energy to do something about the need.[11]

4. THE VIRTÙ AND PRUDENZA OF MACHIAVELLI

We may close this examination of the determinants of
human action with a consideration of the role of judgment.
According to Machiavelli verdicts as to the nature of the
situation confronting man and of the most effective course of
action to achieve his objectives would tend to be correct if
guided by prudence. Hence, one's hopes and desires, the prevailing set of religious and moral beliefs and values, the lack
of an adequate acquaintance with the situation—all those
factors that distort prudence—are causes of mistakes in
judgment. Antidotes would include closer contact with the
events and acts that are to be evaluated and careful analysis
of the experience of others. To provide such antidotes is, of
course, a major reason for Machiavelli's own literary activities. It is perfectly clear from these writings that correct
political judgments do not depend, as they ultimately do for

11. It is well to recall that for Machiavelli there could be no higher
act of political intelligence than to see the need to have one's own militia, and no higher act of political *virtù* than to proceed to establish it.
In addition to the above passage in the *Discourses,* see, inter alia, the
last chapter of *The Prince.*

Plato and Aristotle, on theoretical comprehension. The problem of understanding Machiavelli on this important point lies at the other end of the spectrum from the classic concept of *theoria*. The question is whether the acquisition of such correct political judgments can involve even the slightest generalizations or anything more than the refinement through actual experience of that exquisite discretion that a Guicciardini holds to be the only valid, if very imperfect, guide to action.

> To pronounce absolutely, categorically, and, as it were, by the card, concerning the things of this world, were a great mistake; for nearly all of them are marked by some singularity or exceptional quality due to differences in their circumstances, making it impossible to refer them all to the same standard. These differences and distinctions will not be found set forth in books, but must be taught by discretion.[12]

Machiavelli, too, has the diplomat's and politician's high regard for the skills that only come from experience. But Guicciardini knowingly exceeded Machiavelli's own position on this point and developed it into a major criticism of Machiavelli (see his *Considerazioni ai Discorsi del Machiavelli*). To accept Guicciardini's position is to deny the possibility of an art of politics since there are no general rules that may be taught, and no exercises, including the reading of histories, that one may practice to perfect the skill in applying the rules. The only possible way one can learn is through personal experience in actual situations. Guicciardini's radical skepticism undermines the possibility of learning from the past—not, of course, in every area, but certainly in politics.

Machiavelli shares Guicciardini's disdain for philosophical

12. Francesco Guicciardini, *Ricordi*, tr. N. H. Thompson (New York, 1949), p. 133.

speculation, but he is not about to extend this to the study of history, past or present. In this domain there are ample lessons to be extracted and profitably applied. Judgment can be shaped and, in part, determined by such study.

Machiavelli's concern with judgment figures very dramatically in the *Discourses*. The preface to Book 1 laments the fact that whereas the art of antiquity is both admired and imitated the political deeds and institutions of the ancients are admired but not imitated. After all, Machiavelli observes, not only in art but in subject after subject contemporary practice is nothing but an imitation of the past. Civil law consists of the collection of decisions of the ancient jurisconsults, and medicine of the experience of the doctors of old, "in spite of which in constituting republics, in maintaining state, . . . in forming an army or conducting a war, . . . one finds neither prince nor republic who repairs to antiquity for examples" (p. 124). Machiavelli is quick to offer his explanation for this state of affairs. It is due "to the lack of a proper appreciation of history (*non avere vera cognizione delle storie*) owing to people's failing to realize the significance of what they read, and their having no taste for the delicacies history comprises (p. 124).

This lack of appetite for such things on their part explains why people take pleasure in hearing of deeds of old but never think of emulating them. In his introduction to *Clizia*, Machiavelli indicates that the function of a play is to do more than please: it is to teach. Each event in the play is a lesson because it is an instance of a more general truth that covers many cases. If one can learn from a play, how much more important is it to learn from history. This is the reason, Machiavelli informs us, that he has deemed it necessary to write the *Discourses*. It is time to disabuse his contemporaries of this error of judgment, an error that amounts to people's refusing to recognize themselves—"as if the heaven, the sun, the elements, and man had in their motion, their order, and in their potency, become different from what they used to be" (p. 124). Machiavelli returns to this topic toward the end of the work. After having criticized Florentine policy he pauses to point out the lesson: "These are some of the mistakes which, as I said at the beginning, rulers in our day make when they have to deal with affairs of importance, for they should be ready to hear of how those acted who in olden days had to deal with such problems whereas, instead, so feeble are men today owing to their defective education and to the little knowledge they have of affairs, that they look upon the judgments of their fore-fathers as inhuman in some cases and in others as impossible" (p. 461). It is by regarding history (the arena of politico-military deeds) and not by contemplating themselves that men can come to recognize themselves—to rediscover their capacity for great deeds and also to learn the principles of the sustained greatness of states. For it is in public life that the passions find their most appropriate stage, a stage on which they can act and in turn win public recognition.

To know the world of affairs at any time is at the same time to know one's own world and one's self. The Socratic injunction is sharply redirected. If Socrates gave the inquiring mind a new program when he called upon men to turn from the study of natural and cosmological phenomena and to redirect their gaze inward in an examination of the ethical basis of life, Machiavelli's proposal represents the turning to a third tradition which seeks *vera cognizione* in the inspiration and analysis of politico-historical experience.

From the central principle, echoed in all of Machiavelli's writings, that men are the same in all ages, also derives the prudential or realistic element in Machiavelli's hope that Italy can be saved. This hope links *The Prince* and the *Discourses*. In the last chapter of the former, Machiavelli also tries to dispel the sense of hopelessness that overwhelms people when they are confronted with the enormous task of revitalizing Italy by again arguing that what was possible in the past is possible in the present. The amount of *virtù* and prudence in the world does not change from age to age (an observation also repeated in *The History of Florence*). The *animo* remains as expansive and as capable of greatness as ever. Hence political vitality and greatness are not limited to Italy's past. If the Florentines would only recognize themselves in their ancestors they would soon discover their own political energies and talents.

The *virtù* and prudence of Machiavelli the writer and advisor is to help revitalize this political *virtù* and prudence. Almost unnoticed, Machiavelli has advanced a highly ambitious claim for the political thinker. And to judge by his longevity, Machiavelli, our man of *grandezza d'animo*, has achieved his end—succeeding generations have turned to him to receive the inspiration of political *virtù* no less than that of political prudence.

COMMENTARY
Anthony Parel

I WOULD LIKE to start my remarks with a vote of thanks to Professor Fleisher for opening this conference with so appropriate a topic. The task of introducing us to the "World of Machiavelli" is a difficult one, and we are in Professor Fleisher's debt for undertaking it for us.

The world explored here is of course the world of passion

and politics as seen by Machiavelli: it is the inner world of the human psyche, of which the master of the 'new method' had such an intuitive grasp. Human nature is seen as the focus of several disintegrating drives—ingratitude, ambition, and avarice, to mention only some of the more fundamental ones.

Animo, both in its substantive and adjectival senses, gives impetus to these drives. In trying "to reconstruct" this world (p. 118.) [1] Professor Fleisher uses the method of analysis of specific terms: mainly *animo, ambizione, ingegno, prudenza, inganno,* and *virtù.* This is a very perilous undertaking, though one that cannot be avoided, because Machiavelli, not being a philosopher, did not use terms with a consistency of meaning. To put the sort of clarity that has been put into the meanings of these terms is no mean accomplishment.

I would like to raise one or two specific questions by way of a discussion rather than of criticism. The first of these is the problem of *ambizione* in Machiavelli. Professor Fleisher has succeeded in capturing its dynamic, insatiable aspects, its character as the principle of instability, disorder, and war in history. He points out that *ambizione* is ungovernable by reason (pp. 119, 125–29). However, it is also the principle of greatness, order, and glory (p. 124–5). How are we to resolve this apparent difficulty? The answer, I think, is in the fact that Machiavelli uses the term ambition in two broad meanings. In the first meaning its object is the self, or the sect or both as distinct from the *patria* or the *bene commune.* It is this type of ambition that is "the cause of variations in earthly things," and that "destroys our states." [2] Ambition in this respect is nothing but self-love manifested in avarice, among other things, in factionalism based on family or other quasi-

1. The numbers in parentheses refer to the pages of Professor Fleisher's paper.
2. Machiavelli, *The Chief Works and Others,* tr. A. Gilbert (Durham, 1965), 3 vols., 2: p. 762.

private considerations. This type of ambition ruined Italy, ruined Florence, and, in fact, would ruin any state.[3] Machiavelli dreaded this ambition as one of the fundamental causes of the corruption of political man and political society.

But there is a second meaning in which ambition is used in Machiavelli. According to this the object of ambition is the *bene commune,* the *patria.* This is clearly seen in the Capitolo on *ambizione,* especially lines 91 ff. Though in itself evil, there is some positive purpose to which ambition could be applied, namely the service of the *patria:* "If with Ambition are joined a valiant heart, a well-armed vigor (*virtù*), then for himself a man seldom fears evil. When through her own nature a country lives unbridled, and then, by accident, is organized and established under good laws, Ambition uses against foreign peoples that violence which neither the law nor the king permits her to use at home (wherefore home-born trouble almost always ceases); yet she is sure to keep disturbing the sheepfolds of others, wherever that violence of hers has planted its banner."[4]

The application of ambition for the service of the *patria* necessarily leads to war, to the "disturbing" of other "sheepfolds." Thus while *ambizione* assures, under *virtuoso* leadership, domestic order, it does not, according to Machiavelli, offer any hope of world peace. For war is inevitable. Thus, for Machiavelli, ambition is reprehensible in the self and in the sect, highly desirable in the *patria,* but impracticable for purposes of ordering humanity as a whole. It is in the second sense that ambition becomes a basis for public good—even if, in its processes, ambition is manifested as a tension between the chief elements constituting a state, like the plebs and the patricians of ancient Rome. The directing of ambition for private glory, for making others the means of one's own ends, is the essence of tyranny, of which Caesar,

3. See, ibid., the *Tercets on Ambition.*
4. Ibid., p. 737.

according to Machiavelli, was so guilty. Ambition in the *patria,* but not directed to it, led to civil war. There was nothing that Machiavelli detested more, nothing that he would have banished more surely from the world, were he the prince, than civil war. He preferred war to civil war. The difference between the two lay in the canalization of ambition, brought about by the *virtù* of the leader and/or of the people. In so far as it was the principle of domestic order, ambition was opposed to tyranny; and under favorable circumstances produced the *vivere civile.* But where *virtù* was lacking it led to political decay and foreign domination.

The second question that I would like to raise is the relation of reason (as found in the paper) to *prudenza, ingegno,* and *inganno.* It is not clear, at least to me, whether the paper dismisses reason as altogether irrelevant to an understanding of Machiavellian thought. Is reason a faculty, or just one of the faculties, together with *prudenza, ingegno,* and *inganno?* Or *prudenza, ingegno,* and *inganno*—are they just three different ways of using man's rational power? Professor Fleisher is entirely right when he says that for Machiavelli reason means something different than what it meant to the Stoics, the medieval Christians, and the later rationalists. It was not a source of information about the moral duties of man, about divine purposes in human affairs, nor even about secular morality. After having said this, is it beyond dispute to say that for Machiavelli reason was only a "faculty of means" and not of ends? (p. 129). Granted that in scheming and plotting, in making a politically sound judgment— in *prudenza, inganno,* and *ingegno*—there is some use of reason, does the role of reason end here? Without some conception of the end, first as object of knowledge, how can a scheme be a scheme in the first place, and produce the *verita effettuale,* the actual truth? If reason is not the faculty of ends, then what is? If it is said that Machiavelli has no conception (or *theoria*) of end, then are we designating him as a voluntarist? Surely there is a difference in the role of reason as promoting the vitalistic aspects of ambition and its role as *"ratio practica,"* (p. 133), as *"recta cognito agibilium,"* (p. 134), and as the source of the *"vera cognizione delle storie,"* (p. 138); between "serving" passions (p. 134) and "perceiving" the human world (p. 133). What is the difference between reason as "counsellor or advisor" and reason as "not reigning or ruling" (the passions) (p. 129)? Here we have a good illustration of the difficulty arising from the fluid terminology of Machiavelli: reason does not govern but advises. Does this not imply, first, the ontological reality of reason?; second, the several choices that reason presents in the form of "advice"; third, the explanation of why reason does not "rule"—simply because man, corrupt as he is, refuses to accept what reason suggests? If reason rules, one presumably must accept what it suggests; if reason only counsels, one is free to accept or reject the counsel. In both cases reason does make its suggestions. Knowledge is involved. If the counsel is rejected, the fault is not with reason but with will. A corrupt will, even if it consults reason, would not obey it. The meaning of *inganno, ingegno,* and *prudenza* can be seen as the refusal of the will to accept the advice of theoretical reason, not the absence of *theoria* as such.

We spoke of *"cognito recta agibilium"* and *"vera cognizione delle storie."* What distinguishes *vera cognizione* from *falsa cognizione?* It is much simpler to say, I think, that *inganno, ingegno,* and *prudenza* in Machiavelli are the ways of applying reason without morality; it is the ability to act, in practice, as if the theoretical knowledge did not count, (we do not say, was not known).

The primary concern of Machiavelli in mapping out the inner world was, I believe, to lay the foundations of political action and institutions. Out of the restless substance of *animo,* buffeted as it is by avarice, ambition, deceit, ingratitude, etc., he wished to raise a stable edifice—*lo stato* situated in the *patria*—unified, vigorous, stable, as the *virtù* of a people and of its leaders would permit. In laying such a foundation Machiavelli realistically took note of the unstable elements in life. But he was even more careful to search for the stable elements in life; law, arms, religion, and I would say even reason. I would go a step further to say that he used the stable elements to give discipline and purpose to the dynamic but otherwise disintegrating nature of *animo*. He tried to combine the wisdom and the restlessness of man, which may be defined as the elements of political action and success.

Machiavelli's view of the inner world of man is nearer to Augustine's than to the Stoics': man is a 'sinner'; his reason and will are weakened but not completely put out by corruption. He limps to wholesomeness. The disciplined portions of mankind manage not to get disintegrated. Politics is the art of salvaging, of continual "renovation" and "reform," of a wrecked world, the outer world of institutions and laws, as well as, to some extent, of the inner world of *animo*.

Custom & Grace, Form & Matter: An Approach to Machiavelli's Concept of Innovation

J. G. A. POCOCK

THE INTENTION OF THIS PAPER IS TO explore certain implications that Machiavelli's thought can be shown to bear by means of a reconstruction of patterns of thought inherent in the culture and language of his time. I should like to make it as clear as possible that I do not necessarily impute to Machiavelli himself a conscious intention to deploy all the implications that I shall try to discover in his thought, though as he was plainly an extremely sophisticated thinker and literary artist we should do well to estimate highly his awareness of the full meaning of what he said. But the methodological postulate on which my paper rests is that what we call political thought consists of the use and exploration of the political language—or languages —available to the thinker in his time. It is a characteristic of speech as a social and in a special sense as a political instrument that as we use it we become increasingly committed to patterns of implication which it carries but which we did not necessarily know were there until we embarked upon the adventure of communication. To certain schools of philosophy, these unseen burdens of language are the source of puzzles and confusions that it is the task of the philosopher to clear away; but to certain schools of anthropology, trained to think in terms of conflict, communication, and exchange, it might seem that they ensure that language itself becomes a complex device whereby its users enter into exchange relationships, give themselves away, and give one another hostages and ritual gifts in a commonly recognized currency. A politics of language could certainly be worked out along lines like these. To the historian of thought, however, it is sufficient to recognize that once we begin to employ language we enter a realm of multiverse implications and connotations that it is not expected and is indeed impossible that we perfectly command. The more sophisticated the thinker, we may wish to say, the greater his consciousness and control of the instrument he is using; but at the same time, it must be added, the greater chances that he will press ahead into regions of implication little known or mapped and will carry out changes in the accustomed use of language whose full import may be hidden even from him. It is at this point that we encounter the value of employing contemporary philosophies and other patterns of articulated thought to interpret the writings of some thinker who may not have been practicing philosophy or the activity of constructing whatever pattern it is of which we make use. If we define philosophy (and we are now encouraged to do so) as the exploration of linguistic patterns and puzzles, then a contemporary philosophy, however different its aims, may help us by articulating the structures of implication to which the contemporary thinker found himself committed and the consequent problems in which he found himself involved. Should he prove— as in the case of Machiavelli it is said that he did—to have carried out some drastic revolution in the accepted use of concepts, this approach will help us to see more fully the linguistic structure in which he began to act and so to understand better what it was that was new about what he did and even what it was that he was doing.

The history of ideas, then, can be treated as the history of use and change in what I shall be referring to as paradigmatic structures; but these paradigms exist in contexts of multiple implication and, if for no other reason than that the historian can never hope to tell the whole of his story at a finite number of sittings, it is necessary for him to choose the particular continuum of implication and usage in which he will depict his history as taking place. Selection is necessary; the "history of Machiavelli's thought" I aim to tell is, I believe, a history that can be shown to have actually happened, but it is not the only one that could be narrated. Machiavelli communicated many things to many minds, and for this reason touched off more histories of paradigmatic change than he could have anticipated; and if we assume that he was using a language of whose full burden of implication he could not have been aware, then he was involved in more such histories already going on than he could have known. For this reason we are entitled—in fact we are obliged—to construct linguistic and conceptual contexts in which to interpret the historical roles which his thought played. The only requirement is that our hypothetical constructions shall yield histories of paradigmatic change and persistence that can be shown to have really happened, in a world of real men actually engaged in the activity that we call thinking.

I began some years ago to construct a study of Renaissance constitutional thought and was led early on to ask myself the question of what constitutional thought might be defined as being. I formulated the idea that it was political thought aimed at the understanding of particular political systems—those of Florence, Venice, France, England—rather than political society as an abstract universal. This led next to the reflection that late scholastic thought was very well equipped with concepts for dealing with universals, not too badly off for concepts relating the particular to the universal, but far from well supplied with concepts for understanding the relation, notably the succession or sequential relation, of one particular to another. By "particular" I mean, first, the particular phenomenon or event, next the particular decision aimed at regulating the phenomenon or event and ordering it within a social structure, and finally the particular national or municipal governing system viewed as built up from the tissue of particular decisions and the institutional structures to which they gave rise. I found evidence that fifteenth-century minds were by no means unaware of this perspective upon politics but encountered great difficulty in reducing it to rationality, largely because "reason," as they understood the term, was concerned with universal, abstract, and timeless categories. This suggested the further reflection that the particular was seen very much as the time-bound, as that which had a beginning and came to an end in time, and that time itself was viewed largely as the dimension of this very imperfectly understood particularity. It followed therefore that the kind of intellect I was defining tended to see the succession of particular events and actions in time as non-rational, but that such means as it did possess of rendering the particular intelligible were also the means available to it of understanding the sequence of events in time and of rendering political actions viable and political structures stable in time. At this stage a study of late-medieval or

Renaissance constitutionalism had turned into a study of late-medieval historicism; and I proceeded to construct a model of those means of understanding the particular and time that appeared to me to have been available. These are, basically, the languages or paradigmatic structures which I shall be employing in the remainder of this paper.

The particular decision might be made by adapting universal law to particular time and place; the particular entity might realize its end or nature by participation in universal form. But these were modes of relating the temporal to the timeless, and what I was in search of was the means whereby the time-bound individual might understand and control the time-bound phenomenon in its relation to other time-bound phenomena. There appeared to be two ways of approaching this problem. In the first place, there was use and experience: through reiterated experience of recurrent or consequent phenomena, it was possible to build up patterns of remembered and repeated behavior, extending through time to form traditions of usage, sometimes institutionalized as bodies of customary law. This paradigm had a number of interesting intellectual characteristics. It received epistemological support from Aristotle's observation that the accumulated experience of the many was sometimes more reliable than the wisdom of the philosopher; but another important circumstance was that this kind of knowledge was not without its effects on the personality of the knower. To quote Sir John Fortescue: "All that is loved transfers the lover into its own nature by usage, wherefore, said Aristotle, *Use becomes another nature.*"[1] In addition to his essential nature, that in virtue of which he existed to reach his end, social man could acquire a second nature through use, tradition, and inheritance, the result of his assimilation (we might say) to what he and his ancestors had experienced and learned

1. Fortescue, *De Laudibus Legum Anglie,* tr. S. B. Chrimes (Cambridge, 1949), ch. 5, p. 7.

and become through experiencing.

In the second place, there was faith reposed in divine providence. The succession of particular temporal events might be seen as being directed by an aspect of the divine mind which, precisely because it directed the succession of particulars, was inscrutable and past finding out. The human mind might observe the course of events so directed and within limits learn from it; prudence was the virtue by which men lived in the providential present, just as it was, so to speak, the present tense of experience; but God's ways must remain beyond the reach of the human intellect. From this point, however, it is possible to see two further paradigmatic structures branching out. To begin with, the content of Christian revelation included prophecies of the historic future; and a variety of apocalyptic schemes, some orthodox and some heterodox, had been developed to particularize these foretellings. When a particular event occurred of an exceptionally striking nature, or when a particular secular society found itself cast for an exceptionally dramatic role, it was not illegitimate, though it was always dangerous, to utilize apocalyptic and, by identifying the phenomenon with one of the events, persons or signs of the apocalyptic scheme to account for the uniqueness of its moment in time.

For obvious reasons, appeal to the prophetic scheme could be made very much less frequently than appeal to an unschematized providence. But if the ways of providence were not schematized or spelled out at all, only the purest and most Job-like form of faith could be reposed in them. What would they look like if not regarded through the eye of faith? This was the point at which the medieval intellect, even while finding it impossible to describe a coherent existence without faith, made use of the ancient Greco-Roman symbol of fortune (*fortuna*). Fortune was what providence looked like if we had not faith; but, since once we had, she became providence again, the two concepts tended to approach each other. Moreover, Roman moral thought had developed the concept of a *virtus* by which wise and good men obtained a mastery over *fortuna* and transformed her into a force which operated beneficently; and this, Christianized by the addition of faith to *virtus,* became in the Boethian tradition the idea that the good man's faith in the ultimate beneficence of providence obtained for him a grace whereby, if his external particular circumstances did not become beneficial, nevertheless they became part of the fabric of his redeemed Christian life. When this was restated in Aristotelian parlance, virtue and grace became the agency by which the matter of circumstantial *fortuna* was shaped into the form of a good life. Sometimes prudence could see how the ways of providence operated to this end; rarely it could be seen in terms of the ongoing fulfillment of prophecy; but normally it was left to faith to discern the process of which it was itself part. Finally, there existed a rhetoric of fortune which described the terrible aspect which the providential world must have to those who lacked faith, and this was now and again made use of by those medieval dropouts who lacked it themselves.

I have now nearly completed delineating the model that I hope to apply to Machiavelli's *Prince:* I am saying in essence that the ability to understand time and particularity was important to secular political thought, and that the foregoing paradigms were those available to late-medieval minds which sought that understanding. Machiavelli—I will excuse myself from defending the epithet "late-medieval"—was such a mind; but before applying the model to him, something further must of course be said about the Florentine political intellect in and after 1494. It was equipped with at least one other highly authoritative political vocabulary, and I separate this paradigmatic structure from the others only because it was less universally distributed and because, in the Florentine context, it bore the character of a set of goals or commitments rather than of available instrumental devices. This vocabulary defined the values, procedures and general theory of what I shall take the risk of calling civic humanism. Since this is a controverted term, let me add that I mean no more by it than a vocabulary which asserted that man was a civic or political animal, and that the individual fulfilled his nature and attained virtue and knowledge only if he was a citizen, participant with other citizens in decisions aimed at the distribution of a common good. "Civic humanism" seems the appropriate term for this code of values and other paradigms, and I shall be employing it simply to denote this code whenever it is found, as it very frequently and importantly is.[2]

For theory on how the community of citizens was possible, civic humanist thought drew above all on the *Politics* of Aristotle and, among secondary writers, most notably on the sixth book of Polybius once they were acquainted with it. But even before they knew Polybius's writings, they were familiar with the problem to which he had addressed himself: that of endowing the Aristotelian polity with stability in time, time being seen as a continuum in which the tendency towards instability and decay was very strong indeed. Civic humanism operated to politicize virtue; only as a citizen could man be truly good, since otherwise his goodness was not truly his own; and conversely goodness was that which held him attentive to the good of all men as well as his own. But each man's virtue was now terribly dependent on that of his neighbor; citizenship was a relation between equals (in the Aristotelian sense of the word) and if my neighbor was not attentive to the public good, he might become either my master or my servant, both injurious to my practice of virtue. Virtue became to some extent a man-

2. For further analysis of the problems arising from use of this term, the reader is of course referred to the debates between Professor Hans Baron and his commentators and critics.

made structure, and these were notoriously vulnerable to time and fortune. Indeed, since a republic must by definition be less universal than an empire, it was by that definition doomed to decay; and it might be said that underlying all humanist and Machiavellian thought is the philosophical impossibility of attaining a universal ideal—virtue—in a particular structure, the republic. Now *virtus,* as we know, stood in a special relation to *fortuna,* roughly that of form to matter; but *fortuna* was the name of a deforming force which reduced everything to disorder in time; an important source of her power was the inability of human reason to reduce temporal existence to rationality; and this irrationality of the particular is in my model a cardinal feature of late-medieval or Renaissance thought about politics. The theoretical situation brought about by civic humanist values was this. The form that virtue imposed upon fortune was the republic: the polity of virtuous citizens attentive to universal rather than particular goods, which seemed to be possible only when authority was widely and equally distributed. But this form, the *vivere civile,* was threatened by *fortuna,* subject to an inherent instability arising (1) from the inability of men to control their particular natures or cease setting particular goods above universal, (2) from their inability to foresee and control the particular event or problem. These two tended to coalesce, so that virtue in the technical sense—the ability to impose form upon *fortuna,* including the ability to foresee and control events—became one with virtue in the central sense, the ability to control one's nature and direct it towards its end; and virtue in both senses was realized in the well-ordered republic. *Fortuna* threatened virtue and the republic in part because of the limitations on men's understanding of time; and the only sets of paradigms directing and furthering that understanding, says the model, were those associated with tradition on the one hand and apocalyptic on the other. Yet the republic was neither a traditional nor an apocalyptic community. I propose now to apply this pattern of paradigmatic dilemmas to the antecedents and contents of Machiavelli's *Prince;* but I shall begin with Savonarola.

To explore the structure of the friar's ideas—I shall proceed in analytical order, not that of their historical development—a good point to start is where he considers the question of the best form of government.[3] He concedes with Aquinas that it is in principle monarchy but adds that you have to consider the particular nature of the people for whom you are prescribing a government. In the case of the Florentines, the citizens have inherited from their forebears a bent towards liberty, activity, and participation in their own government, which renders a republic the only political form adapted to their nature. So far, then, Savonarola presents a plain case of the difference between universal and particular, abstract and specific, ideal and actual; and this difference is made by use, wont, and tradition, which supply the particular society with its inherited second nature, that individuality to which the word nature is applied in a different sense from the formal Aristotelian meaning of the word. (In some *cinquecento* writings I notice the word *naturale* used as a noun, where *natura* might otherwise have appeared, and the idea of inheritance and acquired characteristics is usually associated with it.) But when Savonarola begins, in the sermons preached after the fall of Piero de' Medici and the establishment of the Consiglio Grande,[4] positively to recommend the republic as a form of government for Florence, he does not speak of it as a nonideal second-best. It becomes a holy commonwealth, that state of affairs in which *la città* is *una religione,* and its realization in Florence is constantly depicted in an apocalyptic context of imminent divine events

3. This is to be found in Savonarola's *Trattato circa il governo e reggimento della città di Firenze,* composed in 1497.
4. *Prediche italiani ai fiorentini,* ed. F. Cognasso (Perugia-Venezia, 1930).

and a "fifth age of the Church" now at hand. The reconciliation of these ideas, it seems to me, can be effected in the following way. The republic is now the political form of the realm of justice, in which every man really is more attentive to the common than to the particular good; it has become an ideal, reconcilable with the former assertion that the ideal form of government is monarchy only on the supposition, which Savonarola energetically advanced, that Christ is now king of Florence. That is, the republic is the kingdom of grace, which can be realized only in an apocalyptic context. If men live justly, a grace will be given them; but if Florence lives justly and is visited by grace, that event, since Florence is a historical entity, can be visualized only in historical, i.e., apocalyptic terms. Moreover, to live justly and according to divine law is what men were created to do; it is their nature, or *prima forma,* and Savonarola constantly stresses that since *prima forma* is the gift of grace, *reformatio*—the recovery of that form—can be effected only by living in such a way as deserves grace; but if living justly, i.e., attending to the common good rather than one's own, is identified with the life of the citizen according to Aristotle, then the doctrine that man is by nature a political animal or citizen becomes identical with the doctrine that man was formed by God to live justly and according to his law. The republic is the recovery by man of his original nature; it has a political form, but it is the gift of grace and comes about only at an apocalyptic moment in history. Savonarola's apocalypticism, in this respect at least, is perfectly Aristotelian and Thomist. *Gratia perficit naturam,* grace perfects nature; but the nature of man is political and its perfection is an apocalyptic happening.

A specially interesting point in all this is that inherited "second nature" of the Florentines, which, we were told, rendered them incapable of any but a republican government. It might seem on the face of it as if this accidental growth had, by divine prevision, prepared them for the resumption of *prima forma,* and I doubt if Savonarola would actually have rejected this position; but it is observable nevertheless that he constantly speaks of use and custom—*consuetudine*—as that by which man grafts on to himself an artificial nature (formed, as Fortescue reminded us, by loving the accidents that he has experienced) that comes between him and the recovery of his true nature. Nor is there anything in the Florentine past of much value to the city in effecting its present reformation. It is possible that only providentially directed accident, visible in men's inherited natures, can prepare them for the recovery by grace of their original natures; but that recovery cannot take place unless the old Adam—the accidental nature of time-bound fallen man—is burned away in the fires of renewal: burned away, one might add, with the rest of the vanities of Florence. I will not determine whether Savonarola is exploiting ambiguities in the relation of first to second nature; but I will claim that our model has been substantiated in so far as the republic—a political form that raises in an acute way the problem of the relations between universal and particular—has to be visualized in a context either of use and tradition or of grace and apocalypse.

Now let me carry these paradigmatic structures on into the analysis of Florentine thought after the fall of Savonarola and specifically after the restoration of the Medici in 1512. Savonarola had made no use of the concept of *fortuna*—his temporal context was so entirely one of prophecy and grace as to preclude it—but it would be in accord with the model if, after so severe an eschatological disappointment, the idea of circumstance undirected by grace were to reassert itself. But it is more striking still to see how the group of writers who dealt with the reality of 1512 and the subsequent years developed the concepts that they used to explore it. By this group—I say nothing about their connections with each other—I mean Guicciardini when he wrote the early *Discorsi* of 1512–16,[5] the lesser optimate writers whose treatises of the same years have been collected by Rudolf von Albertini, and of course Machiavelli himself, writing *The Prince* about 1513 and circulating it whenever and however widely he did. Now if we look at Guicciardini, or at Paolo Vettori and Lodovico Alamanni as members of the second group,[6] one general assumption catches the eye. This is that the Florentines are by nature a people predisposed to liberty and political activity, inheriting these proclivities from their ancestors, and that the experience of living from 1494 to 1512 under the Consiglio Grande, which satisfied this appetite on a large scale, has made an irreversible difference to them, so that there can be no going back to the state of affairs that existed before it. The *popolo,* it is assumed, will never forgive the Medici for depriving them of the Consiglio; and if an implication dear to the optimate mind is that the Medici ought to treat at least the leading citizens as free and equal, these writers are all more than doubtful if this can be effected in the circumstances.

The question, however, is why the nature of the Florentines is thought unalterable and why the experience of the Consiglio Grande is irreversible. The simplest answer to the first question is that inherited nature is the work of use and custom and that, since no means of understanding or acting upon the world exists other than experience, there is no means of acting upon the change in our natures which experience and usage bring about. The interesting exception here is Lodovico Alamanni, who contends that it is wrong to hold that men's natures and customs can never be changed;

5. The *Discorso di Logrogno* (1512), the *Discorso del governo di Firenze dopo la restaurazione de' Medici* (1513) and the *Discorso del modo di assicurare lo stato alla casa de' Medici* (1516), all in R. Palmarocchi, ed., *Dialogo e discorsi del reggimento di Firenze* (Bari, 1932).

6. Their *discorsi* are printed in the appendices to R. von Albertini, *Das Florentinis che Staatsbewusstsein im Übergang von der Republik zum Prinzipat* (Bern, 1955).

certainly there is nothing to be done with the older men at Florence, who are incurably addicted to civic life and values, but the younger notables can be exposed to an alternative political culture—a way of life *alla cortigiana*.[7] You can make courtiers of them, and they will cease to be citizens. But it is unclear exactly why the Consiglio Grande should have had so strong an effect in addition to that of inherited nature, unless there is at work some idea that it fulfilled and perfected the nature of the Florentines and even restored its *prima forma.* At all events, Guicciardini, who in his writings down to the mid-1520's seems to me constantly trying to depict a popular republic in which the *ottimati* can play a leading part, does in the *Discorso di Logrogno* make a proposal (once echoed after 1512) to burn the vanities. That is, he talks of conducting a general purge of luxuries which distract men's thoughts from the public to the particular good; but the figure he invokes is not that of any Hebrew or Christian prophet; it is Lycurgus. The classical legislator, who rendered it possible for men to live as citizens where they could not do so before, was recognized in antiquity as a being rather divine than human; in Christian Aristotelian thought he restored or imparted form to matter; and Guicciardini uses in connection with Lycurgus the word *grazia*.[8] Certainly, this could mean either grace or good fortune; but that ambiguity is itself no accident.

But the closest link between these optimate writers and Machiavelli is to be found in their concept of innovation. The Medici after 1512 cannot be like the Medici before 1494, because their rule rests on the overthrow of the Consiglio Grande, not on its nonexistence. The people are now used to participation, and a government that deprives

7. Albertini, op. cit., pp. 370–71.
8. *Dialogo e discorsi*, pp. 257–58. Note the proximity of "grazia" to the assertion that the work of a reforming legislator is "più tosto opera divina che umana."

them of it runs counter to their natures as affected by the experience of participation. The key terms are use and experience. Guicciardini, Vettori, and Alamanni all employ the notion that if you deprive the people of what they are used to, all their habits of mind operate to your disadvantage; the people are more conscious of what they have lost than of what they may have gained, because the only relevant form of knowledge is experience resting on memory. In 1516—by which time they may have exchanged ideas with Machiavelli —Guicciardini and Alamanni are pointing out that the Medici rule neither as hereditary princes nor as leading citizens; these writers are setting up the category of innovation, and exploring such pertinent figures as Cesare Borgia, Francesco Sforza, Agathocles of Syracuse, and Oliverotto da Fermo. But innovation is always against use and custom, against acquired second nature, and what renders the innovator insecure is the fact that these things operate to make the breaks run against him. The concept of *fortuna,* though present, is not given central prominence; but here is the thought of *The Prince.*

Machiavelli's thinking in 1513 can therefore be seen as part—I am not of course bothering about questions of originality and who influenced whom—of a style of analysis of the restored Medicean regime, employing the paradigms relevant at the time. But whereas all these lesser tracts are specifically addressed to the concrete question of what is and has been going on in Florentine politics, *The Prince* is not; and as I read it the book surveys a variety of situations of which perhaps none, and if any not the most central, is identical with that of the Medici in Florence after 1512. I take it to be a work at a higher level of abstraction: a work *de principatibus,* or rather, since it is devoted to the subject of new princes, *de innovatoribus:* a typology of political innovators, employing the categories available and appropriate to that study. This is not to deny its relevance to contemporary events, only to define its relation to them.

States are either republics or principalities; principalities are either old or new. In the former case the prince is *naturale*. This adjective is best translated "hereditary and legitimate," but what it primarily means is that the people are used to obeying one of his lineage, so that their inherited responses operate to legitimize nearly everything he does, and he must step very far out of line before this conditioned structure ceases to work in his favor. But the new prince, meaning for the moment simply one who has seized control of a people conditioned to other obedience, has everything running against him; he lacks legitimacy and the presumption is against everything he does. He is bound to displease more people than he pleases with every action. The *principe naturale* has no need of outstanding talent, since all he has to do is avoid committing egregious mistakes like rape and military failure; but the *principe nuovo* needs it desperately, since he has to do everything right without guidelines. Here we are at the antithesis of *virtù* and *fortuna,* and it is important to detect the paradigmatic structure behind them. The new prince is vulnerable to *fortuna* where the old is not, because he has disturbed the fabric of use, custom, and tradition, the acquired and inherited second nature of the people, by which all the prince's acts are assimilated to what is already familiar through experience and all accidents made to operate to his advantage. Having disturbed that, he must fear the consequences of every act of his own and every external accident, since his subjects will react in ways predominantly disadvantageous to him which he cannot control. This is what is meant by the power of *fortuna* over him. Our model is borne out in that use, tradition, and second nature are principal modes of imposing order (not form) upon accidental and chaotic matter.

The *principe naturale* does not need *virtù,* since use and tradition operate in his favor; the new prince needs it badly because they do not. But because they do not, he is exposed to *fortuna,* and of course *virtù* is that by which *fortuna* is tamed and reduced to order so far as this is possible. This was no new statement; Sallust and Boethius had been beforehand with it; what is extraordinarily new is the context that gives it its Machiavellian meaning. *Virtù* is alternative to use and tradition, and since we are studying the case of a usurping single ruler it is alternative to the Aristotelian-Thomist structure of interlocking civic virtue as well. Moreover, once Machiavelli begins to speak of it as a means of the prince's rise to power, *virtù* becomes part of the act of innovation that exposes the prince to *fortuna* and renders itself necessary. In short, what has happened is this. Machiavelli's development of the theme of innovation has caused him, first, to employ the concept *virtù* in its purely formal sense of that by which order is imposed upon *fortuna,* and, second, to do so in a way that separates it from the Christian and Aristotelian, moral and political contexts in which it ordinarily functioned. His decision to use the word in this way was his act of creative genius; we are looking at a genuine case of breakthrough in the employment of paradigms, one of which I abstain from using the analogy "scientific revolution" only because I am not sure who next used the term *virtù* as Machiavelli used it here, or what changes in paradigmatic vocabulary can be said to have come about in consequence of his so using it.

What is new is that *virtù* is necessary because innovation has occurred. Innovation is committed primarily against the traditional structure, though Machiavelli also observes that an innovator who seizes power over a free republic faces a next to impossible task, since once men have been free they never forget it or forgive a usurper. Lodovico Alamanni knew better; but Machiavelli does not tell us why they cannot be conditioned to another *vivere.* According to the language we are employing, and which Machiavelli himself sometimes uses, the answer could be that in such a case the *materia*— he sometimes employs this word to denote the citizen body— has assumed something so like its final form that you cannot change and can only destroy it; but that must be conjecture. If then the innovator's problems are essentially those that follow the displacement of a structure of habit, much of *The Prince* can be read as precepts on how he may survive amongst and manipulate the behavior of men divorced from this structure while still remembering it. But there is another level of analysis that I should like to explore in conclusion.

Chapter 6, it seems to me, presents a typology of innovators arranged according to the degrees to which their *virtù* renders them dependent on *fortuna*. We have to remember that *virtù* is two-faced; it is that by which the innovator imposes form on *fortuna*, but it is at the same time that by which he carried out the original act of innovation that exposed him to her. The new prince is one who has imposed himself on a traditional structure that does not legitimate him, and so far he has been discussed in terms of his relations with his subjects bereft of that structure; it follows, by the way, that Cesare Borgia is an eccentric if highly interesting case, because his dependence on *fortuna* has very little to do with the way his Romagnuol subjects react to his rule but a great deal to do with his father's tenure of life in the Vatican. But since it is possible to compare innovators in terms of *virtù*'s dependence on *fortuna*, the case might theoretically arise of an innovator whose *virtù* owes nothing to *fortuna* at all. Machiavelli now sets up the case of those who owed nothing to *fortuna* "except the opportunity (*occasione*) which gave them matter into which to introduce whatever form they thought good." These were Moses, Theseus, Romulus, Cyrus; they all found their people (and Romulus found himself) in as anomic a condition as can be imagined; and this is a logical necessity, since if there had been a structure of norms and laws before their advent their innovation would have disturbed it and exposed them to *fortuna*. If the precondition of anomie is met, then we can say that they imposed form upon matter in that pure and unconditioned sense that Savonarola had thought required the direct action of divine grace. Moses of course enjoyed that grace, but the others being pagans did not; and unlike Guicciardini, who was prepared to use *grazia* in connection with Lycurgus, Machiavelli insists on the distinction, the better to savor the ironies that result. His mention of Moses leads on to the case of Savonarola himself and to the famous distinction between prophets armed and unarmed; and this, I think, can be very easily misread.

In the first place, our model, by suggesting that the relevant paradigms centered around the ideas of grace and custom, offers an explanation of what Judeo-Christian prophets and Greco-Roman legislators were doing in the same box. Only grace could supersede nature, meaning the secondary nature acquired through custom; but if the legislator was thought of as imposing *prima forma,* he was doing the same work that the prophet proclaimed as the action of grace. This is why Machiavelli deals with them together; that he does so in a way that shows he had no great faith in the actions of a special grace in the field of politics is of less importance than the analysis that shows why he could not ignore the topic. In the second place, the discussion of prophets armed and unarmed occurs in the context of a discussion of the extreme difficulty of innovation. The innovator, Machiavelli says, is always dependent on the behavior of others, which he cannot control; Savonarola was destroyed when men ceased to believe in him, and Moses on the brink of the same moment used the sword. But everybody knew that story, and it was not supposed to detract from the reality of Moses's prophetic mission; it was the people who backslid, not Moses who was a fake. What Machiavelli is saying here, I think, is that the pure case of the prophet or legislator, who finds the people inert matter and molds them into form in a way that owes nothing to *fortuna,* never exists in reality, not even in the world as subject of grace. There is always an antecedent structure of habit and memory, and the inspired or heroic innovator is always exposed to *fortuna;* there were always fleshpots in Egypt, and even prophetic grace must operate on an entrenched second nature that limits its political efficacy.

The model suggests that after Savonarola's failure the question could in principle arise whether *virtù* could succeed unaided by prophetic or apocalyptic grace. Formally, this would mean asking whether a legislator might succeed where a prophet had failed; but contrary to what has sometimes been suggested, Machiavelli does not respond with a portrait of the prince as legislator. He begins at a point alongside, rather than in, the discussion of the changed character of Medicean rule after 1512, which arose when certain Aristotelian, humanist, and Savonarolan concepts were used to interpret the situation after 1494; but instead of discussing the position of the Medici, he discusses the category of innovating princes into which they fall. This he analyzes by means of the *virtù-fortuna* polarity, though it does not provide him with any slot into which the Medici visibly and significantly fit; and it is the category "innovator" that he enlarges by addition of the species "legislator" and "prophet" —ideal types who differ importantly from the species "new prince" with whom the analysis began, though as Machiavelli denies their existence in impure reality their condition reverts towards his. In the penultimate chapter of the book we come back to the question whether *virtù* can do the work in which grace may already have failed, whether it can triumph over *fortuna* and impose form upon matter; and the answer, pretty clearly, is that it cannot. Machiavelli does indeed say that the new principality, when managed in the proper way, is more intense and exciting to live in than the hereditary monarchy; but that is not to say that it will last as long.

The key statement here is the remark that we can never be independent of *fortuna,* because we cannot change our natures as fast as circumstances change. The nature in question is that which we acquire through appetite and usage, love and habit; and if the prince cannot change his own nature, he cannot change that which his subjects acquire through custom and inheritance. In the end, custom is king if grace does not overthrow it; only *prima forma* can take away second nature, and human *virtù* is not superior to traditional conditioning. And yet—once again—Lodovico Alamanni knew better.

This investigation of Machiavelli's thought in terms of paradigmatic change has shown it functioning, precisely where it is most original, within humanist, Aristotelian, and medieval limits. Because the frontiers of thought were those of custom and grace, form and matter, it seemed to Machiavelli and his contemporaries that the Medici of 1512 were innovating and that innovation was a thing next to impossible. *The Prince,* an exploration of that paradigmatic world, develops the concept of *virtù* in the most extraordinary way, without thrusting back the frontiers very far; Guicciardini and Giannotti, the only republican theorists of a stature approaching Machiavelli's in his lifetime, employ *virtù* only in its civic and never in its innovative sense and confine themselves to exploring the question whether the Medici and the Florentine elite can work out their relations within a republican framework—neither can be said to conceive of any alternative. So it was only Alamanni who had thought of a way in which the prince might change the nature of his subjects and had foreseen something of the character of that ducal regime that was to take shape in the 1530's.

If the ability to predict were really the test of a political theory, we should have to say that Alamanni was the greatest political theorist of his generation at Florence; but we know that he is not. The stature of a political theory—insofar as questions of stature should concern the historian—depends on its ability to explore, illuminate, and change the conceptual or paradigmatic world in which it takes shape. Machiavelli's historical renown rests largely on what he did with the concept of *virtù* in *The Prince;* but once he had decided that the innovator could not change the inherited nature of men, his thought turned back to the republic, since the only alternative to the traditional community was now the community of civic virtue. The thesis that in *The Prince* we find the legislator relegated to the category of ideal type is borne out by the fact that the basic theme of the *Discourses on Livy* is how a republic can flourish when there has been no legislator or he has done his work imperfectly. But if the republic is to be neither a traditional community nor a community of grace, it must exist in a world of innovation and *fortuna;* and perhaps the most disturbing suggestions in all Machiavelli's writings are that the republic cannot rest on a simply Christian morality, that it must pay the price of a high incidence of social conflict at home, and that it must pursue a career of war and conquest abroad. But one can trace the ways in which his contemporaries and intellectual peers—Guicciardini and Giannotti—and his most imaginative heirs and followers—Giannotti and Harrington—declined to take up these suggestions, bridged the gap which he had opened up between the ideal of Rome and that of Venice, and employed his ideas to perpetuate a republicanism that rested on the assertions that man was naturally a citizen, that his virtue consisted in a regard for the common good, and that the business of politics was to stabilize the structure in which this virtue could be manifested. It was only in the eighteenth century that the issue between a stable and a dynamic politics could be directly confronted.

COMMENTARY
Brayton Polka

I THINK THAT we may all take pleasure in Mr. Pocock's so-phisticated discussion of Machiavelli in terms of the para-digms of political thought available to him in Italy in the earlier sixteenth century. Mr. Pocock provides us with a most useful framework in which to examine Machiavelli, and I wish to use this framework in examining Mr. Pocock's con-tribution to our understanding of Machiavelli's thought.

As I am myself an historian of what I am wont to call late-medieval and Renaissance thought, I am intrigued and not a little pleased by Mr. Pocock's reiterated claim that Machiavelli is a late-medieval thinker. This he says without apology or blushing. And I congratulate him. Let me recall for you the conclusion to Mr. Pocock's paper—it should still be ringing in your ears:

> This investigation of Machiavelli's thought in terms of paradigmatic change has shown it functioning, precisely where it is most original, within humanist, Aristotelian, and medieval limits. Because the frontiers of thought were those of custom and grace, form and matter, it seemed to Machiavelli and his contemporaries that the Medici of 1512 were innovating and that innovation was a thing next to impossible. *The Prince,* an exploration of that paradigmatic world, develops the concept of *virtù* in the most extraordinary way [i.e., in its "inno-

vative sense"], without thrusting back the frontiers very far. . . .

I agree with the thrust of Mr. Pocock's conclusion, but, in saying this, I wish nevertheless to argue in my brief comments that he did not press his analysis sufficiently far to gain as clear a perspective on Machiavelli's thought as I believe his approach makes possible.

You will recall that in the earlier sections of his paper Mr. Pocock had some very penetrating comments on the lack of interest on the part of medieval thinkers for what we today call the temporal dimension, that is, the realm of particulars. Mr. Pocock declared that the instability of the particular was a cardinal feature of late-medieval political thought. The vocabulary of form and substance, of *telos* and final cause, involved an ontology in which only unchanging, perfect, static universals were real; and these concepts also implied an epistemology in which the only basis of real knowledge was universals, universals conceived as possessing real existence in themselves. It is obvious that that which we today typify as historical and temporal, implying that change is real and that only particulars have real existence, was not real to medieval thinkers like Thomas Aquinas or Dante.

Yet we know that such late-medieval thinkers as Marsilius of Padua, William of Occam, Nicholas of Cusa, natural philosophers like Buridan and Oresme, not to mention the greatest fifteenth-century humanist, Lorenzo Valla, were increasingly attacking this Platonist essentialism, fundamental to the earlier Middle Ages, and that they were increasingly concerned with providing a philosophical framework for time, self-consciousness, and the existence of particulars, about which St. Augustine one thousand years previously had written so evocatively in his *Confessions*.

When Mr. Pocock, late in his paper, addresses himself

specifically to Machiavelli's concept of innovation, he does not point out that it was in fact quite impossible for Machiavelli to have a coherent theory of innovation. Machiavelli did not challenge the typical early-medieval fusion of Christianity and Aristotelianism which the civic humanists had, for the most part, simply continued. And it is this tradition which was unable to provide an ontological, not to mention epistemological, basis for innovation—for innovation implies that the temporal dimension is real and that change is inherent in the human condition. A theory of innovation assumes, in other words, that man is an historical creation.

Because of his concern to elucidate Machiavelli's concept of innovation, I am puzzled why Mr. Pocock did not care to comment on what I feel to be the passage in which Machiavelli most clearly indicates his fundamental values: the Preface to Book 1 of the *Discourses*. In this passage Machiavelli clearly reveals to us his attachment to the medieval fusion of Christianity and Aristotelianism, for he disdainfully rejects values attached to the historical or the temporal, the novel or the innovative.

> On account of the envious nature of men, it has always been no less dangerous to find ways and methods that are new than it has been to hunt for seas and lands unknown, since men are more prone to blame than to praise the doings of others. Nevertheless, driven by the natural eagerness I have always felt for doing without any hesitation the things that I believe will bring benefit common to everybody, I have determined to enter upon a path not trodden by anyone; though it may bring me trouble and difficulty, it can also bring me reward, by means of those who kindly consider the purpose of these my labors. And if my poor talents, my slight experience of present affairs, and my feeble knowl-

edge of ancient ones make this my attempt defective and not of much use, they will at least show the way to someone who, with more vigor, more prudence and judgment, can carry out this intention of mine, which, though it may not gain me praise, ought not to bring me blame.

When I consider, then, how much respect is given to antiquity and how many times (to pass over countless other examples) a fragment of an antique statue has been bought at a high price in order that the buyer may have it near him, to bring reputation to his house with it, and to have it imitated by those who take pleasure in that art, and when I know that the latter then with their utmost skill attempt in all their works to imitate it, and when I see, on the other hand, that the most worthy activities which histories show us, which have been carried on in ancient kingdoms and republics by kings, generals, citizens, lawgivers, and others who have labored for their native land, are sooner admired than imitated (rather, they are so much avoided by everyone in every least thing that no sign of that ancient worth remains among us), I can do no other than at the same time marvel and grieve over it. And I marvel so much the more when I see that in the differences that come up between citizens in civil affairs, or in the illnesses that men suffer from, they ever have recourse to the judgments or to the remedies that have been pronounced or prescribed by the ancients; for the civil laws are nothing else than opinions given by the ancient jurists, which, brought into order, teach our present jurists to judge. And medicine too is nothing other than the experiments made by the ancient physicians, on which present physicians base their judgments. Nonetheless, in setting up states, in maintaining governments, in ruling kingdoms, in organizing

armies and managing war, in executing laws among subjects, in expanding an empire, not a single prince or
republic now resorts to the examples of the ancients.

This I believe comes not from the weakness into which
the present religion has brought the world, or from the
harm done to many Christian provinces and cities by a
conceited laziness, as much as from not having a true
understanding of books on history, so that as we read we
do not draw from them that sense or taste, that flavor
which they really have. From this it comes that great
numbers who read take pleasure in hearing of the
various events they contain, without thinking at all of
imitating them, judging that imitation is not merely difficult but impossible, as if the sky, the sun, the elements,
men, were changed in motion, arrangement, and power
from what they were in antiquity. Wishing, then, to get
men away from this error, I have decided that on all the
books by Titus Livius which the malice of the ages has
not taken away from us, it is necessary that I write what,
according to my knowledge of ancient and modern affairs, I judge necessary for the better understanding of
them, in order that those who read these explanations of
mine may more easily get from them that profit for
which they should seek acquaintance with books. And
though this undertaking may be difficult, all the same,
aided by those who have encouraged me to take up this
burden, I hope to carry it in such a way that only a short
journey will be left for some other who will bring it to
its destined place.[1]

In light of these ideas, it should not be difficult to see why
Machiavelli never really analyzed in any depth the tradi-

1. Niccolò Machiavelli, *Discourses on the First Decade of Titus
Livius*, in *The Chief Works and Others*, tr. Allan Gilbert (Durham,
1965), 3 vols., 1:190–92.

tional notion of custom and experience, or what Mr. Pocock calls "second nature." If Machiavelli believed that the inherited nature of men could not be changed, we can only suppose that his concept of custom or experience or second nature was still so fundamentally Aristotelian that he simply was not able to appreciate the fact that, if it is true that nature is but custom and experience, its very essence is change.

Not only does Mr. Pocock not make clear that Machiavelli did not possess a theory of innovation, but I find his treatment of Machiavelli's concept of innovation ambiguous. When he states that Machiavelli's use of the term *virtù* is two-faced, he should rather say, I would think, that it is contradictory. You will recall that Mr. Pocock told us that *virtù* is both that by which an innovator imposes form on *fortuna* and that by which an innovator carried out an original act of innovation which exposed him to fortune. I think Mr. Pocock's analysis of Machiavelli's use of the term *virtù* is accurate—the conclusion he draws from his analysis is, in my opinion, inadequate. Working within what Mr. Pocock himself calls a medieval, that is simultaneously Christian and Aristotelian, framework, Machiavelli is unable to conceive of real temporal change, for *virtù,* on the one hand, presupposes innovation, in that the innovator imposes form on fortune, and yet, on the other hand, *virtù* is the source of innovation, for the new prince acts boldly, through his virtue, and thus finds himself exposed to fortune.

I want to conclude these brief comments with two additional remarks. I would like to suggest that it is not as a political thinker that Machiavelli is novel, not to mention revolutionary. He did not pierce the framework of traditional Christian and Aristotelian political thought by challenging its fundamental ontological and epistemological values. It would be a political theorist like Hobbes who, on the basis of a new ontology radically founded on the individual, created a new political universe. Mr. Pocock's paper is particularly welcome in this respect, for it suggests how very timid Machiavelli was and how unable he was to create a new, comprehensive framework in terms of which the concepts of innovation and of change would become meaningful.

The second remark that I wish to make is that, for all Machiavelli's discussion of politics in his major works, his genius lies in his tentative but precise discernment of the ethical dilemma which is the hallmark of the modern condition: the division between public and private, between subject and object, between different concepts of the good which cannot be related one to the other hierarchically but only existentially. When Machiavelli asks us to look to the end, he is really asking that we be aware of the peculiarly delicate relationship of means and ends: their relationship is not hierarchical or static, but, rather, dynamic, for our choice of ends will affect the means we employ, and the means we choose will affect the end we have in mind. So far as I am aware, Machiavelli is the first thinker in the West to posit, philosophically, the collision of aims, each good in itself. Thinkers like Plato, Aristotle, Cicero, St. Augustine, St. Thomas Aquinas were all keenly and realistically aware that it was frequently the case that men did not pursue the good and that, thus, action was in conflict with the good. Cicero could even advocate that it might be essential to pursue a purely utilitarian goal. But always lurking in the background was the comforting notion that, ideally, the realm of the good was still there to be entered by the virtuous man. Machiavelli returns, I suspect unconsciously, to the myth of Adam and Eve, the myth that tells of man's alienation from paradise, of his knowledge of good and evil, of his existential dilemma as he undertakes to create a kingdom of man which is essentially temporal.

In his brilliant study *Shakespeare's Doctrine of Nature,* John F. Danby examines the Elizabethan's gnawing recogni-

tion of the perilous fault that lay beneath the temporal kingdom of man: when this kingdom was rocked by earthquake,
raison d'état did not call for Christian piety. In the following
passage Danby discusses the meaning of Machiavelli for the
Elizabethans in the context of analyzing the passage in which
Shakespeare describes the murder of King Henry VI by
Richard of York in the third of the Henry VI plays:

> Henry VI is the regulating principle of traditional soci-
> ety. He is mercy, pity, love, human kindness, reinforced
> by God's ordinating fiat. It is this which Richard
> kills. . . .

> Right up to Henry's murder Richard has been a typical
> member of the Yorkist group. His pre-eminence in fact
> has been due only to his having the approved qualities
> of the York family in a larger measure than his broth-
> ers. Up to this point, too, the conflict about the throne
> has been conducted as a dynastic rivalry. There have
> been rights and wrongs on both sides. No one has made
> claims as an individual merely. Everything has kept
> within the limits of the medieval code. The killing of the
> King marks the transcendence of this code. The dynastic
> issue is left behind, and it is now a question of Richard's
> personal ambition. Up to now, from the observer's stand-
> point, there has been war, bloodshed, treachery, lacera-
> tion of the body of *Res Publica:* but all as the outcome
> of debated primogeniture. With Richard the war, blood-
> shed, treachery and laceration continue: but Richard jet-
> tisons the idea that only a discussion of primogeniture is
> sufficient to justify it. Nothing external is changed or
> needs to be changed. However, the whole inner mean-
> ing of what is happening before our eyes has been
> transformed completely.

> This, I think, is the prime significance Machiavellianism
> —the mere idea of it—had for the Elizabethans. There
> is a new sense of the fissuring of man, of a gap between

the external and the internal, a possible dichotomy between the social and the spiritual. We can see it even
in Hooker's contradiction: man must be thought of as a
reasonable creature if we are to justify the unity of law
and love, yet for reasons of government it is best to
think of him as a lawbreaking beast. The new element
is not merely the thought of appalling wickedness. It is
rather the uneasy feeling that 'wickedness' might be a
social advantage. What is morally wrong might be socially expedient, a strong ruler who is bad better than a
holy King who is also weak. 'Pity, love and fear' may
be governmental handicaps. There is no doubt in the
chronicle cycles that Henry VI, by all concerned, is regarded as an irrelevance. Pity, love, and fear are not socially usable as things are. Yet they are the ideal for
man, and living together on any other terms than on an
assumption of unifying kindness is scarcely reasonable.
This honest enigma underlies everything else in the
machiavel-figure. It provides the sober basis for what
would otherwise be flesh-creeping pantomime. If pity,
love, and fear have become socially irrelevant, then
are they true, or do greybeards merely say they are divine? If they are not true, then the whole façade of society is a mask. The man conscious of this will be the
hypocrite—a man superior in degree of consciousness to
his fellows: one able to convince his fellows by his mere
existence that they are the mask and he the reality. Behind the mask there is not an angel but a devil—and
notwithstanding a more reliable and efficient regulator
of *Res Publica.* This man, aware of how things really
work, aware of the mockery of moral claims, aware of
what men really are motivated by as opposed to what
they pretend to themselves, will kill the King.[2]

2. John F. Danby, *Shakespeare's Doctrine of Nature: A Study of
King Lear* (London, 1961), pp. 60–62.

This is the world of the individual, or solipsism, a world in which the good is relative to individual need and perception. Machiavelli stumbled upon this world, looked into the abyss, and withdrew to the solace of the ancients who had denied the existence of the abyss. For, as Machiavelli told his friend Vettori in his famous letter of December 1513, he would return home in the evening, remove his everyday clothes, and, having put on royal and courtly attire, he would enter the ancients courts of ancient men where, beneficently received by them, he would dine on that food which alone was his. Machiavelli told Vettori that, no longer mindful of the human condition, he would return to his courteous ancients: *Tutto mi transferisco in loro*—"I give myself up to them totally." [3]

3. Niccolò Machiavelli, *Opere,* ed. Mario Bonfantini (Milan-Naples, 1954), p. 1111.

The Time Motif in
Machiavelli

ROBERT ORR

IT IS THE WAY OF CIVIL PHILOSOPHERS
to draw man in society as dwelling in some kind of abstract world. The world selected may be one of inescapable,
but not ungovernable passions, as with Hobbes; a cosmos of
the intentions and purposes of an identifiable Creator, as with
St. Augustine; or a world impregnated with law, as with St.
Thomas. The world drawn is always abstract, because, as a
starting point for a system of ideas it must necessarily be an
irreducible *principium,* taken out of the unexplained chaos
of concrete life. The point, or one point, of the exercise of
political philosophy is to demonstrate the behaviour and the
morality which fit the condition of man specified. Further,
this inferred behaviour and morality is in itself an abstract
world of hypothetical relationships which offers us, not
moral 'guidance'—it is a world away from that—but a set

of categories that compose a theory of behaviour and of ethics.

The appeal of such philosophies is, of course, as diverse as the possibilities they offer. Some people, including their authors, see in them opportunities for the furtherance of non-philosophical, often persuasive, purposes. A philosophical system might be made to serve rhetorical ends by supplying a demonstrative model or, more modestly, a mere vocabulary. The *philosophical* appeal of philosophical writing, however, unless it excites a purely passive admiration for a well-turned hob, is the provocation, or the excuse, it offers for further philosophy.

In this respect, the classical 'systems of philosophy' are at a potential disadvantage which is, paradoxically, the concomitant of their achievement. The very completeness implicit in a system can be a detraction from its value as an agent of further philosophical thinking. Where the parts are seen to interlock with apparently unimprovable perfection, there is little encouragement to undertake a construction, or even a demolition followed by reconstruction. A system of thought, if it existed, in which nobody could find a creaky joint or an incoherence, would become more heavily embalmed than it is bound to be anyway by being in print.[1] In all probability it will be found to have turned into a doctrine, the entombment of genuine philosophical thought. The increased philosophical interest in Hobbes's writing during the last decade is surely attributable to a renewed awareness of the ambiguity in which he wraps his account of the source of moral obligation. Not all political philosophers share this posthumous fortune of Hobbes. Their philosophical and paedagogic employability is liable to be confined to fringe logical nit-picking, or at worst some straightforward construing—a process also more suited to doctrine than to philosophy.

But there are some writers who would not even describe

1. Plato, *Phaedrus*, 275.

themselves as philosophers, whose work suggests, though it never achieves, a system; whose thoughts carry a subtle interrelatedness which invites philosophy. Such writers may be said to leave enough material lying around for others to do their philosophy for them. Montaigne is an example among moralists, Pascal among theologians. But among political writers it is Machiavelli who catches the eye. His advice, his histories, his military texts, his plays, his correspondence tantalize with their systematic suggestiveness. His diverse observations and recommendations upon the themes of ruling, citizenly virtue and state-building, have provoked others to detect various unifying principles: of moral hedonism, of secularism, of political utilitarianism, of historical recurrence. Each of these interpretations has attributed to Machiavelli what might be called a set of definitions of certain roles or occupations—those of ruler, citizen, soldier, etc. In other words, he has had extracted from his various subsystems of thought—'a philosophy of power,' 'of statecraft,' 'of success,' etc.

What I wish to attempt here is an outline of a rather more generalized philosophy of moral and political life which might be constructed out of Machiavelli's writings; to suggest that he does have, and implicitly recommends, a distinctive way of looking at man in his universal setting, which gives a philosophical 'coloring' to his particular prescriptions without, of course, making these prescriptions any more or less wise, or even plausible.

Philosophical thinking always tends towards a monism, and a fully developed system will be a resolution in terms of a single central principle. But not all philosophies achieve this end. It is characteristic, particularly of political philosophies which are often originally conceived in terms of an antithesis, e.g. the individual versus the collective, to be left resolved in terms of a dualism, which is a more generalized version of the original antithesis. I believe that Machiavelli's writings lend themselves more convincingly to a dualistic rather than a monistic form of philosophical construction. The initial idiom of his political thinking is that of government and society; that of his moral thinking is that of a man and circumstances. His writing sustains this contrapuntal character.

Man, as Machiavelli sees him in society, inhabits a world ruled neither by fortune, nor by himself, but by time. The image of human life in his mind is that of a man or a society completing a span of life from birth until it becomes something else, i.e. death. Problems and miseries stem ultimately neither from a deficiency of man's nature, nor from external impediments to his natural development, but from the fact of his being a temporal creature living in a world of temporal events. "It is a well established fact that the life of all mundane things is of finite duration." [3] Temporal boundaries are natural to a man's world, and this world is not an artificial hiatus in a natural eternity, nor is it a will-o'-the-wisp shadow of a world of timeless essences. [4] This condition of things is seen as unavoidable while we are in this life, and no escape save death is envisaged. Even religion, as officially interpreted, can give no escape; Christianity offers only the distracting drug of humility. [5]

But time, as Machiavelli conceives it, not only governs our lives by way of providing us with a terminus, but it is itself the events which fall between the margins of our existence, coming to us from the future, claiming our attention, then passing into the record. It is time, "said to be the father of all truth" which makes and manifests human characters. [6] By time, he understands the succession of events, not of moments or of other regularly measurable intervals. A metaphys-

3. *Discourses*, 3:1.
4. Cf. St. Augustine, *De Civitate Dei* 11 5, 6.
5. Ibid., 2:2, 6.   6. *Discourses*, 2:3.

ical doctrine that defines time as extension, as "the number of motion according to former and latter" is the artificial creation of philosophers, not the time which they or anybody else inhabits. This sort of time knows only two measures, those of remoteness and immediacy; events know only one relationship, that of antecedent and consequent. *A* is the antecedent of *B*, which is consequent to *A*, but the antecedent of *C*. Further, these events are not all of the same magnitude. Death is an event, but in the life of a state the untimely death of a great leader, e.g. of Lorenzo de Medici at the age of forty-four, is a 'larger' event than the death of Machiavelli himself; though for him, considered as a private person, the order of magnitude would probably be reversed. The 'size' of an event is its consequences.

The life of a man or of a society is not *one* series of events (e.g. the series of solar or lunar movements by which we calculate the arrival of other events and keep them manageable) but many. In this respect the life of a man and of a state are formally similar. Both have a physical life, which has a beginning, a middle and an end; but neither restricts its life to the time-series of physical events. There is the series of conscious thoughts (the succession of mental events), the series of chemical events, of legal events, of defensive or military events, likely more if anyone wanted to discover them.

A man's life is up to a point comparable to a person standing astride a narrow channel, through which a river carrying many objects has to pass. He has to do something with each, and to do so effectively, he has to keep an eye upstream. The analogy has at least two limitations:

(1) Time is not just a river-like medium carrying the events, it *is* the events themselves.
(2) There are good reasons for looking at a man himself as a passing event, enjoying no privileged point of arrest in the process.

Events do not usually appear singly; they may come in constellations. Then we say we have a 'situation on our hands.' To get it off our hands we need both a relational and a particular awareness; we need to see both the pattern and connectedness of events, and have to divide and manage them in turn.

Nothing we know existed 'prior' to time: the beginning of the world was the beginning of time, and ideas of 'morality' and 'justice,' i.e. general principles of human relationships, are the progeny of time.[7]

If events yield themselves into antecedent and consequent, it follows that each event has a past, comprising all antecedent events, and a future, comprising all consequent events. But men speak of themselves as having a 'present existence.'[8] In a world divided between "what has to be," and "what has been,"[9] what place is there for a present? Machiavelli speaks of the 'present' as the immediate future, of what needs to be done 'presently,' that future which asks urgent attention and which arises out of the *immediate* past, in contradistinction to the *remote* past.[10] 'The present' is a subclass of the two established categories, past and future. A genuinely categorical 'present' could only be man's awareness of having a past and a future, but this awareness is itself resolvable into a series of mental events, each with a past and future. To speak of the present as something like a point of arrest in the flow of events is to speak of an intrusion of eternity into time, for only something which was not itself an event could interrupt the flow of events. And this is not a recognizable feature of our world, in which 'time waits for no man.'[11]

But a man sees himself, not as an event in a series—a link in a chain of ancestors and offspring, nor his acts as items in a sequence of antecedents and consequents, but as occupying

7. Ibid., 1:2.
8. Ibid., 3:43.
9. Ibid., 3:4.
10. Ibid., 1:39.
11. Ibid., 3:4.

a distinctive position in the passage of time. Whether he is self-conscious about it or not, he views his intentions, purposes and choices as composing at least a special class of events. What he is thereby doing is distinguishing between mental and nonmental events. Mental events have their own sequence; but they register other sequences which they cross and connect with at various points, and between which they construct hypothetical linkages. They 'see' nonmental events that lie in the future as possibilities, those that lie in the past as facts.

The mental events with which Machiavelli is concerned are those that are responses to events that still lie in the future, i.e. to possibilities. A response will be followed by another event, the consequent event being one which may range in magnitude from making a mental note to buy strawberries to blowing up the world. All responses are immediate, i.e. they are provoked by what is to hand; but some are remote as well, because they are a response not only to events which are before us but also to others as yet some distance ahead. For instance, the opening of a bank account is a response both to the immediate availability of cash and to more remotely anticipated needs. In statecraft, the supreme example of a response that is both immediate and remote is the creation of a constitution. A constitution is a temporal device —it is itself an event—made to regulate the sequences of legal and political events. Its value is its permanency, and in order to last it has to take account both of foreseeable and unforeseeable possibilities. The virtues of the Roman republican constitution and of the laws given by Lycurgus to Sparta lay in their capacity to survive and to regulate the events of several centuries.[12] And a mixed constitution possesses a staying power superior to that of a monarchic, aristocratic, or democratic one.

12. Ibid., 1:1,2.

The response that men make to a possibility is not itself the resultant event. It is exactly half of that, the other being what is given to them by Fortuna, the disposer of their immediate futures; she it is who makes the immediate sequences which men have to face.

Human responses are of two kinds, necessary and chosen. Necessary responses comprise those in which we have no free will, as when we die after injury, and those (with which Machiavelli is mainly concerned) in which we retain our free will, but are deprived of free choice (*libero arbitrio*). We have free will but no free choice when any response save one will apparently be followed by ruin. Ruin can mean loss of office,[13] of means of sustaining life,[14] of territorial integrity,[15] or of reputation.[16] Once chosen, the response will be followed in due course by success or failure. We do not deliberately choose failure, but we may choose an immediate disadvantage in the expectation of a greater later advantage. There are those who want success only in eternity and believe it necessary to choose a temporal life of renunciation, one of admitted failure, a choice which does not earn Machiavelli's approval.

Where there is no necessity (either physical or of ruinous alternative), a man makes a chosen response, in which he exercises his powers of judgment, foresight and concentration. In choosing, he is neither like a traffic policeman preventing or permitting events nor a selector picking the event out of a range of alternatives, but a *turner* of events. Whatever the precise shape of his response—and the variety possible here is infinite—he can turn events in only one of two ways; either right side up or wrong side up, to his advantage or disadvantage. He may turn a man into a friend or an

13. *The Prince,* ch. 15, 18, 25; *Discourses,* 3:3.
14. Ibid., 1:1,3.
15. Ibid., 2:12.
16. Ibid., 2:27; 3:10.

enemy, a battle into a victory or a defeat, a state of public restiveness into chaos or order. After his response, the event is history, standing in the record as a success or a failure, which are in time what good and evil are in eternity. A success for most men means winning rather than losing and being honored for your win. But success is not limited to triumph (whether splendid or niggardly) or scrambled superiority; it may mean losing gloriously rather than ingloriously—as Hannibal reckoned when he decided, despite inferior forces, to attack Scipio in Africa.[17] Neither a success nor a failure marks a terminus, or even a check in the passage of events. Both success and failure are subsequently open to further failure or further success; the outcome will depend on the combination of Fortuna's disposition of events and human response to that disposition. It is even possible for glory to follow the capitulation of one's armies, though this is exceptional enough to be unlikely without the active assistance of Fortuna, such as the Roman Consul Postumius enjoyed following his surrender to the Samnites.[18]

Such is the life of a man or of a state: a treadmill of happenings in which responsive movement while it lasts and a closure in death are the only inevitabilities. It would indeed be a desperate delineation if there were nothing but inevitabilities. But there are possibilities as limitless as the number of potential responses.

How are these to be realized? Clearly some skill or aptitude is called for, and Machiavelli has his own version of the doctrine that virtue is knowledge. It is *foreknowledge* that earns merit and brings such success as is deserved. Foreknowledge means perceiving the shape of events before they are upon you, in such a way as to recognize their eventual possibilities. But it is possible to recognize only something that you have seen before, either with your own eyes, or that has been de-

17. Ibid., 3:10.   18. Ibid., 3:42.

scribed to you by somebody else. Whether you rely upon your own experience or that of another, your knowledge of the future can be found only in the past.[19] To recognize something that is not yet fully manifest is, therefore, to identify it, to see it as something you have seen or had described to you before. Life, however, is constantly bringing events that invite us to treat them as entirely novel, a temptation to be resisted if we are to shape events our own way. But how can novel events be made to disclose an identity? It can only be possible by shaping future possibilities into types of past events—and on the verisimilitude of the outline our success in handling the event will ordinarily depend. Military history shows pointedly the importance of a correct identification of the situation before you. How many field commanders have misread enemy activity to the extent of seeing defeat near, and packed up for the night, when another hour's fighting would have secured victory? [20]

Types of past events are available for both the general and detailed characteristics of emergent possibilities. Even something as idiographic and detailed as new terrain will submit to identification by somebody with prior experience of any countryside. 'The lie of the land' before you will be familiar if you have already been over similar terrain— hence the value of hunting as a sport if you plan a military career. "Consequently, great men look on this sport as honourable and necessary." [21] Closer to politics, the practices of medicine and law are the practices of identification of emergent events in terms of those that are in the records.

The accuracy or inaccuracy with which you identify a possibility will be revealed when it has become a fact. The important thing is to see past the surface of events, to find the character that later developments, including your own response, will show.[22] A ruler must identify remote elements

19. Ibid., 3:39, 43.   20. Ibid., 3:18.
21. Ibid., 3:39.   22. Ibid., 1:3.

of discord which lie behind an apparent social tranquillity. This is admittedly hard advice to follow, for history is full of accounts of surface social harmony concealing elements of trouble which only time has later revealed. The harmony that prevailed in Rome after the expulsion of the Tarquins masked a fundamental discordance, which only the eventual death of the Tarquins made manifest.

How far ahead will a correct identification of an event enable us to forecast? With respect to politics, Machiavelli has extremely modest expectations for one who accepts the Polybian cycle as a description of long-term constitutional sequences. At the beginning of the *Discourses,* he describes the six-phase constitutional cycle, taken from Polybius without notable alteration or even acknowledgement. While endorsing the idea of cyclic patterns of events, however, an inspection of the relevant passages discloses how little predictive value he placed upon it. The only expectation a man might reasonably derive from the cycle is that no form will last forever. And he insists that the cycle is not impervious to interruption. It may suffer the intervention either of what he calls external accidents, e.g. the defeat of Rome at the hands of the Gauls, or of internal occurrences, such as the advent in political life of a constitution that can serve to stabilize or renovate the state, or of a "good man who arises in the midst, and by his example and virtuous deeds produces the same effect as does the constitution." [23] In Book 5 of the *History of Florence,* his last book, the recurring sequences of government are drawn in even more generalized terms, an "ebb and flow" from order to disorder, returning to order: "thus things always descend from good to bad, and ascend from bad to good." The time-sequence of social fortunes is "a constant succession of prosperity and adversity in all human affairs." *Virtù* tends to promote peace, which begets idleness,

23. Ibid., 3:1.

which in turn breeds contentiousness and faction which may bring ruin and confusion. But here Machiavelli is writing history, not tendering advice; these were "the vicissitudes that Italy experienced, first, under the dominion of the ancient Tuscans; and then under that of the Romans; sometimes flourishing and powerful and sometimes reduced to misery and distress." Apart from reminding us that nothing in this world is constant, that everything is liable to show its other face, the passage is richly explanatory but short of predictive suggestion. The theory of recurrent cycles is a device to explain the past, rather than a formula for identifying the future in the past. It may organize our understanding, but it does not disclose to us how to decide on a response to what is on hand.

If the Polybian cycle does not rank prominently in Machiavelli's idea of how men face the contingent future, still less does the Augustinian so-called 'straight line' theory of events. St. Augustine's theory does not, in any case, flatly contradict the cyclic theory since it depicts a divine, not a secular, programme of events; the world of secular fortunes may well display ebb and flow, the rise and fall of earthly kingdoms. It is, in fact, a theory of necessary, not contingent events, i.e. events that demarcate epochs of a divine time-schedule. St. Augustine's intention in writing was to dissuade people, as strenuously as he could, from identifying recent temporal events of great magnitude with 'events' in the divine plan, by showing that human institutions and empires, existing in secular time, might well rise and fall. But neither the sack of Rome, nor any other event in secular time, however decisive it may look, may be used to forecast the return of Christ, which was the next event due in the divine scale. The Augustinian 'straight line' theory may be said to be intended to encourage hope while forbidding prediction—a clean reversal of Machiavelli's understanding of what men must make of events in secular time. Machiavelli had a crude theory of how contingent time is organized; he had no theory at all of necessary time.

The past in which we are to detect the future need not be immediate; it might well lie in antiquity, particularly if antiquity is well stocked with types and examples, as Machiavelli believed it to be. What will edify us and forewarn us in those records is not so much recurring cycles as recurring successes and errors. And where we see a general proneness to a particular error, our ability to detect and identify our own situations will be sharpened.[24]

Up to a certain point, there is no limit to the number of past happenings, whether drawn from your own life, or from the records of somebody else's, that you may use to find the possibilities of your own future. The hint of limitation is as follows: any knowledge of the past which is even moderately extensive will disclose two general maxims about the succession of events, maxims which heavily qualify a simple reliance upon precedent to elucidate the identity of what is ahead.

One maxim is that human feelings about what is remotely past are qualitatively different from feelings about what is immediately past and immediately ahead. The difference is to be found in the promiscuous capacity of ancient records to reveal what we wish them to reveal. We can let our imaginations create unbounded pictures and satisfactions from what is well behind and we need never fear harm from our ancestors. This past, because it stokes the imagination of the remote future, offers a ready escape from the immediate future. But the ease with which the past lends itself to be praised (at the expense of what is before us) is a limitation on its predictive serviceability.[25] Time plays tricks with everybody's memory, and Machiavelli himself confesses to being a victim of the temptation to create a dream-world out of the records of the ancient Romans, even to the extent of dressing himself up in clean clothes for the occasion of reading about their great deeds. But despite this disarming frank-

24. Ibid., 3:10.   25. Ibid., Bk. II, Preface.

ness, he sticks to the contention that "the virtue which then prevailed and the vices which are prevalent today" are as clear as the sun.[26] Hence the peculiar value of antiquity as a guide to an honorable and virtuous future.

The other qualification is the operations of the agent he comprehensively calls Fortuna, allusions to which occur throughout his literary works. The Roman goddess of chance had been pictured and sculptured in antiquity as a composite of these emblems: the cornucopia, representing prosperity—a meaning similar to that which the Old Testament Jews understood by the 'blessing' of God; the rudder, guiding human destiny, akin to the Homeric idea of fate; and the wheel, which betokened the constant flux and movement, up or down, the ebbing and flowing of events.

Now for Machiavelli, Fortuna is primarily neither a cornucopia nor a rudder, but a wheel; the motive force of contingent events, capable, not of an infinite number of directions, but of only two—either up or down, bringing men, not riches or famine, nor their ultimate destiny, but an ascendant or a descendant movement in relation to other men.

The image of Fortuna had suffered diverse interpretations from its origin in the ancient world up to the sixteenth century. For Boethius, whose exposition of the Christian conception of Fortuna dominated medieval thought, she was a minor agent of the Deity, working to turn men's eyes away from this world where there is no justice, no correspondence between merit and reward, towards the eternal world which *is* regulated by dependable rules and principles. But she was still a directive force, as the Romans had thought of her, to be heard and heeded with regard. For Boethius, and for Dante later, Fortuna is not to be challenged, but to be studied, for the lessons she teaches of the deceptiveness of all

26. Ibid., Bk. II, Preface.

terrestrial honor and reward. The point of it all is to encourage men to lay up treasure in heaven.

Machiavelli, familiar with the writings of Dante at least, gives a new turn to the idea of Fortuna. She is neither a goddess herself, nor an agent of God employed to provoke the otherworldly virtues in human beings. He sees her as an active sharer with men in the making of events. She appears to humans always as the producer of what they have not foreseen. In his plays and stories Machiavelli speaks of her in a fashion that implies merely chance—that which is fortuitous and therefore inexplicable—not only as that which men cannot predict, but that which they cannot retrodict, an event that they can neither foresee nor account for even after it has happened.

In his political writings, however, he makes a more pointed and meaningful use of Fortuna. She is certainly not a goddess to be worshipped and pleased (men, not being gods, can hardly 'pound,' 'beat,' or 'chastise' a Goddess), still less is she an emissary of eternity, directing human perspectives away from the world of secular events. She is commended, in fact, as capable of being treated as a partner with men in arranging the sequence of events in secular time. And the relationship is understood as implying anything but passivity on the part of men. Fortuna is not all powerful on earth. Her operation is in any case limited to secular kingdoms—she holds no sway in ecclesiastical principalities, whose affairs are subject to the intervention of God only.[27] More relevantly, she is subject to the limitations of human foresight, prudence, valor. This does not mean that she may not win in an encounter with men's better qualities; but it means that human *virtù* and Fortuna are able to practice mutual frustration as well as mutual furtherance. Machiavelli's strong criticism of Plutarch and Livy for crediting the

27. *Prince,* Ch. 2.

Romans' acquisition of an empire to Fortuna rather than to *virtù* was executed by a detailed attribution of what was claimed for Fortuna to Roman military and diplomatic skill.[28]

Any relationship may be either continuous or intermittent, and although Machiavelli inclined on occasion to speak of Fortuna as a *principium universalitatis,* he predominantly speaks of men's relation with her as not continuous but fluctuating, even spasmodic. Fortuna is a temporal—and temporary—visitor; when she comes, it usually, though not always, means trouble, or at least greater difficulty in managing affairs. A visit by Fortuna is not an occasion on which we might reasonably expect foresight to be rewarded and plans to be fulfilled. For this reason men see her on the whole as an unwelcome caller, though she does sometimes operate to their advantage. When she is active, events seem to accelerate—the wheel spins faster, or, to revert to the earlier metaphor, the current of events flowing past us seems swollen; at times it reaches flood proportions, carrying all before it. Events are not, of course, moving faster; they only seem to be because we have not foreseen them. They then engage our attention with a close-range intensity.

Fortuna, then, operates in time, and from time to time bringing 'untimely' sequences. But the changeability of Fortuna bears a lesson for men living in a world of events. Machiavelli has specific recommendations, in the form of maxims, which he advises men to follow in coping with Fortuna's visits. He prescribes three phases of conduct, corresponding to the three stages of the visit, which must be practiced by Fortuna's host—if he is not to be her hostage. He must know what to do well in advance, what to do when she arrives, i.e. when the relationship is immediately before him, and what to do when she has departed. Machiavelli, in short, has a scheme of conduct to match his understanding

28. *Discourses,* 2:1.

of what it is to live in a world governed by time; proper conduct is itself contingent upon the location in time at which it is required.

Since Fortuna is a flood, remote preparation for her advent will mean building ditches and earthworks. How is this to be done? Machiavelli describes the general defensive principles suited to those holding military and political responsibilities. The *virtù* of a captain or of a ruler is in part his stragetic defences against the arrival of Fortuna. "Fortuna favors good order (*ordini*)," and for the military, order means discipline, which has in itself the promise of valor and determination in the troops. An army must have confidence in itself and in its leaders, and it is possible to breed this, as an insurance against misfortune. "True valor, good discipline, and a sense of security are not easily dissipated." [29] The cultivation of a patriotic religion in the army is also a long-term precaution, but the best insurance for any army is a reputation for winning campaigns. This makes other people respect and fear you, and they are thus less likely to become agents of Fortuna's operations against you.[30]

For a civilian government, the prime way of digging in is by establishing a constitution able to meet a sudden spate. This had been done in France, Spain, and Germany, but not in Italy. Again, as a ruler you will refrain from undermining respect for laws and customs, and not be seen to flout the laws yourself, especially if you are an hereditary prince. Preparation means securing the support of your population while things are quiet, before you need to call upon active assistance to fight an invader. You will not give hostages to Fortuna such as refusing in advance to negotiate with your enemy. You will never relax your watch for hazardous developments, especially conspiracies. This is what is

29. Ibid., 1:4; 3:33.
30. Ibid., 2:1.

meant by the exercise of *virtù* in statecraft; it is not to live for the immediate future but to sacrifice some short-term advantages to contingency planning. The *virtù* of the Roman Republic was her constitution, her military organization, the qualities of her outstanding men, and the love of liberty of her citizens. *Virtù* is the intelligent precautions men can take to mitigate and soften the impact of events. Fortuna's powers are only magnified "where men have little *virtù*." [31]

Lastly, you will not imagine that the present quiet procession of events will last; the tempo will change with little notice; you will expect a visitation at any time. You are in the position of a man anticipating, but anticipating what he does not foresee.

The second phase is confronting Fortuna when there is little distance between events and yourself, when your response must come immediately, and everything seems to be happening at once. Here there is little scope for detailed advice; indeed, a man might be forgiven for supposing that the only advice of any use would be something akin to that given by Marcus Camillus to his fearful troops: "Let each man do what he has been taught to do or has been accustomed to do." [32] But Machiavelli does describe alternative reactions to a situation when Fortuna descends, the choice of stances available when the answer has to be almost automatic.

The possibilities are: First, you may lie low and do nothing. This is a posture or a response that may bring success; it is only likely to do so if it represents a conscious policy of waiting for the guest to depart, when things will become more controllable. While lying low you remain watchful. But it may represent a slothful trusting of oneself and one's responsibilities to Fortuna. If so, you may still enjoy success as did Numa, the second King of Rome; but this is not gen-

31. Ibid., 2:30.
32. Ibid., 3:31.

erally to be expected, and in any case you deserve no honor.[33] Those who command an army or conduct a conspiracy are particularly liable to be ruined if they trust Fortuna.[34]

Second: You may place yourself in a position to use Fortuna, to catch events and run with them. But this ability presupposes an amplification of the ability to identify singular events and forecast what they portend. The descent of Fortuna is itself an event, and your ability to second her visit to your own design requires the greater and rarer capacity to identify, not just one happening, but which way things are currently going, and the type of general reaction called for.[35] To recognize 'the quality of the times' is to know whether cautious patient tactics, like those of Fabius Maximus, are needed, or bold decisive action like that of Hannibal or of Pope Julius II. Such effective recognition demands constant watchfulness, in order to ascertain who is currently profiting, who is losing by the visitation; the spinning of the wheel takes some up, some down. To have a good prospect of rising, it is helpful to know who else is rising, who is falling. The image here is that of a man moving back, or recoiling from events, 'playing for time,' so that he can see them at a slight distance and thereby employ the onrush to his own purposes.

Third: Instead of either lying low, or recoiling slightly, you may move forward in an attacking posture, aiming to grab Fortuna before she grabs you. This is what Machiavelli means by audacious action in the face of events. The essence of an audacious act is its speed; it takes place before anybody, including Fortuna, has time to predict it and dispose themselves accordingly. Not surprisingly, most of Machiavelli's eulogies of bold action are exemplified in military terms. There are times when a correct assessment of events

33. Ibid., 1:19.
34. Ibid., 3:6.
35. Ibid., 3:9.

will reveal that boldness is not just best, but necessary—it provides the only prospect of victory—as when a general knows that the advantages (or perhaps the financial resources) he holds cannot last, and he must necessarily strike now.[36] When Hasdrubal was threatened by Claudius Nero and Livius, he attacked immediately—an action commended by Machiavelli even though Hasdrubal was defeated.

Boldness, in fact, is the one advantage of character that men hold permanently over Fortuna. Up to a point we have to fight her with her own female weapons—variety, flexibility, evasiveness. But we hold an additional weapon which, if we did but know it, can be made an ace. She is a woman, but we are men, able to move with speed, which carries with it a certain quality of determination and even some negligence of consequences. But it is dangerous to rely exclusively on any one weapon, even your master one. You must, if you have it in you to do so, be ready to move forward, or backward, or temporarily to let events pass over you. Only one stance is excluded: steady and prolonged *resistance* to the direction of events.[37] This must bring disaster, because it is an attempt to place yourself right outside the flow of events; a form of behavior that reflects the illusion that your intentions and wishes are immune to the conditions of living in time.

The third phase is when Fortuna has departed. The disposition recommended when the guest has gone is equanimity. If foresight is needed when in a state of remote anticipation, flexibility when in immediate contact, a certain fixity of attitude should be apparent after the event. As the consequent events reveal the truth of antecedent events, so the departure of Fortuna is the revealer of the human character who has confronted her. Men of exceptional character are just those who are not altered in their judgment of their demeanor by

36. Ibid., 2:10.
37. Ibid., 3:9.

a visit of Fortuna. "If Fortuna changes, sometimes raising them, sometimes casting them down, they remain ever resolute, so resolute in mind and in conduct throughout life that it is easy for anyone to see that Fortuna holds no sway over them." [38] Fortuna leaves a weak man changed; he is either intoxicated with self-esteem for the windfall which Fortuna has brought him, or abject with self-pity for her depredations. Among individuals, Machiavelli's type of the equable character is Marcus Camillus, who said: "The dictatorships did not elate me, nor did exile depress me." Among peoples, the Romans are the exemplars. "No bad luck ever made [them] become abject, nor did good fortune ever make them arrogant." [39] After a severe defeat at Cannae, they neither lost heart nor sued for peace but kept their armies in the field. Contemporary Venice, by contrast, exemplifies the instability of peoples who indulge in grandiose illusions while Fortuna has left them high, but turn unnecessarily abject when she has left them dry. The maxim to remember is: whether Fortuna has frustrated or furthered your designs, remember that the wheel will turn again. Keep on your feet, or if you have been knocked off balance, pick yourself up and be ready for the next visitation. Either to despair at failure or to imagine that your recent success will insure your future is to assume a timeless world. Fortuna's ends are as unknown as the ways she takes to those ends; there is no ground for either despondency or elation, but only resolution and continued watchfulness.

Such are the formal conditions of success in a world composed of contingent events. But there is something more to note. Conduct, disposition, and an attitude that conduce to success are not necessarily moral, and Machiavelli's picture of human life would be disproportioned if it contained no ethical coloring, i.e. no intimation or hint of what is thought of as

38. Ibid., 3:31.
39. Ibid., 3:36.

an admirable human character, "the kind of man it is good to be." On Machiavelli's concrete moral recommendations the literature is not scarce, and his views on what is hypothetically and circumstantially desirable are in general not obscure. But there are as well unmistakable indications of a view of what morality means for the temporal creature we know man to be. It is a life that implies recognition of its own contingency, that does not attempt to slip out of the time scale we know into some other, rooted in eternity or in some foreordained schedule of events.

The estimable character lives in the future, accepts responsibility for it—anticipating, preparing, confronting, making provision. The contemptible human being is the one who evades the future, who, as he himself usually puts it, 'lives in the present.' To live in the present is an impossibility in a life in which what is conveniently called the present discloses either an immediate past or an immediate future. To attempt to live in an illusory present is to try to escape the life we know without effectively achieving the life we don't know, i.e. eternity. The virtues of "abnegation, humility, and contempt for mundane things" are only virtues in a life of which the end is paradise, and this is not a life that consists of trying to turn events right side up.[40] Those whose only anticipation is of heaven are attempting to have eternity in time; their morality is that of men who accept themselves as failures but who are unwilling to surrender life. It is suitable for no one else.

Now most men are not self-admitted total failures, essaying to resign from life without dying. Even when people speak of 'living for the day' they mean the day to come—not the week or year. But neither are they willing to strive for the supreme emblems of moral recognition, which are honor and glory; these are only to be earned by the ceaseless

40. Ibid., 2:2.

exercise of energetic foresight. And the man who manifests the intellectual virtue will also be capable of the moral virtue of magnanimity. The confident spirit which results only from a clear sight of the future is the precondition for honorable and generous actions.

Complete failures are few; but so is the other class of men who are capable of the highest services which can be given for the State. Most moral theories recognize two classes of virtue, that of sufficiency and that of excellence. The first is the supreme virtue in a world of denizens who expect peace, order, and necessities of physical existence, who are generally content to back the favorite for a place. The second is the crowning quality of "magnanimity, bodily strength, and everything else that tends to make men very bold." [41] This is the morality of those with a penchant for long odds, for demonstrating their strength while scorning to injure those weaker than themselves. They are not saints—sainthood has in any case no moral standing in the temporal world, where it is a mere profession. They are men prepared to give generous protection in return for honor, whose imaginations serve them as a morning bulge, not as a fading nocturne.

These qualities are as rare as is the exceptional foresight which is their prerequisite. In a letter to Vettori(10 August 1513) wherein he urged that the apparently unmenacing Swiss, who had just occupied Lombardy, should be seen as portending a threat to Tuscany, Machiavelli named the three "natural defects" which afflict the generality of men: they like to live from day to day, they do not believe that what has never been can ever be, and they "always tend to judge people after the same pattern," i.e. they rely excessively on handy precedent, drawing no lessons from the known activities of Fortuna.

The profession of ruling is one which not only forbids ab-

41. Ibid., 2:2.

ject or absolute failure (an indulgence which no State can permit to more than a few of its subjects), but rules out moderate or relative failure also. Statecraft is not for those whose virtues do not exceed those of their fellows, in whom is not uncommonly prominent the gifts of *long* foresight, readiness for the unexpected turn of events, and ability to re-create these events as well as to recognize history in them. To display these qualities in the conduct of public affairs is to secure a fame which will outlast your own life—the only immortality available to creatures of time.

Party & Sect in Machiavelli's
Florentine Histories

HARVEY C. MANSFIELD, JR.

M ACHIAVELLI'S FLORENTINE HISTO-
ries resembles a history book of our day in having a
period of narration and in presenting a problem. After the
Epistle Dedicatory to Pope Clement VII, who had commissioned the work, Machiavelli states the problem in the Proemium. Despite his commission, he calls the *Florentine Histories* "my undertaking"; and "my purpose," he says, was to
write on "the things done inside and outside by the Florentine
people," especially on the former, "the causes of the hatreds
and divisions in the city." If any republic has notable divisions,
those of Florence are "very notable." Most republics have had
one division between the nobles and the plebs, as Rome or
Athens, but Florence has suffered from many divisions dividing the winning party which have produced "as many deaths,

as many exiles, as many ruined families as ever appeared in any city of which we have record." [1]

Machiavelli's undertaking, then, is to seek the causes of the divisions in Florence as contrasted to those in Rome or Athens. Yet in the rest of the work we are given only two explicit statements on the causes. In the first chapter of the third book Machiavelli says that whereas the Roman people desired to share supreme honors together with the nobles, the Florentine people fought to govern themselves without participation by the nobles. The refusal of the Florentine people to share supreme honors with the nobles is puzzling, however, because Machiavelli began the chapter with the remark that popular men do not wish to obey and the implication that they do not wish to rule. What makes the Florentine people thirst for partisan victory?

In the first chapter of the seventh book, Machiavelli gives his only explicit characterization of the Florentine parties. Some divisions, he says, are harmful to republics; others are beneficial. Harmful ones are "accompanied by sects and partisans," while beneficial ones are not. The founder of a republic cannot prevent enmities; he can provide that there not be sects. The enmities of Florence were always sects or "mixed with sects." But what are sects? Nowhere in the *Florentine Histories* does Machiavelli define "sect." He uses the word in several meanings, but always in connection with religion; and the religion of Florence was Christianity.[2] We

1. *Florentine Histories,* F. Flora and C. Cordié, eds., in *Tutte le Opere di Niccolò Machiavelli,* 2 vols. (Milan, 1949–50), hereafter cited as *F. H.* Machiavelli's *Discourses on the First Ten Books of Livy* will be cited as *Disc., The Prince* as *P.,* and numbers in parentheses will refer to this edition.

2. This is true even of the "two sects of armies" in 5:2 (Vol. 2., p. 221); see note 47. The word "sect" occurs thirty-five times in the *Florentine Histories* in fourteen different locations; the seventh location is 3:7, and the word occurs in a sequence of seven chapters, 3:3–9. The only book whose first chapter contains "sect" is the seventh. In *The Prince* and the *Discourses* taken together, "sect" occurs twenty-one times, in seven locations in the *Discourses,* first in the seventh chapter where it refers to the "sects" of Savonarola and of his opponents, and seven

are led to the suggestion, which this study will develop, that Christianity is responsible for the special character of the parties in Florence.

Christianity, with its otherworldly understanding of "supreme honors," and its consequent superpolitical claims and transpolitical organization, is a sect essentially different from the ancient sects. It could not be managed or controlled by the Florentine princes in the way that the Roman Senate was able to manage the more political sects of pagan priests. The Christian sect (in the sense of "religion") became the context of the modern sects (in the sense of "parties"), and determined the play of modern politics by deprecating its prizes. In a work commissioned by and dedicated to a Florentine Pope, Machiavelli does not make this point directly. No man acquainted with politics would expect otherwise, and since the publication of that fundamental work of Machiavelli scholarship, Leo Strauss's *Thoughts on Machiavelli*, scholars have begun to explore Machiavelli's methods of indirect statement. In the *Florentine Histories* he makes his point indirectly both in the form of the work (sections 1–4 of this study) and in the content of his narrations (sections 5–9). To begin with the form of the book, one must consider its period of narration.

THE MEANING OF 1434

In the Epistle Dedicatory Machiavelli excuses himself for the things he will say against the Medici by pretending that, contrary to the instructions of the Pope (formerly

---

times in the body of one chapter, 2:5. It does not occur in *Disc.* 1:26, as one might expect from 2:5. When "sect" means "party," it is never used to refer specifically to the ancient parties, and in the *Florentine Histories* Machiavelli uses the expression "Guelf sect" but never "Ghibelline sect"; cf. *P.* 20. It is some indication of the difference between the *Florentine Histories* and the *Discourses* that in the former he speaks of Catholic or heretical sects within Christianity, since the context is Christian, and in the latter of the "Christian sect" as opposed to the "Gentile sect."

Giulio de' Medici), he may have seemed to flatter them. Thus he forestalls the charge of hostility by denying the charge of flattery, and in the Proemium he says that it was "my purpose" to begin "my narrative" at 1434, when the Medici had become the most powerful family in Florence, because "two most excellent historians" had told of the things that happened before that time. But on examination, their works proved inadequate on "the civil discords and internal enmities" and indeed, because of the importance of these matters, altogether defective.[3] This is the kind of examination that ambitious young princes of scholarship apply to the established authorities, and it might seem that Machiavelli was merely enlarging a gap in the scholarly literature to make a place for himself as a narrative historian. The *Florentine Histories* is often translated *The History of Florence* as if this were his intention, whatever his success in it.

The *Florentine Histories* is the only work of narration that Machiavelli wrote, but its resemblance to a modern history book is merely superficial. He speaks of "my narrative," "my narratives," and "our narrative"; once when he inter-

---

3. Neither of these two historians, Leonardo Bruni and Poggio Bracciolini, in fact ended his history at 1434. They did not adequately discuss civil discords in the past, Machiavelli says, because they feared to offend the living; but their fear was unnecessary. They did not consider that "actions that have greatness in them, as have those of governments and states, however carried on, and whatever outcome they have, always appear to bring men more honor than blame." *F. H.* Proemium (vol. 2, p. 7). In cruder words, these writers overestimated the power of morality in determining reputation, and their inadequacy is the result of a deep and general mistake. This mistake is indicated in Bruni's assertion that the Florentine people is a free people "not conquered in wars outside but oppressed by internal and civil discords." Bruni does not appreciate the connection between inside and outside things, *Historiarum Florentini Populi, Libri XII,* "Rerum Italicarum Scriptores," E. Santini ed., vol. 19, Part 3, p. 22; E. Santini, "Leonardo Bruni Aretino e i suoi *Historiarum Florentini Populi Libri XII,*" *Annali della R. Scuola Normale Superiore di Pisa,* vol. 22 (1910), pp. 121–22. See note 71. Cf. the writers discussed in *Disc.* 1:4 who "condemn the tumults between the Nobles and the Plebs," (vol. 1, p. 104).

rupts the narrative briefly he speaks of returning to "our order." But he also speaks of "our history" [*la istoria nostra*], of "my history," which he determined to begin at the beginning of "our city," and of "all parts of my history," which include "speeches and private reasonings, direct as well as oblique." [4] The "history" is not identical with the "narrative"; it determines where the narrative begins and contains invented speeches and reasonings that mere narrative would not include.

Moreover, the "history" has parts; as we know from the title of the work, it is divided into "histories." The obvious divisions are the eight books, of which seven begin with a discussion of some general political topic in the first chapter, in five cases an explicit comparison of ancient and modern practice. Perhaps it would be better to understand these "histories" as in the classical sense "inquiries." [5] The master inquiry, stated in the Proemium, would be "to show the causes of the hatreds and divisions" in Florence as opposed to Rome or Athens, and the seven following inquiries would serve this end. The master inquiry is not an historical problem in the current meaning, since its end is not to characterize the "history" of Florence but to use narratives of events in Florence to characterize certain parties and sects. It does not assume, as historians do today, that "history" is a thing to be studied or an aspect of reality as well as a certain kind of study. Correspondingly, the seven inquiries do not each introduce an historical period whose course of events illustrates some general human propensity in favor or in demand at that time, like the periods that make chapters in our his-

4. *F. H.* Epistle Dedicatory, Proemium, 1:10 (Vol. 2, p. 21). Of thirty-four quoted speeches in the *Florentine Histories* twelve are introduced with the formula *in questa sentenza* and one, in 3:11, of which Machiavelli says the words are true, with *in questa forma*. There are also seventeen indirect speeches.

5. Herodotus, 1.1; Aristotle, *Rhet.* 1360a37; Aristotle, *Poetics* 1451b3; Polybius, 1.1.4; Cicero, *De Oratore*, 2.12.52–14.58; Cicero, *De Legibus*, 1.2.5.

tory books. Machiavelli's inquiries (to which we shall return) overlap and do not seem to begin or end a course of events.

Most important, the narrative does not proceed without interruption or complication. It is constructed to and from 1434, the date of Cosimo de' Medici's return to Florence from exile, which was the coming to power of the Medici in Florence; and it is divided in four parts according to a distinction between things inside and things outside Florence. In giving the plan of the work in the Proemium, Machiavelli divides his task at 1434, before which he will, in view of the scholarly literature, discuss "particularly" things that happened inside the city and those outside things necessary to know the inside things. After this date, he will describe both the one and the other. Then he says that before dealing with Florence, he will show how Italy "came under the powers that governed it in that time"—a guarded expression suggesting the wide scope of things outside Florence. Machiavelli then gives an outline of the first four books; the first book describes "briefly" events in Italy to 1434 and the second to fourth books on Florence also close at 1434. From that time, he will present things happening inside and outside Florence "up to our present times." In fact, he tells first of things outside Florence to 1463 in Books 5 and 6, and then returns to 1434 at the beginning of Book 7 to catch up on things within Florence. From the seventh chapter of the seventh book, that is, from the death of Cosimo de' Medici, Machiavelli relates events inside and outside Florence together.

The reader thus expects 1434 to be a crucial year.[6] It seems

6. "1434" occurs eleven times in the *Florentine Histories,* and first appears as "the year of the Christian religion 1434." Proemium (Vol. 2, p. 5) To show the power of sects in establishing the narrative of events, Machiavelli begins forty-nine chapters with parts of the verb "to be," thirteen of them in Book 1. There are 107 dates in the work in

214

to be connected to the distinction between things inside and things outside Florence, for the narrative is told in such a way that the things outside Florence are brought ever closer to the things inside. In the first book, only events outside Florence to 1434 are narrated; in Books 2–4 (before 1434) only those outside events relevant to events inside Florence are narrated; from the beginning of Book 5 to Book 7: 6 (after 1434), outside events are assumed to be relevant to inside events but are narrated separately; and from 7:7 (1464) they are narrated together. 1434 divides exactly in half not only the eight books but the 286 chapters of the *Florentine Histories.*[7] The precise difference, as given, is this: before the coming to power of the Medici, it is necessary to distinguish between things outside Florence necessary to know the inside things and things outside unnecessary to know for that purpose; and afterwards it is no longer necessary to make this distinction. With the return of Cosimo, things outside Florence are automatically relevant to things inside, and this result is given emphasis by the change in narrative method used after the death of Cosimo.

The meaning of 1434, though not obvious, seems surely grand. But when we turn to Machiavelli's description of this event in the last chapter of the fourth book and the first chapter of the fifth, we find no discourse on "the meaning of 1434." Instead we find a trifling turn of fortune caused by impotence and foolish confidence.

---

seventy-five locations; 35 dates are given with the formula "the year. . . ." In the *Discourses* there are 26 dates (all at least partly in Machiavelli's lifetime) in twenty-three chapters.

7. The first four and the last four books have eleven × thirteen chapters; the first book has three × thirteen chapters, and the last seven books, nineteen × thirteen chapters. Machiavelli's *The Prince* has twenty-six chapters; and his *Art of War* has 182 (thirteen × fourteen) speeches. The *Discourses* has 142 chapters, but this is the same as the number of books in Livy's *History*. It would have been praeternatural for Livy to have anticipated Machiavelli's need. Leo Strauss, *Thoughts on Machiavelli* (Glencoe, Illinois, 1958), pp. 48–49, 52.

It appears at the end of Book 4 that the Medici did not first become prominent in 1434. In that year Cosimo de' Medici was restored from exile to Florence in triumph over the chief of the opposing party, Rinaldo degli Albizzi, himself now sent into exile. "Rarely has it happened that a citizen, returning in triumph from a victory, has been received by his fatherland with such a concourse of people and so great a demonstration of good will, as he received when he returned from exile." But how did he get the victory and what was the nature of the triumph?

Cosimo had been sent into exile by a party of "nobles" whose divided counsel had allowed him to bribe his way to this easy fate, leaving his own party strong in Florence.[8] When Cosimo's partisans captured the *Signoria* by the usual method of lot from elected or prearranged eligibles, Messer Rinaldo and his party were again divided and irresolute. Though aware of the danger, they could not decide to prevent the new *Signoria* from taking office. As soon as it showed its intention of restoring Cosimo, Messer Rinaldo took arms, but those of his party who had argued against precipitate action, as they called it, had no stomach for fighting an opponent who by their inactivity had won public authority. Messer Rinaldo upbraided them for their sluggishness, receiving a feeble excuse from one and muttered incoherence from another. He took the time to declare to them that if disaster followed he would have the satisfaction of having given advice of the danger and of having been present at it with force. But in fact, Machiavelli says, Messer Rinaldo had sufficient force to capture the *Signori,* and lost his opportunity by waiting for more. In the time he spent in upbraiding his friends, the *Signori* recovered their spirit, made preparations for their defense, and sent some citizens to Rinaldo to exhort him to lay down his arms, assuring him the *Signori*

8. This was a mistake of the nobles; see *Disc.* 1:33; *F. H.* 4:3, 27. Niccolò da Uzzano's foretelling, 4:19 (end), foretells Rinaldo's foretelling in 4:30 because it indicates the division of the Florentine nobility.

had no intention to restore Cosimo. One of Rinaldo's lieutenants accepted this assurance, and went with his followers into the palace of the *Signoria* to signify his acceptance. Rinaldo saw his own followers begin to lose their warmth of spirit.

At this point the Pope intervened. He was staying in Florence because he had been chased from Rome by the Roman people. "Seeing these tumults and believing it his office to quiet them," he sent for Rinaldo and persuaded him, with a guarantee of the good intentions of the *Signoria,* to disarm himself. Whereupon the *Signori* secretly arranged to seize the city's fortresses, and having done so, brought back Cosimo and exiled Rinaldo. Pope Eugene, seeing the ruin of those who "at his prayer" had laid down their arms, was "very ill content." He lamented the injury "done under his faith" and asked Rinaldo to have patience and to hope for the good "because of the variability of fortune." Rinaldo accepted these priestly condolences in the spirit with which they were offered: he blamed himself more than anyone else, he said, for putting too much faith in the Pope and for believing that "you who have been chased from your own fatherland, could keep me in mine." [9] He said that he had had much experience of the senselessness of fortune, and that if fortune did not show herself favorable to him, he did not desire anyhow to live in a city where the laws were less powerful than men. Rinaldo stalked out of Florence in high dudgeon, and Cosimo returned "in triumph." [10]

9. Just before Rinaldo died, he tried, Machiavelli says, "to gain his celestial fatherland, since he had lost his terrestrial"; *F. H.* 5:34 (Vol. 2, p. 271). His failure to see that one cannot have both—that all men are "exiles" from one or the other—was the source of his credulity. Cf. 4: 22 and 4:26 for Rinaldo's naïve request for protection against "false calumnies" and 5:8 for his naïve request for aid from the Duke of Milan.

10. Lorenzo was able to claim, in 1478 after the failure of the Pazzi conspiracy, that Cosimo returned from exile "not with arms and violence, but with your consent and union." *F. H.* 8:10 (Vol. 2, p. 394). For another ludicrous triumph, see 8: 23.

Machiavelli's *Florentine Histories* thus turns on what may be called the comedy of 1434. The contrast of Cosimo's triumph with a Roman triumph is humiliating for Italy, Florence, and Cosimo himself. Cosimo's triumph established the hegemony of the Medici family, but a Roman triumph brought glory to the individual and acquisitions to the republic. A Roman triumph could not occur in Florence because the Florentine nobility, disunited and weak, was unable to manage Cosimo; it thought only of exile or death for him and could not find a task that would attach his interest and glory to the common good.[11] In the end Cosimo was permitted to back his way into power in a kind of "restoration."[12] He did not have to gain power with his own arms.

Cosimo's triumph, therefore, was "Roman" in the modern rather than the ancient sense. It was accomplished partly by "the authority of the Pope,"[13] who at the time was staying in Florence and who thereafter was united with Florence as members of the Medici family became Popes. In submitting the *Florentine Histories* to a Medici Pope Machiavelli asserted that Florence remained divided "until it began to be governed under the protection of Your House [*Casa Sua*]." "Your House" contains the ambiguous reference to both the Medici and the papacy that is needed to confirm the "Ro-

11. *F. H.* 4:27. Niccolò da Uzzano, a noble who opposed the use of "extraordinary ways" against Cosimo, gives a discourse, accurate in its view of future events, that perfectly exposes the impotence of morality in its "ordinary ways." His discourse concludes in a prayer and with the advice to "live neutrally," as if men in need of God's help could forget the cause of their need, their natural partisanship and self-interestedness.

12. Cosimo's party ordained, after he was restored, that others could be restored only by a vote of thirty-four in a college of thirty-seven, which would be a nearly miraculous margin of assent. For the meaning of Cosimo's "restoration," see *F. H.* 7:5–6 (Vol. 2, pp. 336, 340), where Machiavelli's "extraordinary" method of praising Cosimo is perhaps more effective for being seen once, and not always. Cf. *Disc.* 1:52; *P.* 7 (Vol. 1, pp. 26–27); Machiavelli's letter of 30 August 1524.

13. *F. H.* 4:31 (Vol. 2, p. 216).

man" triumph of Cosimo.[14] We may wonder what made that triumph possible. What cause but the character of the Christian sect makes possible the authority of the Pope and establishes his "office" as a regent above human politics and as intermediary and peacemaker between human parties? We shall find a similar explanation for the obvious fact that the Medici house was made more prominent by its ecclesiastical attainments. A private house like the Medici was enabled to rise above public control because Christianity had weakened or destroyed the basis of public control.

THE "EXTRAORDINARY FORCE"

The account of Cosimo's triumph is immediately followed, at the beginning of Book 5, by a discussion of "nature" and man's place in nature. Machiavelli says that "nature does not allow worldly things [*mondane cose*] to remain fixed"; hence order is followed by disorder, and disorder by order, unless men are stifled by "an extraordinary force." This "extraordinary force" outside the working of "nature" and superior to the "worldly things" that move makes one think of the supernatural. Elsewhere in this work Machiavelli describes a whirlwind as driven by "superior forces, whether natural or supernatural"; thus an extraordinary force outside the natural would seem to be the supernatural. One recalls a statement in the eleventh chapter of the *Discourses* (ambiguously titled "Of the Religion of the Romans"):

14. In *F. H.* 8:36 (Vol. 1, p. 431) Machiavelli says that the cardinalate received by Giovanni de' Medici at age thirteen was "a ladder to enable his house to rise into heaven, as happened in time following." After his son Giovanni died, Cosimo said: "This is too great a house for such a small family. . . ." Machiavelli almost omitted this "necessary" saying of Cosimo's; 7:6 (Vol. 2, pp. 338–39). Lorenzo, speaking to the *Signori* and certain citizens, said "our house . . . has always been exalted [*esaltata*] by you"; 8:10 (Vol. 2, p. 393); see the untruth in note 10 above. Cosimo in his magnificence built churches and private houses for his family, but no public buildings, 7:4–5.

"And truly there has been no orderer of extraordinary laws in a people who did not have recourse to God, for otherwise they would not be accepted." [15] Perhaps the "extraordinary force" that keeps modern men in disorder results from having recourse to the Christian God. If we suppose rightly, this is the only chapter in the *Florentine Histories* that considers the contrast of the natural and the supernatural, though without mentioning the supernatural. The chapter on the whirlwind (6: 34), which mentions the natural and the supernatural, does not contrast them. Machiavelli makes one point at a time, in its place.

This chapter (5:1) is also the only one in which the Tuscans, as distinguished from the inhabitants of the region of Tuscany, are mentioned.[16] The Tuscany of the Tuscans (or, as we would call them, the Etruscans) is pre-Roman Italy, hence not only pre-Christian Italy, but considering that ancient Rome is partly continuous with modern Rome, pre-pre-Christian Italy. It recalls the context of "nature" in which the Christian sect is only one among many sects. Machiavelli does not say what the "extraordinary force" could be that has prevented the return of virtue and order out of the ruins of the Roman empire. He merely wonders at the ease with which "weak and poorly administered armies" have held in check "so many very noble peoples." He remarks that since philosophers corrupt "the strength of armed spirits" with honorable laziness, Cato introduced a law that "no philosopher be received at Rome." [17] What is the laziness, hon-

15. *Disc.* 1:11 (Vol. 1, p. 126); *F. H.* 5:1, 6:34; cf. 3:16 (Vol. 2, p. 190). See "external force" in *Disc.* 3:1 (Vol. 1, p. 331). "Extraordinary" means "supernatural" in *P.* 26 (Vol. 1, p. 82).

16. One would expect them to be mentioned in *F. H.* 2:2.

17. *F. H.* 5:1 (Vol. 2, pp. 220–21). This consideration could never apply against Machiavelli himself, who teaches men to use or seize their own arms. Perhaps it takes an "extraordinary force" from this philosopher-captain to overcome the customary oscillation of virtue between quiet and glory and to rescue a people kept in ruin by means of another "extraordinary force."

orable or pious, that prevails in modern Rome? If it arises from an "extraordinary force," can it be controlled by political authority? These high thoughts on order and disorder in nature follow a domestic comedy in Florence and introduce a criticism of the conduct of modern "princes, soldiers, and chiefs of republics" in warfare.

We have, then, a transition from domestic to foreign affairs at the beginning of Book 5, as accords with Machiavelli's plan. The foreign policy of Florence becomes necessarily relevant to its domestic policy after the Medici achieve power in Florence through the agency of the Pope, who could not manage his own domestic troubles and yet thought himself qualified to pacify Florence. Because he does not recognize the distinction between domestic and foreign, he meddles where he can in the domestic affairs of princes and republics.

Thus the meaning of "foreign" is also ambiguous. It refers to the external relations of men with men and of men with God. The ambiguity is implied in Christian doctrine, which says that men live as friends with one another in peace, as they live at peace with God: the brotherhood of man under the fatherhood of God. Machiavelli might have supposed from this that man's distance from God, which he thought too great for gratitude or filial piety on the part of man to God, makes God a foreigner to man,[18] and is ultimately responsible for the distances between human societies and hence for the distinction men make, in "ordinary" usage, between domestic and foreign affairs.

Christianity is the context of the *Florentine Histories,* since Florence, as Machiavelli shows in Book 1, was from

18. Even Cosimo, who spent continually for the building of temples and in charity was never able "to spend as much for the honor of God as was said to be due him in his books." *F. H.* 7:6 (Vol. 2, p. 337). For the connection between magnificence and religion, see Aristotle, *Nic. Ethics,* 1122b20. Florence is a city of beautiful buildings partly because Christianity turned its princes from magnanimity to magnificence.

its beginnings a Christian state. Christianity is not the open theme of the work, however. As compared to the *Discourses,*[19] Machiavelli says little in the *Florentine Histories* about Christianity. Although he states the problem of the work in a comparison of ancient and modern politics, he never describes Christianity, as he did in the *Discourses,* as the decisive difference between ancient and modern politics. The only book without an inquiry, the first, is the book that discusses Christianity, and it does this only by describing the activities of Christians and Popes. Machiavelli remarks here that men are now Pieros, Giovannis, and Matteos instead of Caesars and Pompeys, and he gives some idea of the effect of "the Christian religion" by discussing the effects of its heretical (as opposed to its catholic) sects.[20] The reader is left to surmise the meaning of "catholic sects" just as he was forced to discover the meaning of 1434.

In a book on his own city, commissioned by a Florentine Pope, Machiavelli could not speak as boldly about Christianity as he did in *The Prince* and the *Discourses;* and he does not claim for this work, as he did for those, that it contains everything he knows. But he constructed it with a division in the middle suggesting a thought that points directly at the Pope in Florence and indirectly at a Medici, i.e., Florentine Pope. Machiavelli's rhetoric more than his historical accuracy is at issue here. But which is his historical argument? Did Cosimo capture Florence and then did the Medici capture the papacy for Florence, or by capturing Florence did he and Florence become unconscious tools of the Pope, or was neither of these the case?

Cosimo was a "disarmed man," and he proved unable to expand "Florentine power with an honorable conquest." To

19. *Disc.* I pref., 12; 2:2, 5.
20. *F. H.* 1:5 (Vol. 2, p. 16); in 2:2 the first book is called "our universal treatise" to indicate that Christianity, not nature, is the context of the *Florentine Histories.* See Strauss, *Thoughts on Machiavelli,* p. 307, n. 22.

capture Lucca, he had put his faith in the "mercenary and faithless arms" of Francesco Sforza. He had great authority in Florence, but it was left to his "descendants" to acquire authority in all Christendom. Yet if his "descendants" include the Medici Popes, they too were forced to depend on faithless mercenaries. It seems that under Christianity it is difficult for a prince to acquire anything, whether he is a "secular prince" or a Pope.[21] Because Christianity is above politics, the prince must be disarmed either of this world's weapons, like a Pope, or of the other world's weapons, like a mercenary captain. Cosimo seems to represent the modern prince whose "greatness of spirit" is reduced to private "magnificence," whose ambition is restricted to peacemaking in his own city, and whose authority is dissipated in the ecclesiastical attainments of his "descendants." At his triumph in 1434 and again at his death Machiavelli quotes the epitaph on Cosimo's tombstone, *padre della patria.* Since both *"padre"* and *patria* are ambiguous, this is both a lower and a higher designation in the sacred, as compared to the secular, hierarchy.[22]

THE ABSENCE OF SAVONAROLA

The importance of Christianity is openly slighted and covertly emphasized. In view of this rhetorical tactic, it is significant that Machiavelli fails even to mention Savonarola in the *Florentine Histories.* He says in the Proemium that he will describe things inside and outside Florence "up to our present times," but he ends Book 8 at the death of Lorenzo

21. *F. H.* 1:23 (Vol. 2, p. 40); 7:5 (Vol. 2, p. 335); 7:6 (Vol. 2, pp. 338–39); 6:20 (Vol. 2, p. 300); 8:11 (Vol. 2, p. 396); 8:17 (Vol. 2, p. 404).

22. *F. H.* 4:33 (Vol. 2, p. 218) and 7:6 (Vol. 2, p. 339). Of numerological interest are the facts that these two chapters are separated by seventy-eight chapters, when the two chapters out of narrative order are removed, 5:2–3; that Cosimo is first mentioned in 4:11; and that he succeeds his father in 4:16. See note 9. On Lorenzo, see 8:36.

in 1492. Lorenzo, he says ominously, was mourned with just cause, for after his death those who were left found no way to satisfy or check the ambition of Lodovico Sforza, a situation "which began the growth of those evil seeds that, in a short time, since no living man knew how to destroy them, have ruined and still ruin Italy." [23] Thus Machiavelli quickly shifts his gaze from Florence to Italy, overlooking the then-imminent rule of Savonarola, whom Lorenzo had already invited to Florence. Since he apparently does not keep his promise to carry the narrative "up to our present times," it is easy to conclude that the *Florentine Histories* is unfinished. Yet the arrangement of chapters indicates that it is not simply unfinished.[24] Machiavelli submitted it as finished and surely polished his first draft.

In the Epistle Dedicatory he offers an apology for not writing up to the present: "And since in writing I have come to those times which by the death of the Magnificent Lorenzo de' Medici have changed the form of Italy, and since the things which followed this have been loftier and greater, and are to be described with a loftier and greater spirit [*spirito*], I have judged it well that all I have described up to this time be assembled in one volume and presented to Your Most Blessed Holiness, so that in some part you may begin to taste the fruits of your seeds and my labors." [25] It is as if a second volume were promised that would contain a full description of everything "loftier and greater" than the contents of the first volume. Yet the first volume is a fruit that may have a taste of the second volume, and it seems to end in a way that suggests the loftier and greater things of which Machiavelli could not speak explicitly.

Machiavelli had said in the *Discourses* (in the eleventh

23. *F. H.* 8:36 (Vol. 2, p. 434).
24. See notes 2, 6, 7.
25. *F. H.* Epistle Dedicatory (Vol. 2, p. 3); cf. 5:1; 8:9, 29. Roberto Ridolfi, *Vita di Niccolò Machiavelli* (Rome, 1954), pp. 298–9, 309–10, 466, n. 17.

chapter, discussed above) that one must speak of "so great a man" as Savonarola "with reverence," but he did not hesitate to display "his life, doctrine and the plan he undertook" as an example to confirm the feasibility of bringing new orders even to civilized men, such as the people of Florence supposed themselves to be.[26] Surely a *Florentine Histories* completed "up to our present times" would describe the new order of Savonarola, unless we are to impute reverence to Savonarola in Machiavelli's mention of the "loftier and greater" things to come after Lorenzo. At the end of Book 8, he speaks only of the calamities to come after Lorenzo, the evil seeds whose growth would begin, in the absence of Lorenzo, through the ambition of Lodovico Sforza.[27] This passage must refer to the invasion of Italy by Charles VIII, King of France, in 1494. Now these calamities were signified, Machiavelli says in the same place, by a bolt of lightning that struck the cathedral of Santa Reparata.[28] In the *Discourses*, however, in the chapter devoted to signs (1:56), he mentions this event as occurring before the death of Lorenzo (1492) but without saying what it signified and with the prosaic remark that it caused "very great damage to that building." He must have known Savonarola's interpretation of the event, also as a sign of calamities, but of domestic calamities in Florence. They were the scourge of God—*Ecce gladius Domini*—to punish the Florentines for their sins.[29] Just before he mentions this event without its interpretation, he tells "how much was predicted by Brother Girolamo Savonarola before the coming of King Charles VIII of

26. *Disc.* 1:11 (Vol. 1, p. 128).
27. *Disc.* 2:15, 3:11; *P.* 3.
28. *F. H.* 8:36 (Vol. 2, p. 434); 5:15; 8:5,6; letter of 9 March 1498.
29. *Disc.* 1:56 (Vol. 1, p. 215). Roberto Ridolfi, *Vita di Girolamo Savonarola*, 2 vols. (Rome, 1952), pp. 73–74. Another sign of impending calamities was that the princes *through their spokesmen* [*oratori*] declared their sorrow to Florence at Lorenzo's death; *F. H.* 8:36. Spokesmen of princes are like interpreters of signs. Cf. *F. H.* 7:28 for Machiavelli's prose version of a sign.

France into Italy. . . ." So in the *Florentine Histories* he uses the wrong sign of the two available, the one referring to domestic calamities rather than foreign invasion; and he omits any connection with Savonarola by failing to mention either his name or the domestic changes in Florence that would put him in mind immediately.[30] Machiavelli leaves a false trail that points away from Savonarola and therefore, after the proper "inquiries," leads back to him.

We are at first confused by the fact that the *Florentine Histories* ends with the foreboding of a foreign invasion, when we expect, in a work whose theme is internal divisions, the foreboding if not the discussion of a striking change of government in Florence. But in the refined meaning of "foreign," the coming of Savonarola rather than the King of France constitutes a foreign invasion. In 5:1, Machiavelli says that by the cowardly wars in Italy, "as will be made clearly known by what we shall describe from 1434 to 1494," a new road was opened to the barbarians and Italy put herself back into slavery under them. But Savonarola, in 1494, hailed the coming of the French king as the purgation of Florence and the Church. In consequence of the invasion, the Medici were expelled from Florence and Savonarola seized the opportunity of bringing new orders to men who thought they were civilized. Truth is stranger than fiction, and Machiavelli did not have to make the metaphor of "foreign" that he could find in events.

THE INQUIRIES

To understand the *Florentine Histories* one must make the importance of Christianity explicit. To do this for 1434, the crucial event of the work, it was necessary to consider the inquiry on order and disorder at the beginning of Book 5 as a transition rather than an introduction. At the beginning

30. He does mention Lorenzo's patronage of a rival of Savonarola's; Machiavelli, *Istorie Fiorentine* ed. F. Gaeta (Milan, 1962), p. 575, n. 14.

of Book 8, Machiavelli says that it would seem proper, "wishing to follow our custom," to speak of "the quality of conspiracies and their importance" between the narrations of two actual conspiracies. This he would do, he says, if he had not done so in another place or if he could do so with brevity.[31] So these things will be put aside, and he will turn to "another matter"; the seventh inquiry, it seems, will be omitted. But in fact it is not omitted. Machiavelli does speak of "the quality of conspiracies and their importance," and in such manner as to suggest the quality and importance of his "inquiries."

Passing to the other matter, he says that after "the state of the Medici" had overcome all the hostilities of those who opposed it openly, it had to overcome those who schemed against it secretly.[32] Such conspiracies succeed with difficulty, for they usually bring ruin to "those who move them" and greatness to the man conspired against. Unless the latter is killed, which rarely happens, he rises to greater power. Then he often becomes wicked, as these conspiracies by their example give him cause to fear; fear causes him to secure himself; securing himself causes him to injure; injuring gives birth to hatreds "and many times his own ruin." Thus, Machiavelli concludes, such conspiracies quickly crush "those who move them" and with time, harm "those against whom they are moved."

These remarks serve as a prelude to a fascinating narration of the Pazzi conspiracy against the Medici brothers Giuliano and Lorenzo. The conspiracy was executed inside Flor-

31. *F. H.* 8:1 (vol. 2, p. 379). See references to the preceding or following book in 1:39, 3:1, 3:29, 6:38, 7:1, 7:34. Machiavelli treats of conspiracy in *Disc.* 3:6 and *P.* 19, each the longest chapter in the work.
32. *Occultamente* and *secretamente* are used interchangeably (vol. 2, p. 379). Opposition to the Medici in Machiavelli's day would still have to be secret; Felix Gilbert, *Machiavelli and Guicciardini* (Princeton, 1965), p. 239. See the letter of Donato Gianotti (written in 1533), quoted in Machiavelli, *The History of Florence*, ed. Myron P. Gilmore, (New York, 1970), pp. xxvi–vii.

ence and by a last-minute change of plan inside a church, and it failed because the executioners, lacking "a great and firm spirit [*animo*]," killed only Giuliano and not Lorenzo.[33] Lorenzo, rid of a brother who was bound to cause him trouble, did indeed rise to greater power in a city "that judges things by success and not by counsel." [34] Why, then, did Machiavelli make so much of the indirect consequences of conspiracy, since apparently they did not follow from the Pazzi conspiracy? His discussion hints that not every conspirator need "move" his conspiracy. It suggests the possibility of an indirect conspiracy which uses other conspirators to "move" the conspiracy and make the first—ordinarily unsuccessful—attempt. Then the patient master conspirator can watch the indirect consequences develop. In fact, there was a master conspirator behind the Pazzi conspiracy, the Pope—and he was foiled by the refusal of one executioner "to accompany treason with sacrilege." [35]

It would be prudent to suppose that Machiavelli considered himself a master conspirator who intended, however, not to be hoist on his own petard. He remarks mildly that this Pope was "the first who began to show how much a pope could do. . . ." The first words of the *Florentine Histories* are *"lo animo mio"* ("my purpose") and the last words are *"la Italia."* The chapter on the "extraordinary force" that stifles a return to order ends with a recommendation to study modern things as well as ancient, for while "free spirits [*liberali animi*]" can imitate the latter, they can avoid and abolish the former.[36] Having an aim at least partly practical and reforming, the *Florentine Histories* must have

33. Machiavelli is more explicit in *Disc.* 3:6 (vol. 1, p. 349).
34. *F. H.* 8:2 (end), 8:22 (vol. 2, p. 411).
35. The alternative of patience and conspiracy in 8:1 (vol. 2, p. 379) is false. Both conspiracies related at length had master conspirators; see 7:31, 7:33, 8:2, and cf. *Disc.* 1 pr (end), 9 (on Agis); 3:6 on Alexamenus (vol. 1, p. 345), Pelipodas (vol. 1, p. 352), and the two cautions at the end (vol. 1, p. 358).
36. *F. H.* 5:1; 7:22 (vol. 2, p. 360).

been written not with the methods of scientific history but with the devices of reformers or "new princes." Like any new prince, Machiavelli began by being weaker than the existing princes, and he must have been forced to express himself disingenuously, or as he says, with fraud.[37] If he could have said openly all he intended against "this corrupt world," he would not have had to say it. In the *Florentine Histories*, his method of fraud is to conduct the reader by stages in histories or inquiries that bring him to understand what is wrong with the modern world. Each inquiry considers an aspect of the modern world and offers an opinion that points beyond itself to a better understanding; the inquiries overlap each other because each is provisional and hence transitional. Machiavelli makes his hostility to the modern world plain and clear so that everyone, at whatever level of understanding, can find a reason for changing it, but only at the last stage of the conspiracy, as befits a prudent conspiracy, does one learn of the extent of the conspiracy or even that he has joined a conspiracy. Thus the inquiries of the *Florentine Histories*, being transitional from and to the matter surrounding them, are transitional to each other; and they culminate in an inquiry on conspiracy which impudently claims to be omitted.

The first inquiry (2:1) compares ancient and modern policy on colonies: "Among the great and marvelous orders of ancient republics and principalities that in our times have

37. *Disc.* 2:13; *P.* 7 (vol. 1, p. 26); *F. H.* 3:13 (vol. 2, p. 144). In 5:23 Niccolò Piccino makes an escape from his enemies inside a sack carried on the back of his German servant. This adventure of Niccolò's— for Machiavelli keeps calling him Niccolò in this vicinity—occurs between accounts of two strategems of war that worked because the enemy thought them impossible; and it must be compared with the mistake of another Niccolò in 1:31, who tried to escape to the German emperor. Perhaps our Niccolò will escape from his enemies with an impossible trick, by hiding inside a sack carried not by the emperor but by the Pope (who commissioned this work). At any rate *The Prince* and the *Discourses* were first published under papal authority together with the *Florentine Histories*. Cf. *Disc.* 2:33 and Strauss, *Thoughts on Machiavelli*, pp. 106–7.

been extinguished was that by which many lands and cities were built anew and at every time." This statement equates colonizing with new building and implies that political vitality demands growth. Yet Machiavelli conceals the harshness of imperialism by attributing it solely to a defect of "nature." Nature (and its contrary), not "history," is the problem of Machiavelli's "histories." Nature does not provide an even fertility of land, and in the absence of human "industry" or "culture" fertile lands become crowded and poor, while unfertile lands remain desert. This explanation does not account for the phenomenon of conquest, although Machiavelli refers to the policy of colonizing in lands "either conquered or empty." And why do the moderns not send colonies? ". . . [B]ecause princes have no desire for true glory and republics no order that deserves to be praised." The defect of the moderns is political, for Machiavelli condemns modern princes and republics impartially and separately. We note that the moderns are not lacking in industry or in the pacific art of farming but it may be that they somehow place too much confidence in nature, as though forgetting its failure to provide the most elementary necessities and the consequent need for human "culture" or cultivation.[38]

The second inquiry (3:1) discusses "the serious and natural enmities . . . between popular men and nobles" in Rome and Florence. In the description of *natural* enmities we have an intimation that nature is not to be understood simply as distinct from human culture nor human culture simply as supplying the defects of nature. Within human culture, among "human things," these natural enmities are "the cause of all the evils that grow up in cities." Yet "diverse effects" can be observed in Rome and in Florence; in

38. Note "industry" as opposed to "force" in *F. H.* 6:2 (vol. 2, p. 275); cf. the chapter preceding, 1:39: the Florentines "had through many divisions destroyed her nobility and that republic was now in the hands of those brought up in trade." See *Disc.* 2:8.

Rome, the enmities were brought to an end by disputes, in Florence, by fighting; in Rome, they ended with a law, in Florence, with the exile and death of many citizens; in Rome, they always increased military virtue, in Florence, they destroyed it entirely; in Rome, they brought very great inequality out of equality, and in Florence, they reduced inequality to a "wonderful [*mirabile*] equality." [39] For the cause of this difference Machiavelli, as we have said, blames the Florentine people. Unlike the Roman people, who wished to enjoy supreme honors with the nobles, the Florentine people fought to govern by themselves without the participation of the nobles. Their desire was "harmful and unjust," but it is not fully explained. Why did the Florentine people wish to govern by themselves, despite the fact that the people do not naturally desire to command? The consequence of their rule has been to destroy in Florence "that virtue in arms and generosity of spirit [*animo*]" possessed by the nobility, with no stated advantage to themselves.

Machiavelli shows in the next inquiry (4:1) that he does not accept the partisan view of either the people or the nobles. Cities, especially (but not only) such as are not well ordered, and that are administered under the name of republic, "often vary their governors and their state not between liberty and servitude, as many believe, but between servitude and license." The ministers of license, he says, are the people, and the ministers of servitude are the nobles; both claim the name of liberty. Thus the alternative of liberty and slavery would be the popular view that "many believe" and that Machiavelli chooses to expose as partisan. Then how can a city be free? A city "can be called free" when by good fortune a good, wise, and powerful citizen orders the laws so as to quiet the humors of the nobles and people or to restrain them so that they cannot work for evil. Founded on good

39. *F. H.* 3:1 (vol. 2, p. 122).

laws and orders, such a city would not need to be maintained, as other cities are, by the virtue of one man. "Many ancient republics," Machiavelli says, had this good fortune, but cities where such laws and orders are lacking "vary between a tyrannical and a licentious state." Now since the tyrannical state does not please the good and the licentious does not please the wise, these cities have to be maintained by "the virtue and fortune of one man."

Natural enmities, it seems, can be repressed with impartial laws and orders established by a "good, wise and powerful man" who makes the "virtue of one man" unnecessary thereafter. Such a man is "the good fortune of the city": good fortune would then seem to be the solution for natural divisions. How likely is this good fortune? By moving from the division between nobles and people regarding liberty to the distinction between a tyrannical state that does not please the good and a licentious state that does not please the wise, Machiavelli indicates the existence of a natural division between the good and the wise regarding good laws and orders. If a powerful citizen appears who is both good and wise, he must have coincidentally two qualities not only different but contrary.[40]

Thus the problem of natural divisions between the nobles and the people continues among those who might be thought above the quarrel; it cannot be solved by the legislation of an impartial man. Yet "many ancient republics" were gifted with good laws and orders and long lives. Perhaps they used "the virtue of one man," as opposed to goodness, and with good laws and orders managed not to depend on "the virtue and good fortune of one man," like the modern states. Machiavelli's regime is impartial, while his conception of virtue

40. See the contrary advice of good men and wise men in 7:13. Rinato de' Pazzi was "considered a wise and good man" (for all the good it did him) because he was lacking in pride, i.e., in the desire to make himself powerful. See note 42.

emphatically is not. The regime achieves impartiality by using the virtue of many men, each of whom is partial to himself, for virtue is always "the virtue of one man." Since Florence failed to restrain the conflict between nobles and people with the proper mixture of rewards and punishments, the city could not make use of its supply of virtuous men, as each was dangerous to every other.[41] It became dependent on the good fortune, as well as the virtue, of one man. The reason for this failure is not explained, but a lack of tolerance for the partiality of virtue, for the desire of princes for true glory, is suggested.[42] Machiavelli does not mention the possibility, dear to Aristotelian political science, of a mixed regime sustained by an impartial middle class, but the reasoning that separates the good from the wise would bear against this possibility.[43]

41. See *F. H.* 2:29 on Ramando di Cardona; 6:6–7 on the murder of Baldaccio.

42. See *F. H.* 3:17, 22 on Florence's ingratitude to Michele di Lando. Michele was both prudent and good. His goodness consisted in "never allowing a thought to enter his mind that was contrary to the general good"; his prudence "allowed him to conduct things in such a way that many of his party yielded to him and the others he could overcome with arms" 3:17 (vol. 2, p. 152). His partisan thoughts clearly were not contrary to the general good, in Machiavelli's view; cf. Epistle Dedicatory (vol. 2, p. 4). Giovanni de' Medici told Rinaldo degli Albizzi that because men are quicker for revenge than gratitude, "the duty of a wise and good citizen, he believed, was not to change the customary orders of the city" 4:10. Then, knowing his man, he advised Rinaldo to follow the policy of his father and gain the gratitude of the people by benefitting them. Rinaldo never considered this, and shortly afterwards Giovanni took his own advice, changing the orders of Florence to benefit the people and himself. Giovanni was a man "of very great prudence," and his prudence consisted in departures from his goodness and a seeming lack of ambition. Florence, i.e. the Florentine people, showed more gratitude for his benevolence, done at the expense of the rich, than it would have shown for conquests taken from enemies, 4:14, 16. Cf. "the grace mixed with power" characteristic of Cosimo and Neri Capponi, 7:2 (vol. 2, p. 331).

43. Party conflict in Florence was for a time moderated by intermediaries using arguments to calm the zeal of both sides, but the arguments said nothing about justice or impartiality and the conflict began anew five years and two chapters later, *F. H.* 2:14, 16.

The central inquiry has been considered. It seemed to show the contrast between the natural order of "worldly things" in movement, within which men contrive their own order and suffer through its decay, and the supernatural, which can stifle at least the return to good order with an "extraordinary force." This contrast modifies the farmer's view of nature given in the first inquiry, that nature and culture are distinct, in the direction suggested by the second inquiry, that natural order applies to human things, especially the divisions in human societies. But now we have a reason why "natural divisions" can have "diverse effects" in Rome and in Florence: not the chance of a good and wise lawgiver, but a supernatural force or the belief in a supernatural force. Virtue needs arms to bring forth "quiet," a kind of disorder to create order. Since order does not create itself, men can be held in disorder by an opinion, a belief in the extraordinary force of the Christian God, which keeps virtue disarmed.

In accordance with his introduction of the supernatural in contrast with the natural, Machiavelli now blames princes rather than peoples; for it is princes who introduce new orders and new ways of life.[44] "With wonder," he says, it will be seen "how so many very noble peoples were held in check by such weak and poorly administered armies." "Princes, soldiers, and heads of republics" were able to maintain their reputations only by the use of frauds, tricks, and arts.[45] This criticism is continued in the next inquiry (6:1) on the costly indecisiveness of modern wars. Modern wars are as expensive for the victors as for the vanquished because they are fought by mercenaries; these take the spoils if they win and wait to be reequipped if they lose. In either

44. "And it is more true than any other truth, that if where there are men there are not soldiers, this arises through a defect of the prince, and not through another defect of the site or of nature," *Disc.* 1:21 (vol. 1, p. 149). Cf. 2:29, sixty-eight chapters later; and Strauss, *Thoughts on Machiavelli*, p. 178.
45. *F. H.* 5:1 (vol 2, p. 220).

case, the prince must take money from his subjects. Victory brought nothing to the benefit of the people and only made the prince more pressing and less respectful. "Ancient and well-ordered republics with their victories used to fill the treasury with gold and silver, distribute gifts to the people, remit tribute to their subjects, and entertain them with games and majestic festivals; those of the time we describe first empty the treasury, then impoverish the people, and do not protect you from your enemies." [46]

It is no wonder, then, that the Florentine people did not wish to share "supreme honors" with the nobles; there were few of the worldly kind to be shared. Why were there few such? Why were mercenaries, "the two sects of armies" which Machiavelli describes in Books 5 and 6, allowed to engross the profits of victory and live comfortably in defeat? One cannot help but recall Machiavelli's remark in the *Discourses* about "our religion . . . which makes us esteem less the honor of the world." [47] For a Christian people, the "supreme honor" is salvation in the afterlife, in which all men may share a "wonderful equality"; but the desire for this honor is consistent only with the nature of a people, since it does not desire to rule. Mercenaries, who play their own game while holding the fate because they hold the arms of the prince, remind one of other intermediaries who set themselves up as necessary to salvation and who thrive in good times and bad.

The sixth inquiry returns to domestic matters after 1434,

46. *F. H.* 6:1 (vol. 2, p. 274); cf. 1:39.
47. *Disc.* 2:2 (vol. 1, p. 237). In *F. H.* 5:2, where Machiavelli mentions the "two sects of armies," he relates an instance in which the Pope preferred a dishonorable peace to a dangerous war against Francesco Sforza. Sforza, having seized some lands of the Pope, sent him a letter with an insolent Machiavellian salutation punning on an ecclesiastical greeting, *invito Petro et Paulo.* At the invitation of, or despite, Peter and Paul: Christianity, despite its best wishes, needs worldly armies, and because of its best wishes, cannot profit from them. Its rootless priests give rise to rootless warriors.

although the narrative on the "two sects of armies" (Sforza's and Piccino's) in the two preceding books had touched on Florentine internal divisions when necessary.[48] Machiavelli begins his inquiry by stating that he wishes to explain "why those who hope that a republic can be united deceive themselves very much in this hope." This is surprising, because he himself had seemed to plant and nourish this hope in his readers. In the Proemium he promised to show the causes of the hatreds and divisions in Florence, so that "citizens who govern republics" can keep themselves united; and he had said that if Florence had had a form of government that would keep her united, she would have been the equal of any republic, ancient or modern. Now we are told that unity is impossible and we are given an explanation for the diverse effects of the natural enmities in Rome and in Florence. Florence suffered under harmful divisions, those accompanied by "sects and partisans," as opposed to the beneficial divisions "that maintain themselves without sects and partisans." Until this point in the *Florentine Histories* Machiavelli, while admitting that divisions are natural, has treated kindly the opinion hostile to parties which he dismisses at the beginning of the *Discourses*.[49] He needed the protection of this opinion in teaching the causes of weakness in his own city in his own times, and he did not reveal its inadequacy before he was ready to say that some divisions are beneficial. Even so, he soothes the shock of discovering that republics can never be united with a continued hostility to partisans, if not to all parties.

Bearing in mind that he cannot prevent enmities, then,

48. *F. H.* 5:4, 15, 27; 6:6, 7, 23.
49. *Disc.* 1:4. To be sure, the attack on parties in *F. H.* 3:5 is deflated at the beginning of 3:6; and Luigi Guicciardini's speech against vengeful discords in 3:11 is diminished by the events related in 3:12 and opposed by the speech of the plebeian leader in 3:13. Note the different effect of Luigi's "true" words and the "persuasions" of the plebeian on the *animi* of their listeners (vol. 2, pp. 141, 145), and the lack of effect of true words in 3:27 (vol. 2, p. 169).

the founder of a republic must seek to prevent sects. "There-fore," Machiavelli says to introduce a well-concealed conse-quence, he must know "that there are two ways for citizens to acquire reputation in a city: either public ways or private means." The public ways are "winning a battle, acquiring a land, carrying out an embassy with care and prudence, ad-vising the republic wisely and happily." Private means are "benefitting this or that citizen, defending them from magis-trates, helping them with money, getting them honors un-deservedly, and gratifying the plebs with games and public gifts." From the latter way of proceeding come sects and partisans, but the former way is "not mixed with sects, be-cause it is founded on a common good, not on a private good." This distinction, we note, is between private and pub-lic ways of gaining reputation, that is, of gaining a private end; that is why the public ways are said to be "founded on a common good" instead of "aiming at the common good."

Machiavelli makes this implication explicit by almost abandoning the distinction in the next sentence: citizens who use private means will not harm the republic if they do not have "partisans who follow them for their own profit." On the contrary, they will be useful because to succeed, they must try to effect "the exaltation" of the republic, and "par-ticularly watch one another in order that civil limits [*i ter-mini civili*] not be passed." [50] The founder of a republic must admit the need for honors and use them to unite private advantage with the public good. Machiavelli said in the first inquiry that modern states do not send colonies "because princes have no desire for true glory and republics no order that deserves to be praised." Now he combines the two rea-sons. Praiseworthy order in a republic would encourage the desire for true glory or reputation in its princes, offer prizes

50. The distinction is explicitly abandoned in *F. H.* 7:2, where Cosimo is said to have used his "friends" instead of his "partisans" to oppose his "friends" (vol. 2, p. 331).

to them, and manage the competition.

When the reader understands the need for worldly honor in politics, he will join Machiavelli's conspiracy against Christianity; for Christianity clearly denies the desire for worldly honor. But the precise effects of this denial are unclear, since Christianity despite its intention cannot dispense with worldly honor. Florentine parties may have been "mixed with sects," but the Guelfs and the Ghibellines were not doctrinal parties of priests, and few Florentine politicians were notably pious or easily obedient to sacerdotal authority. In politics, Christianity does not necessarily make men into zealots for otherworldly honor, especially not in its time of corruption. Rather, it prevents the princes who desire worldly honors from pursuing them wholeheartedly, attaining them completely, and enjoying them without a bad conscience. At the same time it offers an illusory protection for the weak that keeps them weak—an excuse for defeat, a consolation in failure, and an avoidance of the natural punishments for imprudence. Christianity keeps men in dependence to God or to themselves, a condition that Machiavelli represents as that of a colony. Florence began as a colony of ancient Rome and now continues as a colony of modern Rome.

THE COLONY OF FLORENCE

Since the Florentine parties took their special character from their origin, it is necessary to attend particularly to the first two books of the *Florentine Histories*. Machiavelli shows that parties arose from the dispute between the emperor and the Pope, between the heir to the vestiges of the Roman empire and the representative of its sanctified spirit. The first book, he says dryly, "tells briefly all the accidents that happened in Italy from the decline of the Roman empire to 1434." [51] Its theme is Rome, not Florence, not even

51. *F. H.* Proemium (vol. 2, p. 7).

the origins of Florence, as we would expect from Machiavelli's decision "to begin my history with the beginning of
our city"; Florence is mentioned only three times and carefully not discussed.[52] Its theme is Rome because Florence had
its origin in Rome, a protected beginning as a colony of
Rome. Thus the first book does not have as its theme "beginnings," for Florence did not have a true, unprotected
beginning, as did Rome. Accordingly, the first inquiry does
not occur at the beginning of the first book, and when it occurs discusses colonies rather than beginnings. The beginnings of Rome suggest the beginnings of any city, as we
know from the first chapter of the *Discourses*.[53] But the origins of Florence must be seen in the decaying empire and
growing Church that gave it protection. Florence is kept out
of the first book of the *Florentine Histories* so that its pro-
tector, Rome, can be examined for the cause and manner of
its protection.

In the first chapter we are told that the Roman empire
was destroyed by barbarians who followed a policy of colonizing their excess inhabitants. They lived up north in a
prolific and healthful region where population often increased to such a multitude that a province would "divide
itself in three parts" and send the lucky third south "to seek
its fortune." It was fitting that to overthrow so great an empire, founded on the blood of so many virtuous men, the
Italian princes not be less sluggish than they were, the ministers less faithless, nor the attacks on it made with less force
and persistence than they were. Then in the first inquiry
(2:1), we are informed of the "great and wonderful order"

52. *F. H.* 1:5, 26, 39. In 1:26 Machiavelli mentions the wars of both
the Visconti against the Guelfs and of Castruccio Castracani against the
Florentines; he adds a digression on the Visconti but not on Castruccio.
He also includes a discussion of Venice "in its place," 1:3, 28, 29, but
not of Florence.
53. Entitled: "What have universally been the beginnings of any city
and what was that of Rome."

of ancient republics for colonizing in the same way, except that Machiavelli here stresses the filling of empty lands rather than the emptying of full lands. Florence, it seems, was a product of this very praiseworthy order, having "its beginning from Fiesole and its growth from colonies." [54] In keeping with his avoidance of beginnings, Machiavelli discusses only its growth as a market town under the protection of the reputation of the Roman Republic, i.e., the Roman Empire; he says nothing here of Fiesole or of the "ancient Tuscans." This protection weakened as Rome lost its power and its opportunity to colonize, and Rome was destroyed by barbarians with the vigor to imitate its "great and wonderful order." To protect is to colonize; to be protected is to be a colony; to be a colony is to be conqueror or conquered.

The Roman Empire was destroyed by barbarians, but they were given the opportunity to destroy by the emperors who abandoned Rome for Constantinople and left the western part of the Empire weak. Later we learn that "the emperor became a Christian and left Rome for Constantinople." [55] The disorder that followed was terrifying because not merely princes or governments were changed, but laws, ways of living, and especially religion. The new religion with its miracles fought the customs of the ancient religion, and men died wretchedly, uncertain to which god they should turn, even to which sect of the Christian God, for the disunity of Christianity caused as much affliction as the cruelty of the barbarians. During this disorder the Popes gained authority. The first Popes after St. Peter, because of their holy lives and their miracles, became respected by the people; Christianity was from the first a religion of the people. Then princes found it necessary to adopt the Christian religion as a way out of "the so great confusion existing then in the world." [56]

54. *F. H.* 2:1 (end); cf. "whatever the cause of its origin," 2:2 (vol. 2, p. 62).
55. *F. H.* 1:9 (vol. 2, p. 21); on the affinity between Christianity and the East, see 1:3 (end).
56. *F. H.* 1:9 (vol. 2, p. 21); cf. 1:25 (end); 2:6.

Still, before the coming of the Longobards, the Popes had no other power than the respect they earned for their habits and their teaching; in secular matters they obeyed the kings and emperors, and were sometimes killed by them or used as ministers. The Pope acquired some power in Rome by default when Theodoric made himself King of Italy in Ravenna, and when the Longobards came, they allowed the Pope to become almost the chief of Rome. But as the Eastern Empire declined and the Longobards grew stronger, the Popes began to seek help in France. The many wars of the barbarians in Italy from those times to the present were largely caused by the Popes' summoning help, Machiavelli concludes.[57] The greatest instance was the Pope's summons for Charlemagne, who crossed the Alps and visited Rome, where he "judged that the Pope as vicar of God could not be judged by men" and was proclaimed emperor by the Pope and the Roman people.[58]

The Popes used the opportunity of barbarian invasions, which Machiavelli fails to call heaven-sent, to create the power that could only be maintained by further barbarian invasions. These two powers depended on each other, the Popes on the barbarian kings for that "kingly power" which true princes supply,[59] and the kings on the Pope to rectify the great disorder and introduce quiet and obedience to their kingdoms. Together, they corresponded to the two elements of ancient Rome or any regime: people and princes. But in decadent Rome, the two elements worked badly and could not act and react against each other in a manner to produce the common good.

Why the ancient Roman system failed in modern Italy could be seen in the actions of the crucial factor in the sys-

57. Invitations of Popes to emperors were paralleled and preceded by concessions of Eastern emperors to Western barbarians, 1:3, 4, 6. Cf. Machiavelli's contrary invitation in the title of *P.* 26: "An exhortation to seize Italy and set her free from the barbarians."
58. *F. H.* 1:11 (vol. 2, p. 24).
59. *Disc.* 1:34 (vol., p. 172).

tem, the Pope. The Pope was head of a religion that, scorning worldly honor and political glory, appealed to the people rather than princes; according to the ancient Roman system, he was therefore in the equivocal position of the plebeian prince, ambitious above his rank yet hostile to all of noble rank. Such a man could be "managed" in the Machiavellian-Roman sense by a policy of co-optation into the nobility, in which the plebeian princes were first made rivals to each other for military prizes and afterwards the best or the luckiest selected for noble rank. The "policy" did not require that the nobles in power stay in power, since no harm was done if the plebeian prince defeated his managers and vaulted into the office where he would have to manage others like his former self. All the system seemed to need was the avarice all nobles hold from nature and the prudence some of them display in rising to the highest offices. But to form the combination of prudent avarice, prudence must be free of hostility to avarice and eager to cooperate with it. This was the difficulty in managing the Pope.

The Pope was a prince of the people, who because of the character of the "sect" that gave him office, could not be bribed or rewarded in the usual way with honors. He and the Church he heads have renounced both the use of arms and self-advancement, and so he can neither be offered nor can he accept worldly honors which require the use of arms in one's own advancement. To accept worldly honors in the spirit with which they are offered would reduce him to the level of the other worldly princes in this world and would require him to renounce his claim to superiority over them; yet his office is constituted by that claim alone. As Pope, he cannot be a prince of any kind unless he is superior to the worldly, or the natural, princes. It is his very "spiritual power" that makes him faithless in his worldly engagements.[60]

60. *F. H.* 8:17 (vol. 2, p. 404).

The Pope exercised his authority "first with censure then with censure and arms," as in time he acquired the inferior status of a worldly prince in addition to his superior status, but he acquired worldly status because he had a superior status. His "censures" could inflict "spiritual wounds," whose importance the Emperor Henry IV was the first prince to learn. It was through the power of censures, however, not through fair or equal competition with worldly princes on their level, that the Pope acquired "arms." Henry IV, suffering the spiritual wound of excommunication, came to Canossa to ask pardon of the Pope because he was "obliged by his peoples." [61]

Spiritual wounds do not hurt the spirit merely, but also undermine the worldly rule of princes through the belief of their peoples in the supremacy of otherworldly salvation. The Pope, therefore, wields arms as a consequence of his censures, but not his own arms. Granted the superiority of the divine, he is only the vicar of God, and God does not choose to make Himself the agent of the Pope's worldly designs as if they were directed by a worldly purpose. Machiavelli gives a this-worldly explanation which accounts for both the Pope's existence as a worldly prince and his failure to prosper in that office: "so much are the things that appear feared more at a distance than nearby." [62]

Not wielding his own arms, the Pope must exercise his authority "at a distance." He must work on princes through their peoples; he does not confront them as the prince of his own people. As vicar, he cannot govern directly. In the

61. *F. H.* 1:9 (vol. 2, p. 25); 1:15 (vol. 2, p. 28); cf. 2:16 (vol. 2, p. 79) for the answer Henry IV could not give to the Pope. Lorenzo's answer is in 8:10 (vol. 2, p. 392). But with all his spiritual power the Pope could not prevent the death by diarrhea of his champion the Magnificent Robert, though he did give "the body" every kind of honor, 8:23 (vol. 2, p. 414).

62. *F. H.* 1:19 (vol. 2, p. 34). Note the discrepancy between the purpose of "the heavens" and that of the Pope, 1:25; and see 8:11 for the Florentines' view that God can oppose His vicar.

matter of Thomas à Becket, he imposed a judgment on King Henry II "that a private man would be ashamed to submit to," [63] but he could not make himself obeyed at home in Rome and often had to live elsewhere. As he himself was unmanageable, so for the same reason, lacking his own arms, he could not manage his own people.[64] Therefore his arms had to be foreign.[65] Urban II, hated by his own people and doubting his security amid the divisions of Italy, "turned to a generous enterprise" against the Saracens, "with all other similar enterprises later called the Crusades." [66]

These were the reason (to distract popular discontent) and the occasion (a foreign expedition) which together built the Roman Empire; but they did not build a modern Roman empire. By the virtue of Saladin and the discords of the Christians, all the early gains were lost. Moreover, the Crusades were only one episode in the use of foreign arms by the Popes. From the beginning it was their policy to summon foreign arms, the descendants of barbarians, into Italy.[67] They governed or managed Italy so weakly, and yet persisted despite their weakness so obstinately, because they had inducements or sanctions sufficient to command foreign arms. Thus their power was based on foreign arms in both Machiavellian senses of "foreign," foreign to one's own country and foreign to this world. Their power could not operate for the common good of Italy or any city of Italy or any city.

The foundation of the common good, according to Machiavelli, is the preference for one's own, as this preference makes it possible for orders naturally disparate to coexist if

63. *F. H.* 1:19 (vol. 2, p. 34); cf. the extraordinary banquet of Frate Piero, 7:31.

64. *F. H.* 1:14, 16, 18, 20, 25, 35, 5:2; 6:29; 8:23, 27, 28; *Disc.* 1:12.

65. In *F. H.* 5:7, a Pope employs a cardinal to command his army, then loses the allegiance of the cardinal, who then loses the allegiance of his army back to the Pope.

66. *F. H.* 1:17; cf. 6:33; 7:9.

67. *F. H.* 1:13.

not to live in union. Nobles and people will coexist when
the city can expand to serve their needs and provide both
glory and security. The common good, to speak plainly, is a
good taken from foreigners that is common to one people
and its princes; [68] it can subsist only so long as human beings
are divided in political allegiance, and understood to be divided by their sects, into natives and foreigners. [69] The Christian Church does not observe this distinction, but the factual
truth of its internationalism is subservience to foreigners. If
the common good is at the expense of foreigners in booty
and glory, princes cannot operate for the common good with
foreign arms; the foreigners, that is, the mercenaries, will
keep the spoils intended for their employers. [70] At the same
time, every Christian prince knows that the people of his
land is not his own, but in some part at some times the
Pope's. The Pope has no home and many colonies, especially
the colony of Florence. [71] The disaffection of his own people
is compensated by the allegiance of other peoples, and his
incompetence as a worldly prince does not receive its natural
punishment.

68. Having lost the war against Filippo Visconti, the Florentine nobles
had neither booty to distribute nor glory to offer; they were unable to
manage the ambition of Giovanni de' Medici, *F. H.* 4:3–7.

69. In *F. H.* 5:11, "an older and wiser" noble of Lucca condemns the
Florentine plebs with the purpose of keeping his own plebs loyal. Even
the Pope must understand "a universal peace" as confined to Italy for the
purpose of war against the Turks, 6:32 (vol. 2, p. 319), 37.

70. *F. H.* 5:2; note that the beginning of 6:1 applies to the Pope.

71. Machiavelli dwells on the relation of Florence to its colony Volterra in order to show the relation of the Pope to Florence. See *F. H.*
4:17, where, by "God's aid" and contrary to the intention of certain noble
Volterrans, Volterra was made a "vicarate" of Florence; and cf. 7:30
(end) and 31 (beg.). In *Disc.* 1:49 (vol. 1, p. 200) Machiavelli says
that Florence began as a slave city, in direct contradiction to Bruni, who
claimed that Florence had a free beginning under the Roman Republic
and who tried to trace the beginning of Florence beyond that of Rome
to the Tuscans, Bruni, *Historiae Florentini Populi,* Bk. I, "Laudatio
Florentinae Urbis," in Hans Baron, ed., *From Petrarch to Leonardo Bruni*
(Chicago, 1968), pp. 244–47. Baron has rightly stressed the importance
of this point in Bruni's thought, in *The Crisis of the Early Italian Renaissance,* rev. ed. (Princeton, 1966), pp. 62–75; cf. p. 465, n. 1.

PARTIES IN ITALY

Machiavelli does not believe that the papacy has become corrupt through its temporal possessions. He objects to its *not* being corruptible in the worldly way. His objection, therefore, goes to the otherworldly essence of Christianity, and could not be satisfied by a Protestant or even a Puritan rearrangement of the sacerdotal hierarchy. The Pope acquired his temporal possessions out of the necessities of ruling, which are the same for all princes in this world, including the princes of a church. In the absence of a direct providence of God, ruling men in this world is necessarily worldly. That is why the Popes stirred up new dissensions in Italy "now through the charity of religion, now through their own ambition."

It is true that Pope Celestine, "being a hermit and full of holiness," renounced the papacy after six months, and on the other hand that Popes have increasingly promoted their relatives to the extent that in the future one may expect the Popes to try to make the papacy hereditary.[72] The ratio of piety to ambition has diminished through the history of the papacy, and the Church could now be considered corrupt in the Christian sense. In this condition the Church is now also perhaps open to attack as never before. But whatever the current mixture of motives, piety and ambition in the Popes tended to the same result of disunion and enfeeblement. Pope Nicholas III was the first to promote his relatives; yet Machiavelli says only that "he was the first of Popes who openly revealed his own ambition." [73] Boniface VIII seems to be criticized for "desiring too much to satisfy his appetite" in using the "weapons" of excommunication and of crusade against the Colonna family in Rome; they might have been

72. *F. H.* 1:23 (vol. 2, p. 38); 1:25 (vol. 2, p. 40); cf. 1:35 on Gregory XII, who renounced the papacy and was merely replaced, and 6:36 on Pius II, who abandoned his "private passions" but got his reward just the same.

73. *F. H.* 1:23 (vol. 2, p. 39).

used "virtuously through the charity of faith" but instead were turned against Christians "for his own ambition."[74] But what other use could he make of his arms? Excommunication is a weapon that cuts Christians only; crusades are directed against foreigners. By confusing the two, Machiavelli seems to indicate that the Pope is compelled to treat all men, including the people of Rome, now as brothers, now as enemies. If pious, the Popes could not ignore the necessities of ruling in this world; if ambitious, they could not obey them. They have "used badly" both censures and arms because they must.[75]

In the thirty-ninth chapter of the first book of the *Histories,* Machiavelli lists the five principal powers of Italy, all of them "disarmed of their own arms." The Pope is in the center of the list, disarmed "because arms are not suitable for him as an ecclesiastic." The other four powers are disarmed for reasons that describe, in Machiavelli's characteristic translation of divine politics into human terms, various features of papal rule. Duke Filippo Visconti of Milan is disarmed; "remaining secluded in his chamber and not letting himself be seen, he managed his wars through his commissioners." The Venetians were disarmed because "when they turned to land, they put aside those weapons which they had used gloriously in the sea" and like the other Italians managed their armies under someone else's rule. Queen Joanna of Naples and the Florentines were disarmed of necessity, the former because she was a woman, the latter because frequent divisions had destroyed the nobility and left the republic in the hands of "men educated in trade." Florence followed "the orders and the fortune of the others" at this time, in 1434.[76]

74. *F. H.* 1:25 (vol. 2, p. 41).
75. *F. H.* 1:9 (vol. 2, p. 23); cf. 1:21, 22.
76. *F. H.* 1:39 (vol. 2, p. 57). The five powers are disarmed partly by choice, predominantly (three to two) of necessity. Cf. 1:29, 5:3. "Men educated or nourished [*nutricati*] in trade" can refer to spiritual merchants.

The system of modern parties is disposed by the influence of the disarmed prince of Christianity and his commissioners. Since modern princes and peoples cannot operate with and against each other for the common good, their parties seek foreign alliances. Whereas the party system of Rome was domestic, based on the common good acquired by common hostility to foreigners, the modern party system is between states or international. It consists essentially of leagues between peoples who favor the Pope as opposed to princes who favor the emperor, aided by exiles expelled by their people. Modern states, incapable of allying their own princes and peoples, are captured by one party or the other in league with its counterpart in a foreign state.[77] The modern parties seek help from those who are like-minded elsewhere, since they cannot operate successfully with their complements at home.

We might say today that the basis of parties had become ideological rather than territorial, but Machiavelli would say "foreign" rather than "domestic," divine rather than worldly. This world, he thought, is divided into lands by differences so exclusive that they can be overcome only by neglecting the interests of this world.[78] But the interests of this world are split, for men are divided by nature into princes and peoples. Thus if a common good in this world is possible only in a territory, it must consider the interests of both the local princes and the local people. Leagues of the like-minded, ignoring the difference between natives and foreigners, produce partisan victories and never achieve a com-

77. *F. H.* 5:6.
78. See *F. H.* 5:8, where Rinaldo, by identifying the holy and the just, argues that the common good of Florence is to be found in justice to its exiles, not locally at home. In a lachrymose and enthusiastic response to Neri Capponi's speech, the Venetian Senate exclaimed that their *patria* would always belong in common to the Florentines and themselves, 5:21 (vol. 2, p. 250). Cf. the distinction between the celestial and the terrestrial fatherland in 5:34 (vol. 2, p. 271), thirteen chapters later. See also the reply of the Pratesi to Bernardo Nardi, 7:26.

mon good.[79] Such victories often wear the appearance of justice because they right a preceding wrong, but, because they also create a new wrong, they must be repeated in series or else in alternation, to the result of misery in the people and death and exile for the princes. The dead are gone and the miserable are not obvious; so the surest sign of corruption in party politics is the crowd of exiles who have suffered partisan defeat. They find themselves in the hard position of being impotent except to hurt the country they love, for the exile without a fatherland can at best attain the reputation of a mercenary.[80]

The Pope, we have seen, needed the kingly power of the emperor to sustain the power of the Church in Italy. He also had to fight the emperor, who could not be expected to serve as a mere subordinate in this design. The dispute between Pope Alexander II and Henry IV, in which the latter suffered "spiritual wounds," was, Machiavelli says, "the seed of the Guelf and Ghibelline humors," the parties of the Pope and the emperor. This single dispute is made responsible, like a seed, for continuing domestic party conflict: Why? The mutual hostility of the Pope and the emperor was sustained and rendered permanent in the modern party system by the mutual dependence which has been explained. Since each power was, as it were, a factor in the regime of the other, neither could destroy or ignore the other as a foreigner; and yet they could not combine in one regime to support a common good.

As a result of the "Guelf and Ghibelline humors, Italy, when without barbarian invasion, was torn by intestinal

---

79. *F. H.* 7:21.
80. Consider the exile's argument of Rinaldo, asking the Duke of Milan to be doctor to Florence's internal ills, *F. H.* 5:8. But why should the Duke of Milan wish to make Florence healthy? In politics the doctor must look to his own health. Cf. the parallel argument of a noble of Lucca, note 69.

wars." [81] Intestinal wars were the disease left by the barbarian cure, for with its Christian constitution, Italy could never unite against a foreigner. In every Italian city the people had a common otherworldly, that is, ecclesiastical allegiance; and in consequence their opponents had a common need to league with each other and with the emperor or some other counterweight to the Pope.[82] If a single prince had succeeded in uniting Italy in one kingdom, he would still have encountered the power of the Church in the extraterritorial allegiance of the people to the ecclesiastical hierarchy within his territory; he would have substituted for Guelf and Ghibelline party conflict the episcopal disputes of the Christian kings outside Italy. But a single prince could not succeed in uniting Italy because of the temporal possessions of the Pope; in Italy, the Pope had a territory, not merely an office, to defend. He therefore brought in foreigners to Italy more readily than he could send one Christian king to enforce his will against another. It was easier to pay the doctors' fees by allowing them to feed on the patient than to get them to collect from each other.

Affairs in Italy were complicated by the number of participants, for there were many powers and both princes and Popes had short lives.[83] The alignment of Guelf and Ghibelline powers was surely not perfect, unaffected by circumstances. At one point the Pope, to keep the emperor out of Italy, deserted the Guelfs and welcomed the entry of John, King of Bohemia, who had been summoned by the Ghibellines. This overturn of established allegiances did not change the system, however; the Pope gained nothing from his faithlessness and the King of Bohemia nothing from his faith.[84]

81. *F. H.* 1:15 (vol. 2, p. 29). Sixty-six Guelf and Ghibelline families are listed in 2:4.
82. *F. H.* 1:21, 22, 26, 27, 28.
83. *F. H.* 1:23 (vol. 2, p. 40).
84. *F. H.* 1:28.

Thus the dispute between Pope and emperor was the prototype, as well as the origin, of the modern parties. In all the events what remains constant as the essence of the system is the inability to achieve a domestic regime. Foreigners were not merely the material of the regime, the booty and the victims of a domestic alliance between princes and people of a common land; they were a factor in the regime itself. Modern government is confused between "things outside" and "things inside," [85] and the cause is a deeper confusion of allegiance between the other world and this. "Barbarian invasion" and "intestinal wars" were fundamentally identical; so it was no wonder that they were politically connected. This bad system was against nature, by which Machiavelli means this world. It denies the claims of this world, in particular the claims that princes make because of their nature. Yet, though unnatural, it continues; the system, as we say today, was in equilibrium, and by the operation of an "extraordinary force."

THE FIRST DIVISION IN FLORENCE

The Florentine parties were modern parties of this description. Machiavelli shows this by separating his account of the origin of the modern parties in Italy, given in Book 1, and his account of the origin of the Florentine parties in Book 2. By this rather artificial separation he gives the Florentine parties a chance to begin, as it were, on their own, in conformity to the natural partisanship of men. When the characteristic modern corruption appears, as it does very soon, we know it must be attributed to a general context of corruption rather than to a bad beginning peculiar to Florence. "As Florence was late in following the sects of Italy,

85. *F. H.* Proemium; 2:5 (foreign judges), 32 (beg.); 6:8 (beg.); 7:25 (beg.). In 8:10 Lorenzo asks: "If we have then honored strangers, how have we injured relatives?" (vol. 2, p. 393).

so she was more afflicted by them." [86]

Machiavelli relates "the cause of the first division" in Florence, even though it is "very well known" from being celebrated by Dante and many other writers. The cause turns out to have been "the chance" that a young knight could be tempted to break his pledge of marriage to one rich and wellborn girl for another, equally rich and well-born but more beautiful.[87] This act of infidelity brought revenge from the family of the slighted girl, who killed the knight and with "this homicide" divided the city between partisans of the Buondelmonti, the knight's family, and partisans of the Uberti, relatives of the girl. After relating this incident, Machiavelli in the next chapter begins to speak of the Guelfs and Ghibellines in Florence: "[M]uch as our city was divided, so all Italy had for a long time been divided, into Guelfs and Ghibellines." He does not say how the small incident of imprudence and private revenge was absorbed into the grand dispute between the Pope and the emperor. Though he lists the Buondelmonti in the group of families belonging to the Guelf party and the Uberti among the Ghibellines, he does not say why the chance division into partisans of the Buondelmonti and the Uberti became the all-Italian division into Guelfs and Ghibellines, which had its seed in a great confrontation between the Pope and the emperor and its necessity in their mutual hostility and dependence. The sequence of chance incident and great division recalls Aristotle's remark that "factions arise not over small things but out of small things, and they are carried on over great things." [88] But what is the precise connection be-

86. *F. H.* 2:2 (vol. 2, p. 62); cf. 6:9.

87. *F. H.* 2:3 (vol. 2, p. 63); the temptation is in the first quoted speech of the work.

88. Aristotle *Politics* 1303b18–19; cf. 1303b39–1304a4. See the "little changes" of *F. H.* 2:5 (vol. 2, p. 15) and the "little things" of *Disc.* 3: 33 (vol. 1, p. 415). Bruni merely adds the force of the Italian parties to this incident without attempting to see a connection, *Historiae Florentini Populi,* Bk. II, p. 49.

tween the small matter and the great?

When the Uberti party was meditating revenge, some of them feared the evils that might result from their retaliation; but one man, Mosca Lamberti, stilled these doubts, saying that those who think of many things never finish them, and he concluded with the adage: "What's done is ended" (*Cosa fatta capo ha*). He could not have been more wrong, but why? Why did the sense of injury linger in the form of party rivalries? In Dante's version of the story, this incident is called "the seed of ruin and misery" for Italy, while for Machiavelli Canossa was the seed of the Italian parties and this incident merely the cause of the first division in Florence. Dante quotes the adage in the mouth of Mosca, who now knows he forgot about divine retribution.[89] Machiavelli carefully says nothing of divine retribution, and we note only that Florence had no institution for public retribution to replace private revenge. As in the case of accusation and calumny,[90] it lacks the practice of management which could focus punishment on the faithless young knight, his bride's mother, who tempted him, or Mosca Lamberti, who loosed the revenge. Christianity is responsible for this lack both because it weakens public authority and because it excites and sustains private revenge. The sin for which Mosca suffers in Dante's *Inferno* is not injustice but too much justice and not enough prudence. Machiavelli seems to agree, and in regard to a later division of parties he implies that the blame for this sin is on Christianity itself.

The Albizzi and the Ricci families had long hated each other when in 1353 they nearly clashed as the result of a false rumor to each that one was using the opportunity of a general call to arms to attack the other. Uguccione de' Ricci, head of his family, then decided to gain superiority

89. *Inferno* 28:103–10; cf. 13:144; *Paradiso* 16:136–44.
90. *Disc.* 1:7, 8; in *F. H.* see especially Proemium; 1:11; 2:12–14; 3:3–11, 19, 20, 25; 4:19–22, 25–27; 6:30; 7:10.

"through the ordinary way" by the renewal of an old law. This law was established after the victory of the Emperor Charles I in 1267; it reserved authority to the Guelfs over the Ghibellines.[91] In time, Machiavelli says, through various accidents and new divisions, this authority had so nearly fallen into oblivion that many descendants of the old Ghibellines held the chief magistracies.[92] Uguccione proposed to renew this law against the Ghibellines, since it would exclude the Albizzi, who "many thought" were descended from Ghibellines. Piero degli Albizzi discovered this intention and decided to favor it, thinking that if he opposed it he might be declared a Ghibelline. Those who were declared Ghibelline and excluded from office were called "the admonished." "Admonishing" then became a regular institution in Florence of purging through calumny; so the renewal of this law was "the beginning of many evils."

"No law more damaging to a republic can be made than one which looks back a long time," Machiavelli says without elaboration.[93] Since he rarely commits himself in this way without possibility of escape, it will be worthwhile to see what he is saying; and to do this, it is necessary to translate in the usual way from human politics to divine or divine-human politics. The most damaging law might be the one that looks back the longest time; in any case that law is of the class of the most damaging. It is the law of obedience to God by which all men are sinners because they are involved in the original sin.

Original sin is *the* cause of divine retribution; it is *the* reason why, in the Christian doctrine, what is done by men is

91. *F. H.* 2:10.

92. This was not true, but Machiavelli wished to draw attention to the descendants of evil-doers and the descent of partisanship; see F. Gaeta, ed., *Istorie Fiorentine*, p. 215, n. 3.

93. *F. H.* 3:3; this chapter begins seven consecutive chapters in which "sect" occurs. Looking backward is of course unfavorable to the nobles, 4:14 (vol. 2, p. 188); 7:10; *Disc.* 1:37 (end).

not ended for God, and consequently not for men. Since original sin makes all men sinners, it justifies an absolute revenge or retribution which appears in the minds of the godly or those who have persuaded themselves they have been forgiven their sins. Belief in divine retribution, since it confers grace on the godly, gives a sterner cogency to human retribution, instead of the patience with human weakness one might otherwise expect.[94] If every injury must be paid for, men are more rather than less eager to exact the payment.

When this belief in divine retribution reaches back to the sin of the first men, and so includes the present rulers no less than the meanest subject or strangest foreigner, it becomes politically unmanageable.[95] Only the transpolitical priests who bear no arms can absolve, and their interest is not that of the princes nor of the republic. Indeed, they can defend their worldly status only by dividing their enemies, and for this purpose they can never allow old wrongs to lose their stink. The freedom of priests and the fervor of the godly set the ends and means of politics among politicians who were in neither category but had to accept the condition of unmanageable partisanship. As these were the great majority of rulers, and as they were condemned and opposed not only by Machiavelli but also by reforming priests like Savonarola, it took a sharp eye to discern overmuch religion as the cause of the many evils of Italian politics. Machiavelli had a sharp eye.

Florentine partisanship feeds on the Christian spirit, as Machiavelli sees it, of absolute revenge. This revenge may not have been intended by the religion which endorses the state-

94. *F. H.* 6:20; 7:4, 19, 21; 8:10. On the connection between revenge and "inside and outside," see 2:37 (vol. 2, p. 114).

95. The characteristic difference between the nobles and the people in regard to vengeance is portrayed in *F. H.* 2:26–27. The nobles argued against a vengeful pursuit of Castruccio Castracani because it was unnecessary; then the people broke their promise to the exiles helping them against Castruccio because it was unnecessary to keep it, and turned their vengeance against the nobles.

ment "judge not that ye be not judged," but the natural desire for revenge in men is too powerful. If this desire is condemned and denied, it will expand and find expression in the belief that God has judged in favor of oneself or one's party.[96] It is much safer and more humane to control this desire than to deny it, for men will feel it themselves and must incur it in others. Human necessity operates through the movement of human things as new dangers and new attractions come to view. When men see these things, for instance a more beautiful girl, men separate themselves from their old loves and hates; they are faithless.[97] They incur the revenge of their old loves or of their fathers. Since one's faith is to one's own as formerly understood, or to one's *old* own, the fundamental distinction in Machiavelli's thought is not between one's own as the customary and the good (as for the classical political

96. See the speech of the Milanesi to Count Francesco Sforza, *F. H.* 6:20. Though outwitted by the Count, they tell him that God will punish him if—and they give the two conditions of divine retribution—faithlessness offends God and if God does not decide to befriend the wicked for some hidden good. Cf. 3:11 (vol. 2, p. 139), 27.

97. On a Florentine embassy to Venice, Neri Capponi pretended that Florence was helping Venice out of liberality and not necessity, and he boasted to the Venetian Senate: "It is not possible that an old love or an old hate be easily cancelled by new merits or new offenses," *F. H.* 5: 21 (vol. 2, p. 249). The next year he besieged and captured the territory of the Count of Poppi, who seeing himself "abandoned by God and by men," surrendered. He begged Neri to leave him the state that his fathers had held for nine hundred years and from whom Neri's fathers had received "countless benefits." Neri replied that he must be deprived of his state "necessarily" for the sake of "example," which was not the "eternal example of your clemency" that the count had spoken of in 5:35. Neri here used necessity as an argument when none existed, and before, when necessity was present, he did not mention it. Besides, the "old hatred" of the Florentines for the Duke of Milan was sustained by their present fear of the Florentine exiles, 5:10 (vol. 2, p. 248) Book 5 tells of Florentine successes that came about because Florence understood its own necessity, though imperfectly, as is made clear in 5:18, the central chapter of the central book of the Florentine section of the work. 6:29 contains a parody of the Last Supper to illustrate the necessity of infidelity. 6:30 contains a Machiavellian view of the same infidelity disguised in the infidelity of Gherardo Gambacorti, who despite his oath abandoned his son to his enemies; cf. *Disc.* 3:3–5.

philosophers) but between one's own as the customary and one's own simply.[98] "One's own simply" is expressed in Machiavelli's phrase, "one's own arms." Necessity rightly understood and properly accepted forces men to place faith in their own arms rather than "with mercenary and faithless arms." [99] This principle limits the desire for revenge because it teaches men to avoid the revenge that promises the consequence of "many evils." Indeed, it could be stated in the adage "what's done is ended," because properly applied by Mosca Lamberti that adage would have precluded revenge against a youth who broke his faith by falling in love with a more beautiful girl. But the principle also justifies revenge to the limit of prudence, for men cannot afford the humility of placing their lives in the hands of foreigners.[100]

Parties in Florence had evil effects because they were used, under the influence of the Christian religion, as instruments of private revenge. This transpolitical religion does not distinguish between domestic and foreign affairs; it keeps modern princes from seeing the distinction clearly, and its priests, so far as they can, prevent princes from acting on the basis of the distinction. But the distinction between domestic and foreign affairs, as we have seen, is necessary to the distinction between public and private affairs, for the public is based on the common good of two disparate orders of men who happen to inhabit a locality together. They will ally if they have enemies to oppose; and if they ally, they will sustain the public good against private interests within. There will be no

98. After his father's death Piero de' Medici received the insincere advice, under which "his ruin was hidden," to collect his father's old debts. Piero did this and fell into popular disfavor for failing to appreciate the difference between what was his own father's some time ago and what was recently and hence truly his own, *F. H.* 7:10 (vol. 2, p. 343); cf. 6:5, 17; 7:12, 16, 18. Note *Sogliono* at the beginning of *F. H.* 5:1, at the beginning of the speech in 6:20, and at the beginning of *The Prince.*

99. *F. H.* 6:20 (vol. 2, p. 300).

100. *F. H.* 6:12.

natives if there are no foreigners, and no public good if there are no natives. The very universality of Christianity causes it to support private attachment to one's own against public control. When this universality is applied to the belief in absolute revenge, the result is violent excitement of a private passion.

Machiavelli shows the necessary condition for the primacy of the public good in his discussion of the two conspiracies in Books 7 and 8. Both took place in churches, and with encouragement from Christian offices that Machiavelli relates in detail; and both were directed for private revenge against allies of the moment and enemies of the Pope, Duke Galeazzo Sforza and the Medici brothers. Both were moved by men of frustrated ambition, the first by ardent youths and the second by a family of high position that could not bear continued injuries from the Medici. Christianity, Machiavelli seems to say, lets revenge loose but holds down ambition. It imposes on the human spirit (*animo*), and especially on the princes whose character is spiritedness, a goal of vengeance that can be traced ultimately to divine vengeance for the original sin; at the same time it denies the value of the worldly honors and rewards by whose attraction human spiritedness can be made to serve the needs of mankind. "So our Italian princes feared in others that virtue which was not in themselves, and destroyed it." [101] Machiavelli does not take a high view of the public good; he does not suppose it to be nobler than private goods. He frowns on revenge, but not on ambition; and in this, as in many other ways, he argues the reverse of Christianity.

FLORENTINE AND ITALIAN PARTIES

Machiavelli mentions three separate divisions which produced the Florentine parties. The first division was the

101. *F. H.* 7:8 (vol. 2, p. 342); cf. 6:4, 7, 21.

dispute between the Buondelmonti and the Uberti, which began, as we have seen, with a broken pledge of marriage and became accidentally involved with the Guelfs and Ghibellines when Emperor Frederick II used the Uberti to strengthen his power in Tuscany against the Church. In time the Uberti were defeated, and by 1298, though some anger and suspicion remained between the nobles and the people, "everyone was living harmoniously and in peace." [102] Then arose the division between the Cerchi and the Donati families, or the Whites and the Blacks, as they called themselves. This division was imported from Pistoia where a card game between members of two families had led to quarrel, injury and harsh revenge. One of these families was related to the Donati in Florence, whose head was Messer Corso Donati, at that time one of the chief men in the city; and in exhaustion and despair, this family came to Messer Corso for support, while the other came to Messer Corso's rival in Florence, Messer Veri de' Cerchi. By these interventions the ancient hatred between the Cerchi and the Donati was so aroused that the Pope sent for Messer Veri and ordered him to make peace.

The result of the Pope's interference was, as always, unfortunate. Messer Veri pretended not to be at war, so that he did not need to make peace, and when he returned from Rome without any settlement, "humors" were so hot that "any slight accident, however it came, could make them burst." [103] It came at a funeral, when both parties came to blows; after this the *Signori,* acting with "the advice and prudence" of Dante, called the people to arms and expelled many of the Blacks and some of the Whites. Messer Corso went to the Pope, and the Pope sent Charles of Valois, brother of the King of France, to Florence to secure the return of Messer Corso and the triumph of the Blacks.

102. *F. H.* 2:15 (vol. 2, p. 78).
103. *F. H.* 2:17 (vol. 2, p. 79).

In the first division the connection between the sects of Italy and the Florentine parties was accidental; indeed, we had to search for a connection in the influence of Christianity between the unmanaged revenge of the incident in Florence and the dispute between the Pope and the emperor. Then in the second division, the domestic incident led to the politics of the Italian sects through the Pope's partisan peacemaking. The third division, between the Albizzi and the Ricci, was simply imposed on Florence through the dispute between the Pope and the emperor. Those families had taken arms and through a false rumor had nearly used them against each other, because they were defending Florence against the menace of a band of mercenary adventurers left unpaid after a war between the Pope and the emperor. Though the old division between Guelfs and Ghibellines had nearly fallen into oblivion, Uguccione de' Ricci revived it, as we have seen, with his proposal to "admonish" the Ghibellines.

Machiavelli thus presents three possibilities: generation of parties from within through uncontrollable revenge; imposition from without of the parties of the Christian system; or the central case of both generation and imposition. From within or without, the Florentine parties received their special character from Christianity. Moreover, Machiavelli moves his explanation from parties generated from within, accidentally (it seems) related to the "sects" of Italy, to parties imposed from without by those sects. As the *Florentine Histories* progress, Florence becomes more and more "foreign," barbarian, Roman. The early separation of Rome and Florence in Books 1 and 2 prepares and displays the gradual overcoming of that separation in a work dedicated to a Florentine Pope.

THE DIVISIONS OF MODERN PRINCES

What distinguishes ancient from modern party conflict, in Machiavelli's first statement, is the number of divisions in modern party conflict. He says the Florentine divisions are "very notable" because they were many; Florence was "not content with one." Of these many he specifies three: among the nobles, between the nobles and the people, and "lastly" (*in ultimo*) between the people and the plebs; and "many times it happened that one of these parties, having become superior, divided itself in two." [104] We are left in confusion about the number of kinds of divisions and the number of divisions, as Machiavelli does not make the distinction. Only the third division is of a new kind, and it apparently exhausts the three kinds, which are not "many." The new division presupposes that the people have won over the nobles; and they have won, we have seen, because the nobles were divided into armed and disarmed princes. The difference between ancient and modern party politics is that in modern party politics the people have won.

Accordingly, Machiavelli says that by repeated divisions the Florentines had destroyed the nobility and the republic put in the hands of "men educated in trade" (1:39); and as he describes toward the end of Book 2 events in the rule of the Duke of Athens, in which the nobility of Florence was finally destroyed, he refers to the "middle citizens" (*i mediocri cittadini*). He also lists three kinds of citizens, the great, the people, and the artisans (*grandi, popolani, e artefici*), and in another place speaks of the great, the lesser people (*il popolo minuto* or *la plebe minuta*), and the people (*il popolo*), a middle class of men.[105] In Books 2 and 3, Machiavelli considers the possibility that modern politics is characterized by a party of the middle, but then afterwards for some reason he resumes his view of the division of all men in politics into nobles and people. He seems to discover a new party division in modern politics arising from the

104. *F. H.* Proemium (vol. 2, pp. 5–6), cf. 2:21 (vol. 2, p. 85).
105. *F. H.* 2:34 (vol. 2, p. 104), 36 (vol. 2, p. 110), 40 (vol. 2, pp. 117–18); 3:18 (vol. 2, p. 154). See "Discourse on Reforming the State of Florence" (vol. 2, pp. 532–34).

victory of the people and then to lose interest in it. In the very inquiry which divides the material on the middle party (3:1), Machiavelli speaks merely of "the grave and natural enmities . . . between the popular men and the nobles," or "between the people and the nobles."

The ambiguity between "popular men" (*popolari*) and "the people" (*popolo*) can be found in Machiavelli's discussion of Roman parties.[106] "Popular men" come from the people but are not of the people; they share the natures but not the honors and titles of the nobility. Machiavelli uses this ambiguity in the *Florentine Histories* to show how "the grave and natural enmities" operate unmanageably in the modern setting. He has a leader of the plebs, "one of the most ardent and of greatest experience," speak to the other "plebeian men," urging them to continue their crimes until they are completed, until "either we shall become princes of the city or we shall have such a share that not only will past errors be forgiven but we shall have authority of power to threaten new injuries." Take no account of shame, conscience, or reputation, the speaker advises, for those who conquer are never disgraced because of the way they conquer; and all who conquer do so either by fraud or force. Then he urges further force against the wealthy and the heads of the guilds. "I confess," he says, "that this plan is bold and dangerous; but . . . spirited men never take account of danger in great things, for those enterprises that begin with danger always finish with reward. . . ."[107] But whose reward? The frank immoralism of this unnamed speaker, whom Machiavelli chose to speak in his account of the year 1378, conceals the purpose of the speaker. We see that he asserts all conquest is by force or fraud and does not mention any fraud in his own plan. The fraud is in the difference between his ardent

106. *Disc.* 1:4–6.
107. *F. H.* 3:13 (vol. 2, pp. 143–44).

nature and the nature of his audience; as he says, the reward comes to the "spirited men" (*uomini animosi*), not to the plebs. When the people conquer, the popular men become nobles.

This speech occurs in Book 3, after the people have won their victory over the nobles and then have divided themselves. Indeed, this division took place immediately. The Duke of Athens had been brought to Florence by the nobles to frighten and awe the people, much like a Roman dictator. But the Florentine nobles were incapable of managing him to their end. On the contrary, they were exposed and punished as the promoters of his odious tyranny; [108] so they went down after him. Yet after "the great" were conquered, Machiavelli notes that three kinds of people, "powerful, middle, and low" (*potente, mediocre, e basso*), remained to share the government.[109] Included among the powerful of "the people" were the Medici and the Rondinegli, and Machiavelli says of the later division begun by the Ricci and the Albizzi that the Albizzi party, the revived Guelf sect, contained "all the ancient nobles with the greater part of the more powerful people." [110]

Thus the new division of modern party politics into people and plebs, which might seem to create a new middle class between the nobles and the plebs of ancient party politics, results merely from the natural differences between princes and people as they appear in the modern setting. The people as opposed to the plebs, or the powerful people as opposed to the low, are merely plebeian princes generated from below, the Tribunes of modern politics, but with the difference

108. *F. H.* 2:32, 33, 37, 39. To expose the arrogance of the nobles was the unconscious role of the Archbishop of Florence, who in accordance with his office and his natural goodness intervened to calm the party dispute and, still in accordance with both his office and his nature, exacerbated it.

109. *F. H.* 2:42.

110. *F. H.* 3:8, 21; cf. 2:11 (vol. 2, p. 72).

that they have defeated the ruling princes, the "ancient nobles." When the "popular men" win, they displace the "nobles," killing many and exiling more, but under the conditions of modern politics, they can manage new plebeian princes or absorb the ancient nobles who may remain, no better than their predecessors. After 1378, they were divided into princes of the people and of the plebs, and the middle had disappeared.[111] This new division is a consequence of the division within the nobility which permitted "the people" to conquer, and the nobility was divided by the interference of Christianity.

The middle class between nobles and people was really a half-armed or disarmed nobility ignorant of the practices of mastery yet by nature incapable of tolerating subjection.[112] Their guilds had been endowed with a kind of political power by the Ghibellines, acting in fear of the Guelfs and their champion, Charles of Anjou. When the Ghibellines tried to take back this gift, and were defeated and expelled, the guilds thereafter supported the Guelfs. From this time (1266), each guild received a magistrate to administer justice to all under its jurisdiction, and it enjoyed the power of presenting armed men under its banner when called upon.[113] In a few years, according to Machiavelli, the guilds took over all government in the city. Indeed, it was they who established the magistracy of the *Signori* from which nobles were excluded. They were themselves divided into more and less honored guilds, called "greater" and "lesser," which sustained the difference between the people and the plebs. The greater guilds were favored by the Captains of the Guelf party, who had acquired rights to certain magistracies at the time of the expulsion of the Ghibellines and consti-

111. *F. H.* 3:18; 4:2, 27; 5:4.
112. *F. H.* 2:39 (vol. 2, p. 116), 42 (vol. 2, p. 120); 3:17, 18, 21. If the nobles are not arrogant, they are abject; there is no middle possibility of "modesty."
113. Cf. *F. H.* 2:5 and 2:8, 11, 22.

tuted a separate power within the city, somewhat like the Church itself, with a palace of their own.[114]

Thus the guilds did not head a middle class by whose commercial vigor and skill the ancient nobility was displaced and debased; they were, rather, the undeserving beneficiaries of ecclesiastical interference in politics. They replaced the nobility because the nobility had been sapped by the Christian disdain for honors of this world and then had been directly attacked by the Pope, the Church, the Guelfs, and their foreign allies. In replacing the nobility they complicated the nomenclature of Florentine party politics to the point that it became necessary for Machiavelli to refer to "a very noble popular family," [115] yet it was not they fundamentally, but the Church, that ruled the city. When politics is divided into sacred and secular as defined by the sacred, secular politics can fall into the hands of merchants, "men educated in trade." Such men are the remnant of a spirited nobility, not the leaders of a rising class.

In ancient party politics, the plebeian princes, intermediaries between the two natural parties of men, are managed and absorbed by the princely party. But in the modern system, leagues of partisans are managed by the intermediaries, both sacred and secular, who scurry through many complexities and confusions to the business of cunning and bungle. The difficulty is that the modern system puts too great a burden on the princes: they have not only to seek the honors of this world against other princes, but also to maintain the interest of the world itself against those who place the supreme honors in the afterlife. Under Christian politics, one of the two natural parties, the popular as embodied in the Church, advances the argument for the supernatural; the other natural party is left to defend the notion of natural

114. *F. H.* 2:11, 12, 13; 3:10, 12.
115. *F. H.* 3:9 (vol. 2, p. 135); cf. 3:4. On the "signs" of popular nobility, see 2:34–37; 3:1; 4:27.

partisanship, which is to say the desirability of this world's honors.[116] No man can reach for honors while he is considering or defending the very status of honor; nor can he defend honor in general while his own honor is at stake.[117]

The princely party is in the position of a party having to defend partisanship and the party system, for in modern politics the status of honor cannot be taken for granted. Lacking ambition, the people never understand it or appreciate the necessity for it; and when they are fortified in the fortresses of Christianity, they can succeed in defeating the natural party of the ambitious. This party, because of the nature of ambition, is always potentially at odds with itself; it can achieve unity by extending the ambitions of individuals to the highest political glory that exacts attention to the common good, the glory of founding new orders. In the widest sense, these new orders must be understood as "sects," for politics, culture, and religion are connected, and the glorious prince makes everything anew. The "new orders" of *The Prince* and the *Discourses* appear in the *Florentine Histories* as "sects." The disease of modern politics, then, can be summarized as the inability of the princely party to control the making of sects. Sects cannot be made or maintained by being remade because the Christian sect controls the popular party. The remaining natural party, since it cannot make the conventional, must confront the supernatural. In this conspiratorial work Machiavelli tries to show Italian princes how to regain control of the supernatural.

---

116. *F. H.* 2:12 (beg.) makes it clear that the modern parties are not the natural parties.

117. *F. H.* 4:7 offers an excellent example of this predicament. After a Florentine defeat, Rinaldo has to defend the party of disarmed nobles against the popular view that God justly willed their defeat to diminish their power. His advice is to consider God's will as fortune, to show fortune a bold face, to imitate their fathers, and not to lose their spirit (*animo*) against "any prince whatever." In effect, unknowingly and unsuccessfully, he advises the people to abandon Christianity.

COMMENTARY
Mark Phillips

SCHOLARS HAVE generally ignored the *Florentine Histories*. By and large they have posed their questions to Machiavelli with very little reference to this late work or have treated it only as a kind of appendage to the better-known political writings. And within the tradition of Renaissance historiography—itself a neglected genre—the *Histories* have not been given the honorable place they deserve.

I suppose one should be grateful, then, when a scholar of Mr. Mansfield's reputation takes up the *Florentine Histories* in a serious way. Unfortunately, as a student of Renaissance historical writing I find it very difficult to accept much of what Mansfield has to say; at the same time many of the problems in his presentation directly follow on the general neglect of Machiavelli as historian.

I

Given the rather esoteric tone and technique of Mansfield's interpretive essay, I hope he will forgive me for giving this audience a brief summary of the argument. The central question as I understand it is whether Machiavelli saw Christianity as having had a major formative influence in determining the factional basis of modern politics. The answer we are given is clearly "yes."

How does Mansfield arrive at this conclusion? He begins

with a description of Machiavelli's purpose in writing these histories. Machiavelli seeks, says Mansfield, to compare ancient and modern—that is, classical and Renaissance—party systems. The work is organized for this reason not so much historically as topically, as a series of inquiries. Indeed, "it would be better to translate 'histories' as 'inquiries' in the classical sense."

The comparison of classical and Renaissance politics clearly comes out in favour of the ancients: classical political divisions did not degenerate into factions. To the obvious question of what went wrong in the modern period, Mansfield's Machiavelli answers unequivocally, "Christianity."

Given the fact that the text of the *Florentine Histories* is generally silent on the subject of religion, how do we arrive at this conclusion? A number of specific passages are interpreted in light of the "inquiries" that Mansfield believes Machiavelli to be conducting. Probably the central text—central both to the plan of the *Histories* and to the present interpretation—is the opening of the fifth book. Here Machiavelli says that the natural cycle of growth and decay, of order and disorder, that cycle so familiar to any student of Machiavelli, can be disturbed by "an extraordinary force." Mansfield is quick to identify this force with the supernatural and hence with Christianity. The Church is a foreign element which the prince cannot control; yet it holds the loyalty of his people, thus alienating some part of their allegiance to him. The extraordinary force of a supernatural power, or belief in a supernatural power, thus has prevented a revival of Roman virtue amongst the Romans' Italian descendants. Christianity created a disruptive element in any state; the Church—representing a religion that "appealed to the people rather than to princes"—became the basis of one of the factions that divided Italy, the popular party or sect.

The word sect introduces us to another of the major arguments for the Christian basis of factionalism. "The

Florentine parties unlike the Roman," says Mansfield, "are 'sects' and therefore they produce 'partisans.' We may suppose that sects are somehow related to Christianity, but Machiavelli, by remaining silent, has made it necessary to establish that supposition." This kind of argument from silence is repeatedly employed in similar fashion and constitutes, I think, a category of argument in itself. Finally, Mansfield sees the *Florentine Histories* as describing the uniting of Florence to Rome—not classical Rome but Christian ecclesiastical Rome—in the persons of the Medici Popes. In sum, "as the *Florentine Histories* progress, Florence becomes more and more 'foreign,' barbarian, Roman."

Let us now examine the evidence for some of these arguments. A prime requisite of any interpretation, such as Mansfield's, that is based solely on the texts without reference to tradition, biography, or social context, is that no violence be done to the texts themselves. Unfortunately this requirement is trampled on from the very beginning in that Mansfield refuses to recognize the very genre within which Machiavelli operates. By the time Machiavelli wrote his history at the request of the Medici, there was a rich and mature tradition of public historiography in Florence. As you would expect, Machiavelli modified and extended this tradition, but he certainly did not ignore it. By insisting on labeling the *Histories* as "inquiries," Mansfield is attempting to impose the character and purpose of the *Discorsi* on Machiavelli's historical work—a work which bears the stamp of its humanist antecedents in its rhetorical and didactic forms, its definition of purpose and scope, its moral and political lessons, its literary language, and, last but not least, in its official patronage and public character.

This denial of genre is not casual; it is in fact necessary to the argument that Mansfield wishes to establish. That Machiavelli intended a comparison of ancient and modern political practice as in the *Discorsi,* rather than simply presenting a sophisticated analytic narrative of Florentine history, is the indispensable prelude to the argument that Christianity was the great distorting influence on Renaissance politics. "Each book," we are told, "except the first begins with a discussion of some general topic in politics, including an explicit comparison of ancient and modern practice (except the last book)." Unfortunately this is not quite true. I find no mention of the supposedly ubiquitous ancients in the argument to the seventh book. So we are down to five out of eight books, and even in the remaining five the reference to ancient politics is often only brief or rhetorical. Only by a great exercise of the imagination can classical politics be taken as a major theme.

To reiterate, Mansfield's argument violates the integrity of the text by refusing to recognize the historiographical convention within which it operates. Similarly, specific textual fragments are badly mangled in this breathless search for the supernatural key to modern politics. The passage in which Machiavelli talks of the "extraordinary force" is a crucial text to which the argument frequently returns. Let us take a closer look. "Machiavelli says that 'nature does not allow worldly things (*mondane cose*) to remain fixed'; hence order is followed by disorder, and disorder by order, unless men are stifled by 'an extraordinary force.' This 'extraordinary force' outside the working of 'nature' and superior to the worldly things that move makes one think of the supernatural." Mansfield here fixes on two phrases—worldly things and extraordinary force—and arbitrarily assigns them values in opposition to each other. In fact, however, there is no indication that the extraordinary force is to be contrasted with worldly things. Quite the contrary. There is nothing in this passage—whose importance Mansfield quite rightly underlines—that in any respect touches on the supernatural or otherworldly.

Here in Book 5 the historian stands at the very center of

his work and at the introduction to the second, Medician phase of Florentine history; quite naturally he looks ahead to the second half of his task. "Thus the military energy, which is in other countries exhausted by a long peace, was wasted in Italy by the contemptible manner in which hostilities were carried on, as will be clearly seen in the events to be described from 1434 to 1494, from which it will appear how the barbarians were again admitted into Italy, and she sunk under subjection to them." As 1434 is the date of Cosimo de Medici's takeover in Florence (the point at which the narrative would now resume) and 1494 is the date of the French (barbarian) invasion that had devastated Renaissance Italy, the context in which Machiavelli meant the extraordinary force to be understood should be quite clear. The extraordinary force that interrupted Italy's natural cycle of order and disorder, far from being supernatural, was the misshapen little king of France, Charles VIII, and his massive invading army. For Machiavelli, just as for Guicciardini, 1494 was the great symbolic divide in Italian history: for Machiavelli recounting the story of the "golden age" before the great catastrophe, as much as for Guicciardini who analysed its humiliating aftermath, the invasions saw the rape of the Italian cities, the deflowering of their fragile Renaissance culture, the end of innocence. For both of them, the invasions were a fateful revelation of the deep flaws in Italian political institutions. The year 1494, the terminus of the *Florentine Histories,* marked a kind of military crucifixion, towards which all previous actions tended, and from which all subsequent events fell away.

Let me deal now far more briefly with the other principal arguments. Machiavelli's use of the word "setta" or sect certainly cannot establish anything about the religious or secular origins of faction, as Mansfield would have us believe. Then, as now, the word "setta" meant simply something cut off, a body of men or opinion, a faction. Of course it may mean sect in the religious sense, but there is no reason why it should. Machiavelli uses it to refer to the followers of condottieri, surely a secular usage.

The argument about the Romanization of Florence depends on a conjunction of events that took place in 1512, twenty years after the close of Machiavelli's account. In any case, in the notably worldly person of Leo X it would be far more accurate to say that Rome was made over in the image of Florence than that Florence herself was Romanized. The triumph of the profoundly unspiritual Medici Popes seems to me an unlikely focus for an attempt to blame Florentine troubles on too great a faith in the supernatural. On the contrary, here indeed is a clear case of ecclesiastical authority bolstering the prince's rule and not the reverse.

Finally, given the looseness of the paper in interpreting the positive statements of Machiavelli, how much can we hope for from the interpretation of his silences? The great danger of this approach to the text is that one begins to find "obtrusive silences," in Mansfield's phrase, everywhere and anywhere—even where the text seems to speak most loudly. I am afraid this is the case where Mansfield argues that the oldest law that should not be revived is that of original sin. Surely the effects of the revival of the old law requiring Guelf purity were ruinous enough without requiring the added burden of original sin.

As for the popular nature of the Church party the facts themselves belie the argument. It is quite true that at certain times the pro-Church faction had a popular appeal, but equally there were times—for example, during the War of the Eight Saints—when the opposite held. It is unfortunate that the maze of Florentine factionalism will not sort itself out for us so neatly and so rationally, but we should remember that it was precisely this irrationality and inefficiency that Machiavelli despised in the politics of his age.

II

It should be clear from all that I have said that what we need if we want a clearer understanding of the *Florentine Histories* is the elaboration of a critique that will work with the text and not against it: a critical reading must respect the integrity not only of specific passages within the work, but also such a reading will see the place of the whole book, considered as a work of art, within the historiographical genre. Obviously there is not enough time now to go into this fully, but rather than end so negatively I should like to give the briefest indication of such a critique.

Some time ago I was doing some work in the chronicle sources on the revolt of the Ciompi, perhaps the most violent factional disturbance in Florentine history. After having made myself familiar with the relevant chronicles, I came to Machiavelli's extended narration of the revolt. I was surprised to find that it is quite clear when Machiavelli is using one of these chronicles almost without comment or embellishment, and when, on the other hand, the real source of his account is his own historical imagination. By this I do not mean that in some places Machiavelli was being truthful and in others simply making it up as he went along; rather, it seemed to me that by careful reading one can distinguish between areas of the text in which Machiavelli was content to let the sources speak for themselves and other areas in which he speaks clearly and fully with his own voice because his imagination is actively engaging the materials. This separation—very much like the effect the modern historian achieves through the use of quotation and citation—was clear to me and may very well have been clear to Machiavelli's first readers. It may, in other words, have been a conscious device, a convention understood by his intended audience.

273

Machiavelli's narrative technique—conscious and conventional or not—makes possible a more refined approach to his text in that it allows us to spotlight those areas of the book where he speaks in his own right. Clearly, he was fascinated by the whole affair of the Ciompi tumult because it gets such disproportionate attention. But there are two areas within his account where the narrative voice is strikingly his own. The first is in his descriptions of Michele di Lando, the barefoot plebian who ultimately pacified the city by virtue of his talents alone and who thus "deserves to be enumerated among the glorious few who have greatly benefitted their country." This exaltation is to be found in none of the chronicles and even goes beyond Leonardo Bruni's admiration for Michele. And perhaps Machiavelli, a man clearly gripped by a passion to be known as a benefactor of his country, felt kinship with this man Michele who, like himself, was "more favored by nature than by fortune." And both men, you will recall, were rewarded by their countrymen with disgrace and exile.

The other area in which Machiavelli is independent of his sources are passages in which he adopts a more analytic stance. Perhaps most interesting is one of those much mocked "conventional," "rhetorical," invented speeches which he adopted from the humanists and they in turn from the ancients. In one of these (it is referred to in Mansfield's paper so I shall not quote at length) the leader of the pleb mob harangues his following, saying; "All men having had one common origin, are all equally ancient, and nature has made us all after one fashion. Strip us naked and we shall be found alike. Dress us in their clothing, and they in ours, we shall appear noble, they ignoble—for poverty and riches make all the difference." He explains in the best Machiavellian fashion that having taken certain calculated risks they must carry through what they have begun. He explains the disunity and weakness of the enemy; he reminds them of past injustices, of hunger, of the rewards to be gained. In sum, the anonymous leader of Machiavelli's creation provides his following with a calculated plan as well as a rationale for action. And his focus is selfish, material, and decidedly unspiritual. It is a conventional argument, but the point is that nowhere in the contemporary chronicles on the Ciompi do we find the plebs endowed with a capacity for rational calculation or in possession of a programme (it is still too primitive to be called an ideology). Even the unique chronicle written by a Ciompi sympathizer never uses such arguments.

In summary, then, Machiavelli's specific contribution to the history of this event was to provide in the words of this unknown orator a plebian rationale for action, because like later historians, but unlike earlier ones, he could not see men engaging in faction and revolt without plan or articulated programmes. His analysis of faction thus resolves itself to a calculus of self-interest violently pursued. On the other hand, we discover that to the chronicler's already well-developed descriptions of disorder he adds nothing. What engages the imagination of Machiavelli, on the contrary, is the attempt by an unlikely, barefoot savior to reestablish order in Florence. This, surely, was a reflection of the historian's own deepest purpose.

COMMENTARY
J. A. Gunn

I QUESTION the emphasis in Harvey Mansfield's paper because it conflicts with two of my prejudices, one relating to the substance of the argument, another to the form. Setting out to explain Machiavelli's views on factions (*parti*), Mansfield notes both the famous justification of the divisions in republican Rome and the fact that Machiavelli counselled princes to avoid such dissensions. All of this is clear enough, for unlike later Machiavellians who frequently advocated the cultivation of faction and especially courtly cabals, Machiavelli consistently denied their usefulness in a principality. The making of factions he dismissed as the resort of a weak prince—a position amply expressed in *The Prince, The Art of War* and even the *Discourses*. But *The Florentine Histories* shows Machiavelli as hostile to parties in a republican setting. Why?

We are told here that religion has poisoned that natural contest between the "people" and the "rich" which was the glory of Rome—perhaps. My first reason for resisting this answer, in the absence of compelling textual support, is the knowledge that Mansfield has previously committed himself to the opinion that the waning of the great religious parties of seventeenth-century England was a necessary prelude to the emergence of that party system defended by Burke. My own examination of the doctrine of party in England leads me to assign a much more positive rôle to religious feeling, particularly as it appeared in the struggle of English Dissent for full civil equality. The story of Shute Barrington and the first defence of party government is far removed from Florence and Machiavelli; but it allows me to record my predisposition to see religion as not necessarily inimical to an acceptance of party. I can, of course, speak with far less confidence of Mansfield's opinions, but I seem to detect some continuity between his perception of the influence of religion in England and his present argument about its rôle in coloring Machiavelli's attitudes toward parties. This directs us to the evidence presented in the paper, and so to my second prejudice.

This looks to the form of the Mansfield argument. Frequently ingenious, his approach still leaves me feeling that the discovery of an esoteric message is far less satisfying and conclusive than one that is explicit, given a choice. But in Machiavelli's writings we are given a choice. Mansfield records Machiavelli's concern, in the *Histories,* about the practise of imposing outside quarrels on the Florentines. Other works by Machiavelli attest to the disfavor with which he greeted such a strategy wherever it occurred. On a number of occasions he observed how dangerous it was to rule subject cities by fomenting internal divisions, if only because the policy was likely to redound to the disservice of the metropolitan power. This was so because factions formed in a colony were likely to be reproduced at home, and it made no difference whether the colonies belonged to a prince or a republic—*divide et impera* would equally damage both. In fact, Florence herself had ruined Pistoia by such measures, while simultaneously reducing her own fragile unity (*Discourses* 2:25; 3:27). The example of Pistoia shows that the migration of quarrels from one jurisdiction to another might harm both, while other examples in the *Histories* indicate that these quarrels might move in either direction, either escalating a private and local tension or bringing a major one on to a smaller stage.

In this way the situation of Florence could be subsumed under a general rule of prudence—creating factions in any sort of polity was undesirable and the products unnatural. Healthy divisions arose without artificial assistance. Were we seeking esoteric meanings, it might not be amiss to suppose that Machiavelli was applying to Florence those counsels about the dangers of importing faction into a subject city. In the *Histories* Machiavelli does not labor the point that Florence had been the creature of outside powers, Italian or transalpine, but this had obviously been the case. What else was Florence at the time of writing but an annex of the papacy? The fact of foreign intervention, from whatever source, was enough to deny to Florence the experience of Rome. The baneful influence of religion thus becomes a particular instance of foreign intervention and the imposition of faction—one symptom of an endemic complaint.

The part of Mansfield's argument that I find most plausible is his careful and illuminating interpretation of the extraordinarily complex collection of parties and classes in Florentine politics. Certainly Machiavelli's remark in the *Histories* (3:1), that in Florence the people had won, requires some clarification. Perhaps he was saying covertly that it was the spiritual authority that had really triumphed, although the connection between the "people" and the Church, with its dependence on the ambiguous status of the Medici family, is too involved either to assert or refute with ease. Clearly the "people" had not won in any simple sense, for the rule by *popolari* had given way at time of writing to the ill-disguised rule by first a Medicean cardinal, then a Medicean Pope. But the very complexity of Florentine politics suggests that the Church was not wholly to blame.

For various reasons Florence lacked elements of the Roman experience. Whereas in Rome the monarchical principle found constitutional expression in consuls, Italy was faced with an embarrassment of princes who had no exact equivalent in the earlier and better polity. In passing over the crucial differences between Roman nobles and Renaissance princes, Mansfield suggests that the so-called "princely party" was simply the victim of modern religion and was not itself in any way responsible for corruption. But it takes two to make a quarrel, and if Machiavelli loathed the influence of Christianity and regretted the decline of the old nobility, he was no less prepared to condemn the treachery of the Ghibbeline nobles of 1250. As a faithful student of the Roman constitution, Machiavelli was sensitive to the several respects in which Florence failed to capture the classical formula for success. His *Discourse on Remodelling the*

Government of Florence makes the point very clearly when
he says that Florence's troubles stem from the city's being
neither a republic nor a princedom, but something vacillating
uneasily in between. Not being a true republic, its factions,
we can assume, had never been productive of that healthy
conflict which served Rome so well. Roman factions, the only
ones that seem to earn Machiavelli's specific approval, were
between different sorts of men, universal and natural divisions
which could find institutional form in struggles between the
Senate and Tribunes of the People, and hence a legal settlement on particular issues.

What is lacking in Machiavelli's treatment of Florentine
parties is any conclusive evidence that he saw religion,
specifically the Christian religion, as the sole villain. The
assumption that Machiavelli's notorious distaste for the
Church informs the entire structure of the *Histories* rests on
two doubtful pieces of textual exegesis. The introduction of
original sin as the ultimate barrier to pragmatic politics and
limited conflict seems quite gratuitous. This sort of retribution
might well prove politically unmanageable, but Machiavelli's
references to retrospective laws are adequately grounded in
the context of a specific issue in Florentine politics. Since the
exoteric meaning seems clear enough, the passage in question
invites no further probing. The second point is more important: Mansfield argues that the decline of the nobility was
judged by Machiavelli to proceed from a proscription of that
quest for worldly honour which would otherwise have been
their glory and that of the state. However, there is dis-
concertingly little indication that Machiavelli intended to
suggest that ideological divisions according to the rules laid
down by the Church were such an inhibiting force. The only
text cited here (4:7) affords absolutely no support. For all
Machiavelli's feelings about the debilitating effect of Christianity, it seems odd to expect him to accuse the Renaissance
papacy of rendering worldly gain illegitimate. Far better

surely to look to the ascetic Savonarola. But he is absent from the *Histories,* and to attach a nonexistent allusion to a neglected figure places far too great a burden on silence. Where the text is unsatisfactory even for sustaining the existence of allusions as to the nature of honour, the supposed message becomes obscure indeed when applied to the difficulties of defending a party system (Mansfield, pp. 265–66). The message is set, as it were, at two removes from the reader. Furthermore, whatever Machiavelli said, it is simply untrue that one cannot pursue worldly honors at the same time as one defends the pursuit—people do so all the time. To bring the point home in relation to parties it is necessary only to observe that when Englishmen came finally to defend a party system the defence was conducted by partisans, supporters of one party who justified the existence of both. That the sentiment is an odd one in some ways is no proof that Machiavelli did not have it, but it gives further incentive to scrutinize any extrapolation of his actual statements.

In the largest sense one cannot argue with Mansfield's linking of Machiavelli's distaste for both Christianity and modern factions—no doubt they were connected. But there are other factors to consider. Machiavelli was hostile to all divisions imposed by foreign influence, suggesting that colonial status of Florence made it susceptible to unnatural divisions; he appreciated the ways in which Florence differed in social structure and constitutional traditions from Rome, perhaps even to the extent of its not being a proper republic, hence making parties inappropriate. There is then much in Machiavelli, apart from his animus against the Church, which would prevent his giving a justification of faction as it then existed, although, as Felix Gilbert has pointed out ("Bernardo Rucellai and the Orti Oricellari, A Study on the Origin of Modern Political Thought," *Journal of the Warburg and Courtauld Institutes,* 12:101–31) others at this time may be seen as contributing to the evolution of parties in the modern sense. Perhaps Machiavelli was oblique in some of his statements; subtlety has long been associated with his name. However, large portions of Mansfield's interpretation seem over-subtle, falling, in a curious way, between two stools. While the specific rendering of certain passages makes excessive demands on the imagination, the general position is fairly well substantiated from Machiavelli's explicit statements. Esoteric interpretation requires some basis in exoteric statement elsewhere, but if this statement is too obvious the need for reading between the lines may vanish. It is in this sense that I wonder if perhaps Mansfield has employed engines of exquisite refinement to force an open door.

The Value of Asocial Sociability: Contributions of Machiavelli, Sidney and Montesquieu

NEAL WOOD

I

BY WAY OF INTRODUCTION IT WILL BE useful to contrast briefly classical Greek and Roman views of domestic conflict with Machiavelli's theory. In order to clarify the differences, we need a working distinction between competition and conflict. Competition presupposes wide acceptance of ends, and disagreement over means as to the person or the policy that will best achieve the ends. Competition is a game situation; competitors may be athletes on the playing field, candidates for public office, members of a deliberative assembly, business and professional rivals. Though in practice the precise line between competition and conflict is often difficult to draw, conflict is generally characterized by tension, hostility, and defiance that may erupt into violence and warfare. Typically, extensive and intensive disagreement over ends and, frequently, an unwillingness to abide by the rules of the game lead to conflict. Characteristic forms of domestic conflict on an approximate scale from non-violence to violence are: deep-rooted party opposition, mass protest rallies, protest marches, strikes, picketing, rioting, mutiny, insurrection, revolution, and civil war. Classical thinkers condemned social conflict, and in varying degrees accepted social competition. Machiavelli not only accepted social competition but also believed that domestic conflict, short of widespread violence, was beneficial. His notion was a radical break with past thought, and a herald of future theory.

Plato and Aristotle conceived of the polis as an organic whole consisting of different parts, each performing its proper function in relation to the proper functioning of the whole. The proper end or function of the polis or social whole is the achievement of the life of moral excellence postulated by reason. This moral purpose will determine the differentiation of function within the polis and the nature of the relations among the functions in order to maintain an equilibrium or harmony of parts. Such a social balance was thought to be natural and good, in keeping with the cosmic unity and symmetry. Aristotle's teleological conception of both the polis and nature entails the idea of social harmony or social "rest" just as it entails the idea of matter being naturally at rest instead of in motion.

His famous criticism of Plato's ideal polis for being a *unison* instead of a harmony of parts is misleading.[1] Neither

1. Aristotle, *Politics,* tr. Ernest Barker (Oxford, 1952), 1263b, p. 51.

thinker will permit the existence of conflict in his ideal polis. Basic to Aristotle's criticism is a dislike of his master's provision for a community of property, and women and children in the ruling class. Aristotle, who desires much more diversity and variety in the well-ordered polis than Plato, does not favor collectivism. Yet on the question of conflict his ideal is very similar to Plato's. He compares the proper ordering of parts in a polis to the harmony of a musical composition, in which different parts are united to form a pleasing whole. But, and to forget this point is to misunderstand Aristotle, the unity of a musical composition is predetermined by the conception of the composer; the harmonizing end of the polis is the common good defined by a particular notion of human excellence. In both cases, musical and political, the end places very definite limits on the nature of the parts and their relations. Aristotle's harmony, like Plato's unison, precludes dissonance, or the blending of the tonal and atonal. Although he prescribes greater competition and multiformity than is found in Plato's ideal, he never recommends the toleration of fundamental differences, of opposition and conflict within the polis. His view of a social equilibrium prevents him from recognizing the legitimacy of the various forms of nonviolent social conflict. Never would he apply the imagery of war and military conflict to domestic politics, as so many unconsciously do today.[2] His very goal of civic concord, *homonoia,* the union of souls in a way of life, is quite foreign to the modern notion of fundamental social and political struggle. Even in the discussion of the "polity," the most generally practicable type of constitution which consists of a mixture of democracy and oligarchy, Aristotle scarcely suggests a system of conflict and contention between demos and oligarchs. On the contrary, he wants the establishment of an equilibrium between the two social groups by a large "middle

2. Upon the novelty of using military metaphor in the discussion of politics see the comments in my essay, "Some Reflections on Sorel and Machiavelli," *Political Science Quarterly,* 83 (March 1968) : 76–91.

class," either larger than any single class or than a combination of other classes. Such a large middle class of landed proprietors in a timocracy, he thinks, will more than counterbalance the other classes, thus preventing factionalism and dissension.[3] Indeed, the polity is the "political" version of the ethical "golden mean" aimed at a life of moderation and minimal conflict. Again, in recommendations for the prevention of *stasis,* the corruption of the polis characterized by factional strife, he refers to the equilibrium of the human body in order to emphasize the danger of the disproportionate increase of any portion of the polis.[4] Clearly, Aristotle, would permit greater heterogeneity and competition in the polis than would Plato; nevertheless on the question of conflict he agrees with Plato. For both thinkers the central problem of the polis is *stasis* and the maintenance of order. Aristotle's idea of the mixed constitution is largely a static one that ignores the elements of conflict and their interaction. Modern liberal notions of conflict should not be read into his thought; he was not an ancient liberal or Whig in this sense.[5]

In regard to social conflict Polybius and Cicero stood with Plato and Aristotle. They agreed that the Roman republican constitution, a mixture of the "principles" of the three simple constitutions of monarchy, aristocracy, and democracy, was the most ideal civic order attainable. Mixed in this fashion, the force of each of the simple types would be neutralized by the others, so that no single principle could prevail and consequently degenerate.[6] The theory of the mixed constitution rested upon two assumptions: the psychological idea

3. Aristotle, op. cit., 1295b–1296a, pp. 181–183.
4. Ibid., 1302b–1303a, p. 209.
5. A recent example of reading liberal proclivities into Aristotle is found in Bernard Crick, *In Defense of Politics,* rev. ed. (London, 1964), pp. 17–18.
6. On their views of the mixed constitution see Polybius, *The Histories,* tr. W. R. Paton (Cambridge, Mass., 1960), Bk. 6:10–18, 43–58, pp. 289–311, 367–403; Cicero, *De Republica,* tr. C. W. Keyes (Cambridge, Mass., 1951), Bk. 1:xxix, xlv, rlvi, Bk. 2, pp. 71, 103–7, 111–83.

that the corrupting influence of power upon an individual or group could be contained by a system of checks and balances, and the sociological idea that classes might be balanced or stabilized.[7] In respect to the latter, Polybius argued that a mixed constitution "should remain for long in a state of equilibrium like a well-trimmed coat."[8] Checks and balances do not hinder unity in times of danger, and during periods of peace and prosperity they are sufficient to prevent any of the parts from disproportionate growth, thereby disrupting the constitutional equilibrium.[9] Class struggle and party strife are to be avoided just as Plato and Aristotle taught.

Cicero, more clearly than Polybius, exhibits the classical aversion to factionalism and conflict, epitomizing the whole tradition on these matters. With Aristotle, he compares a well-ordered commonwealth to a musical harmony.[10] His social and political harmony constitutes what Charles Norris Cochrane has termed a *concordia ordinum.*[11] In existing commonwealths two "parties" or categories of men are always present, the *populares* and the *optimates.*[12] As Cicero describes them, the former are rabble-rousers who attempt to lead the masses to advance their own interests at the expense of the common good. On the other hand, the *optimates* are the wise, moderate, and prudent men who give priority to the common good over the interests of any particular individual or group. Cicero's ideal of the well-ordered commonwealth is one in which the masses are quietly contented under the leadership of the *optimates,* who are able to maintain their

7. See especially Kurt von Fritz, *The Theory of the Mixed Constitution in Antiquity: A Critical Analysis of Polybius' Political Ideas* (New York, 1954), pp. 80–82.
8. Polybius, op. cit., Bk. 6:10, p. 291.
9. Ibid., Bk. 6:18, pp. 309–11.
10. Cicero, op. cit., Bk. 2:xlii, pp. 181–83.
11. *Christianity and Classical Culture: A Study of Thought and Action from Augustus to Augustine* (New York, 1944), pp. 58–59.
12. Cicero, *Pro Sestio,* tr. R. Gardner (Cambridge, Mass., 1958), Sect. 45–47, 65–66, pp. 167–75, 223–27.

rank, prestige, and honor. This is a condition marked by an absence of class or party struggle, in the *Pro Sestio* called by Cicero *cum dignitate otium,* or public tranquility with honor for the worthy.[13] In a last testament to his son, *De Officiis,* he warns that a government should never favor one interest above the other because the result would be destructive to a state, producing party strife, discord, and sedition.[14] If dissension takes place, it should be without bitterness or animosity. The heroic citizen-soldier in a great state should not display the passion or anger of the battlefield in domestic affairs; his conduct should be marked by clemency, meekness, gentleness, courtesy, affability, and a calm and undisturbed cast of mind. Thus a social harmony with little or no conflict will be established.

If the classical attitude toward conflict can be symbolized by Cicero's principle of *concordia ordinum,* Machiavelli's position is represented by *concordia discors.*[15] His concept of domestic conflict, with all its assumptions and implications, is one of the most novel and neglected features of his outlook. His acceptance of social conflict as a positive good is clearly related to elements of his thought that break with the classical purview, or lower classical standards, or explore new concepts. In the first place, although Machiavelli refers to the common good as the end of the state, he has in mind not so much a moral end as the survival, security, and happiness of the citizenry, in a word, the public utility. Moreover, he never places the state in a cosmological hierarchy or universal moral

13. Ibid., Sect. 45, p. 109. See pp. 302–4 for the informative commentary on *cum dignitate otium* by Gardner.
14. Cicero, *De Officiis,* tr. Thomas Cockman, Introd. John Warrington (London, 1955), Bk. 1: xxv, pp. 38–40.
15. *Concordia discors* is used to describe Montesquieu's concept of social order by Sergio Cotta in his valuable essay "L'idée de parti dans la philosophie politique de Montesquieu," in *Actes du Congrès Montesquieu,* ed. Louis Desgraves (Bordeaux, 1956), p. 261. The term seems just as applicable to Machiavelli's view.

order. Political considerations are distinct from moral matters. Politics becomes a self-contained, autonomous activity. Second, Machiavelli thinks that psychologically man is a mass of insatiable desires with reason their instrument. Plato and Aristotle would have agreed with him that such a concept accounts for actual human behavior. However, while they would consider behavior that could be so explained as a deviation from the natural and the good, Machiavelli would term it natural, but not always good. Human desires, at least the basic ones like self-preservation, become the norm for politics and political arrangements; the state is a human artifice to satisfy human wants. Men wish above all things to preserve themselves and to live happily and securely, free from external domination and from tyranny within; the well-ordered state is designed to fulfill these purposes. Ever an ardent republican Machiavelli is one of the first modern devotees of liberty, and his libertarianism is related directly to his recognition of the beneficial effects of conflict. Finally, his fundamental emphasis upon politics as a means, as a series of techniques, his distinct preference for firm, swift, deft, and vigorous action, in a word, action typified by *virtù*, his condemnation of inaction, of procrastination, and indecisiveness, and his fear of a social tranquility as a seedbed of enervation, indolence, and civic corruption, all place him in the modern tradition. His implication that truth is the consequence of action rather than contemplation and that the wise man is an activist rather than a quietist is at variance with part of the classical position.

Machiavelli's theory of social conflict is formulated in the *Discourses* and the *Florentine Histories*.[16] It rests upon the idea that in every republic two primary social classes exist:

16. Machiavelli's ideas about domestic conflict can be found in *Discourses*, 1:ii–viii, xvi–xviii, xxxvii; and in *Florentine Histories*, 3:1; 7:1. See Machiavelli, *Opere,* ed. Mario Bonfantini (Milan, 1963), pp. 95–115, 134–43, 170–73, 680–81, 874–76.

the *popolo* and the *grandi.* The distinction is more psychological than economic, resting upon a view of human egoism
and the individual desire for power. The people who constitute the vast majority of any republic are those who wish to
be free from the domination of the view and to secure their
lives, families, and properties. The great are the social
minority with an inordinate thirst for power and personal
aggrandizement, those who suffer from an excessive *libido
dominandi.* Out of the clash and struggle of the two groups
in a republic, good laws will be framed, and order and
harmony will thereby become a way of life. He adheres to
the classical theory of the mixed constitution with the idea
of a social equilibrium, but his preoccupation is with the
description and analysis of the process of conflict and struggle,
involving human passions and wills in opposition, from
which the constitutional balance emerges. Because he emphasizes rather than ignores the interaction of conflicting elements, of contending social groups, his equilibrium, unlike
that of the classical thinkers, is never static and mechanistic.
Politics to Machiavelli is a dynamic, dialectical process involving the clash of opposites, a momentary synthesis or
equilibrium, the breakdown of the synthesis through new
conflict, *ad seriatim.*[17] His model is always the Roman Republic. Rome had no lawgiver like Lycurgus to provide from
the very beginning a complete constitution that would
guarantee freedom in the future. It was fortune, the friction
between the plebes and patricians, which made up the
deficiency. The countless quarrels and tumults between the
two classes were the *prima causa* of Rome's freedom for
three hundred years, freedom from autocracy and foreign
domination. These violent struggles which Machiavelli
praised were far more than friendly competitions between
rival social groups, according to the descriptions of his chief

17. Again a suggestion of Cotta, loc. cit., in regard to Montesquieu.

source, Livy. However, the idea that the conflict was beneficial to Rome originated with Machiavelli and not Livy. To those skeptical of this idea, Machiavelli offers several arguments. In the first place, the tumults never led to civil war, to bloodshed, or to extensive banishment and fines. Second, Rome's good fortune and superb military organization depended largely upon the good laws that arose from the almost perpetual conflict. And last, the internal struggles were not merely inconveniences but benefits in the sense of being crucial to Rome's grandeur. Every republic, therefore, should institutionalize social conflict by assemblies, public accusations, and comparable devices. However, remedial conflict can exist only in a healthy republic, free from corruption. In a corrupt republic, conflict degenerates into factionalism, civil war, and anarchy. Conflict in a republic is beneficial only where most citizens retain a sense of civic spirit and duty, and when in times of danger they are willing to sacrifice narrow self-interest for the public utility. Prior to the Punic Wars, Rome was certainly a case in point, according to Machiavelli, beset by external dangers. Sheer survival determined the bounds within which conflict could safely function. On the other hand, the fact that Machiavelli's own city was constantly plagued by factionalism and disorder was due to the corruption of the citizens.

Machiavelli, therefore, makes a number of rather radical suggestions of significance for future social and political theory:

1. The liberty of the citizen depends upon domestic conflict and opposition, and not on harmonious competition.
2. An important measure of the vigor of a state is the level of domestic conflict.
3. A much more vital and dedicated form of civic cooperation will emerge from conflict and opposition

than from a situation of competition in which conformity and orthodoxy are stressed.

4. Politics is a kind of dialectical process characterized by a clash of opposites, their temporary reconciliation in a rather tenuous social balance, and then the need to readjust the equilibrium because of new causes of conflict.

5. Beneficial conflict in a "healthy" state like Rome must be distinguished from the factionalism and instability of corrupt states like Rome after the Gracchi and Florence in Machiavelli's day. In such states there is a breakdown of community, a loss of all sense of civic obligation and cooperation, a universal pursuit of narrow self-interest.

6. A well-ordered state will provide a variety of institutional outlets for conflict.

II

If we are to ask how Machiavelli's theory of conflict was received in England, the answer would have to be that it was largely either overlooked or ignored. The most obvious seventeenth-century sources to scrutinize for the possible influence of the Florentine's theory are the writings of the "classical republicans" like Milton, Marvell, Harrington, Neville, and Sidney.[18] They were republicans who worshipped

18. Still the standard study is Z. S. Fink, *The Classical Republicans: An Essay in the Recovery of a Pattern of Thought in Seventeenth-Century England,* 2nd ed. (Evanston, Ill., 1962). Also see Perez Zagorin, *A History of Political Thought in the English Revolution* (London, 1954); Caroline Robbins, *The Eighteenth-Century Commonwealthman: Studies in the Transmission, Development and Circumstance of English Liberal Thought from the Restoration of Charles II until the War with the Thirteen Colonies* (Cambridge, Mass., 1961). On Harrington, reference should be made to J. G. A. Pocock's excellent essay in *The Ancient Constitution and the Feudal Law: A Study of English Historical Thought in*

classical antiquity, particularly the Roman Republic; they were ardent advocates of the mixed constitution, of a government well prepared for military expansion, even if not overtly bent on imperialistic venture. And to Rome were added other models for emulation: the ancient kingdom of the Hebrews, and various institutional arrangements of modern Venice. And, of course, they were devoted pupils of Machiavelli, finding in the *Discourses* a rare fount of political wisdom. With one notable exception, however, Machiavelli's theory of conflict seemed to have little influence. For example, Harrington and Neville were dedicated to the cause of recommending commonwealths of an immortal nature in which harmony and order might be firmly grounded and party contention, if not eliminated, carefully controlled. Although they felt that parties should be allowed in a free commonwealth, they were never enthusiastic supporters of continual agitations.

The exception was that enfant terrible, Algernon Sidney, second son of Robert Sidney, the second Earl of Leicester.[19] Although Sidney cites Machiavelli fewer times in his monumental *Discourses Concerning Government* (1698) a work much longer than Harrington's *Commonwealth of Oceana* (1656), and in language less adulatory, he seems closer to the spirit of the Florentine than does Harrington.[20] His view

the *Seventeenth Century* (Cambridge, 1957), pp. 124–47; and his "Machiavelli, Harrington, and English Political Ideologies in the Eighteenth Century," *William and Mary Quarterly*, 22 (October 1965): 549–83; also Charles Blitzer, *An Immortal Commonwealth: The Political Thought of James Harrington* (New Haven, 1960).

19. No adequate biography of Sidney or full-scale treatment of his political thought has been written. For details of his life and influence see C. H. Firth's article in the *Dictionary of National Biography;* Caroline Robbins, "Algernon Sidney's *Discourses Concerning Government:* Textbook of Revolution," *William and Mary Quarterly*, 4 (July 1947): 267–96. On his political thought see Fink, op. cit., pp. 149–69; Robbins, *The Eighteenth-Century Commonwealthman*, pp. 41–47.

20. The last English edition has been used, *The Works of Algernon Sidney* (London, 1772). In addition to numerous English and American editions (the last being 1805), there were three French translations in

of human nature tends to be more pessimistic than Harrington's; consequently, he recognized the imperfection of all things human, and the impossibility of creating a perfect commonwealth. To write of an immortal commonwealth would be for Sidney, as for Machiavelli, indulgence in delusion. Moreover, because of the frailty of human contrivances, Sidney was convinced with his master that states must be renovated periodically if they are to endure for an appreciable time and if civic corruption is to be stemmed. In recommending perennial reform, he underscores the need for conflict as the foundation of liberty. To his doctrines of reform and conflict, he adds the idea of the citizens' right and duty of revolution against tyranny.

More than the other classical republicans, Sidney insists upon the fundamental egoism and imperfection of man. He affirms that the "bestial barbarity in which many nations, especially of Africa, America, and Asia, now live, shows what human nature is, if it be not improved by art and discipline . . ." [21] and that "men are so subject to vices, and passions, that they stand in need of some restraint in every condition. . . ." [22] The best and wisest of men are handicapped by a lack of foresight,[23] are prone to err,[24] and consequently the most perfect of human artifacts testifies to "human imbecility." [25] Hence, men are always and everywhere extremely susceptible to corruption.[26] Every human institution is mutable and imperfect.[27] Even the best ordered

---

1702, 1755, 1780, and two German, 1705, 1793. Sidney's explicit references to Machiavelli are 2:11, p. 110; 2:26, p. 225; 2:29, p. 245, 3:16, p. 350; 3:40, p. 479. In addition see two passages in which Machiavelli is not mentioned by name: 2:36, p. 459; 3:25, p. 406. These relatively few references (in comparison, for example, to Harrington's *Commonwealth of Oceana*) are no indication of the tremendous influence of Machiavelli.

21. 3:7, p. 304.	22. 3:13, p. 336.
23. 2:17, p. 144.	24. 3:25, p. 404.
25. 3:25, p. 405.	26. 3:6, p. 298.
27. 2:17, pp. 144–45; 2:19, p. 160; 3:36, p. 461.	

polity will eventually decay. All that can be hoped for is the postponement of the inevitable degeneration. Relations between states are a result of human frailties and egoism leading to a *bellum omnium contra omnes*. Because of this, constant military preparedness is requisite for secure social life.[28] Quite frankly, Sidney admits, the best state is the one most capable of waging war successfully.[29] Of all states, republics are the best because they provide citizens with the greatest liberty, which means the greatest spirit of dedication to the common good, and consequently the greatest military capability.

The end of the commonwealth should be the *salus populi,* defined by Sidney as the equal preservation of man's natural and God-given rights of life, liberty, lands, and goods.[30] Civil society is formed on the basis of a contractual agreement among men to secure these rights; [31] government and law must always observe them, and be subordinate to them. Sidney's most cherished social and political value is liberty, which entails the guarantee of person and property. Liberty is "an independency upon the will of another." [32] *Salus populi* from the external standpoint means "independency upon the will" of any other state and, internally, independency upon the will of the ruler in those matters concerning the rights of the individual, and not prejudicial to the welfare of the community. Liberty does not imply licentiousness but, rather, exemption from all human laws to which the individual has not given his assent.[33] Liberty without restraint is inconsistent with government. Men must submit to some rule, to the natural law, and to a civil law in

28. 2:23, p. 178.
29. Loc. cit.
30. 3:16, p. 351; 2:2, pp. 68–69. On natural rights see 1:8, p. 8; 1: 12, p. 24; 1; 17, p. 44; 2:4, p. 76; 2:31, pp. 263–64; 3:16, p. 351; 3:19, p. 435.
31. 3:16, p. 348.
32. 1:5, p. 10; 3:16, p. 348.
33. 1:3, p. 3.

harmony with the natural law.[34] Slavery is the opposite of liberty, a complete subjection of one's person and property to the will of another.[35] The purpose of man's temporal life, therefore, is the preservation of his liberty and the prevention of his slavery.[36] In the context of society, where the rights of each are subject to the common good, each individual should respect the rights of others. The individual is free only in what relates to himself alone.[37] He may do what he wills with his house, his land, and his goods, so long as he does not interfere with the rights of others to do likewise. Any infringement upon an individual's domain for the preservation of the rights of others, i.e., for the sake of the common good, must entail an equal limitation upon the actions of all individuals. When one's natural rights are violated, without reasonable cause, the individual has both the right and the duty to resist civil authority.[38] Except for the very important natural law and natural rights doctrines, Sidney adheres fairly closely to the teachings of his Florentine master. Another difference is his view that the best guardians of liberty in a republic are the patricians.[39] Machiavelli would argue that in the most viable republic, one that expands, the ablest protectors of liberty are the people.

A crucial teaching of Sidney, the link between his valuation of liberty and his stress upon conflict, is the oft-repeated slogan that liberty is the "mother and nurse" of virtue, of all the virtues: moral, civil, and military.[40] In a flourishing republican atmosphere of liberty, advancement should be proportional to one's contribution to the community. Any failure to serve the community brings an immediate check to preferment.[41] Consequently, virtue is a very popular asset, widely emulated, at all levels of republican society. Because

34. 2:20, p. 163.   35. 1:5, p. 10.
36. 1:5, p. 11.   37. 3:41, p. 482.
38. 3:4, pp. 288–89.   39. 2:24, p. 186.
40. 2:9, pp. 110, 114, 117; 2:15, p. 133; 2:25, p. 126; 2:28, p. 236.
41. 2:25, p. 218.

virtue is so dependent upon liberty, order and stability are relative to liberty. Hence, well-constituted republics are the most stable of all governments, although they may be subject to tumults, to strife and contention.[42] In fact, conflict in a healthy republic is a sign of vigor and vitality, not of weakness and instability.

Sidney's case for conflict begins logically with the axiom closely related to his pessimistic view of human nature, that all civil societies, no matter what their design, will be subject to turbulence and disorder.[43] This is simply a universal fact to be recognized. Again we are close to the spirit of Machiavelli, and quite remote from the Platonic and Aristotelian world of ideas. Any conception of a civil order free from conflict is fantasy. Conflict is natural to the civil order just as it is the norm in all human relations. Hence, we should perceive that conflict is by no means the greatest evil to befall a commonwealth.[44] The civil order under the absolute monarch is nothing more than a "peaceable solution," [45] the isolation and fragmentation of a prison or graveyard. Absolute monarchy is a condition of slavery, the slavery of an oriental despot, for example, productive of far greater vice and cruelty than what may happen under popular or mixed government. Following Machiavelli, Sidney differentiates between disorders in corrupt states and conflict in healthy states.[46] While in the former, tumults and seditions bring intestine disorder and war, in the latter they do no harm, and can, in fact, be beneficial and invigorating. He has in mind the struggles between plebes and patricians in republican Rome, which, he asserts, produced remedies for the city's ills, and fell short of the vices of bloodshed, numerous exiles, or fines.[47] The problem of succession, always the

42. 2:18, p. 148.   43. 2:24, p. 185.
44. 2:26, p. 223.   45. Loc. cit.
46. 2:11, p. 109.
47. 2:13, pp. 123–25; 2:14, p. 126; 2:18, p. 151; 2:24, pp. 214–15.

cause of bloody factionalism under absolute monarchy, is absent in a well-ordered republic.[48] Republics soon recover from dissensions and usually all to the good.[49] Furthermore, Sidney reasons, since all human constitutions are subject to corruption, periodic conflicts of the kind which occurred in Rome are essential for the reformation of the state and its restoration to first principles.[50] But Sidney never stands for the pristine perfection of a changeless, immemorial constitution that periodically must be recovered. Like all things human, constitutions change. Constitutional change can be carefully and wisely guided in the direction of the better, and not left to chance and the worse.[51] Sidney had a rather vague idea of social and political progress. This is the great lesson of Rome, which through the participation of the citizen-body, sometimes in conflict, at other times in harmony, was able to fashion a highly imperfect constitution into a more adequate device for the fulfillment of human desires. From a rather pessimistic psychology with emphasis upon egoism, imperfection, and fallibility, together with an admiration of the Roman Republic, Sidney arrived at a radical republican position of citizens' liberties and the adaptability of government to changing conditions by means of domestic conflict and opposition. Throughout he recognizes the difference between the factionalism of a corrupt people and the conflict of a healthy order. Conflict in a healthy order can become the most effective way of energizing social and constitutional change, of preventing social and constitutional abuses, in a word, a warranty of limited, progressive government. And the ultimate form of domestic conflict, the final resort of the citizen, is revolution. When government proves so stubborn, willful, shortsighted, and despotically minded as to outlaw opposition and resist widespread demands for change, re-

48. 2:24, pp. 185, 204, 207, 211, 214.
49. 2:24, p. 215.
50. 2:13, p. 124.   51. 3:28, p. 421; 3:38, p. 469.

form, and individual security, the citizens are justified in using violence to establish new rulers. Sidney lost his life for his conviction.

III

It was Montesquieu, who having absorbed Machiavelli and Sidney, took to heart both what he read and observed of English party conflict, of the commercial hustle and bustle, and of the struggles for liberty in the somber city of the Thames. The result was a brilliant intellectual justification for a *concordia discors.*

At least, since E. Levi-Malvano's classic *Montesquieu e Machiavelli,* published in Paris in 1912, the great influence of the Florentine upon the Frenchman has been fully acknowledged.[52] In particular, Levi-Malvano stresses the impact of the *Discourses* on the early unpublished dissertation on Roman politics and religion, and offers a detailed comparison by means of parallel passages of sections of the *Discourses* and of the *Considerations on the Causes of the Grandeur of the Romans and of Their Decadence* (1734).[53] Two aspects of the influence are of interest here. The first is the sug-

52. A quarter of a century before, Paul Janet in his *Histoire de la science politique dans ses rapports avec la morale,* 3rd ed. (Paris, 1887), 2:326, referred to Montesquieu's great debt to Machiavelli. For recent assessments see esp. Cotta, op. cit., pp. 260–61; A. Bertière, "Montesquieu, lecteur de Machiavel," in *Actes du Congrès Montesquieu,* pp. 141–58; Badreddine Kassem, *Décadence et absolutisme dans l'oeuvre de Montesquieu* (Paris, 1960), pp. 196–99, 259; Shackleton, op. cit., pp. 22, 127, 142–43, 152, 165, 265–69, 292.

In *L'Esprit de Lois,* VI, 5, Montesquieu calls Machiavelli "un grand homme." Montesquieu's other citations of Machiavelli, following the listing of Bertière, op. cit., p. 143, n. 3, are: *L'Esprit de Lois,* 3:9 (passage suppressed); 29:19; *Pensées,* 184, 1793; *Spicilege,* 472–73, 487, 521; *Lettres familières,* 106. Twice he employs a Machiavellian maxim: *L'Esprit de Lois,* 21:20. *Pensées,* 1506. Montesquieu read Machiavelli in translation and also probably in the original.

53. The *Dissertation sur la politique des Romains dans la religion* was evidently written about 1716. Levi-Malvano, op. cit., pp. 59–96.

gestion of Robert Shackleton that Montesquieu's sojourn in England led him to a more mature view of Machiavelli.[54] His friendship with Lord Bolingbroke and familiarity with the *Craftsman,*[55] his reading of Thomas Gordon,[56] and an acquaintance with William Cleland, father of the author of *Memoirs of a Coxcomb,* taught him that Machiavelli was more than the devil's disciple, and that the *Discourses* were relevant to the eighteenth century. The second aspect of Machiavelli's influence relates to Sidney. Montesquieu, after reading Sidney, must have been the more forcibly impressed by certain of Machiavelli's ideas. Authorities agree that the English author was studied by Montesquieu.[57] One of the *Pensées* is undoubtedly derived from Sidney.[58] Upon his return from England, Montesquieu acquired a three-volume translation of Sidney's *Discourses,* published at The Hague in 1702, for the purpose of taking notes and extracts in preparation for the composition of *The Spirit of the Laws.* The very themes of Machiavelli that are emphasized by Sidney are those Montesquieu makes his own: the passionate advocacy of liberty, the hatred of despotism, the belief that absolutism is rooted in corruption, the prescription of a mixed constitution, a paradigmatic description of the behavior of a free people, the call for a return to first principles, and the necessity of domestic conflict.

54. Shackleton, op. cit., pp. 127, 142–43, 152.
55. Ibid., p. 127, n. 4. Shackleton lists the issues of the *Craftsman* referred to by Montesquieu in his *Spicilege:* 31 Jan. 1729/30; 7, 28 Feb. 1729/30; 9 May 1730; 13 June (5 Sept.) 1730; 31 Oct. (5 Dec.) 1730; 21 Nov. (19 Dec.) 1730; 28 Nov. (1 Aug.) 1730; 9 Jan. (23 Jan.) 1730/31.
56. See Shackleton, op. cit., p. 292.
57. For example, Joseph Dedieu, *Montesquieu et la tradition politique anglaise en France: les sources anglaises de l' "Esprit des lois"* (Paris, 1909), pp. 11, 314–26; and his *Montesquieu, l'homme et l'oeuvre* (Paris, 1943), p. 75; Henry Puget, "Montesquieu et l'Angleterre," in *La pensée politique et constitutionnelle de Montesquieu,* ed. Boris Mirkine-Guetzevitch and Henry Puget (Paris, n.d.), pp. 293–94; Shackleton, op. cit., pp. 234, 268, 270, 276, 284, 292.
58. *Pensées,* 626.

However, with a mind as complex and as subtle as Montesquieu's, it is too simple to argue that he arrived at his own theory of conflict by reading Machiavelli firsthand and secondhand through Sidney. Apart from the logical structure of his thought which might have eventually led him to develop such a view, he was deeply interested by what he had read and observed of English social and political reality. Long before visiting England he had referred in *Persian Letter* 136 to "the English historians, who show liberty endlessly issuing from the fires of discord and sedition, the prince always tottering on an immovable throne." [59] The language is striking; these are not the words normally used to describe mere competition. Here, at an early stage in his intellectual development, is the motif of his later thinking on the subject. In perusing the *Considerations,* written in the years immediately following his return from London, one wonders how much of the English experience Montesquieu is reading into his version of Roman history.[60] The ninth chapter especially suggests a kind of synthesis of Rome, England, and Machiavelli, first and secondhand. The full impact of English practice is found in one of the most important, and often forgotten or overlooked parts of *The Spirit of the Laws,* Chapter 27 of Book 19, which should always be read immediately after Chapter 6 of Book 11, containing the famous exposition of the separation of powers.

In turning from speculations about influences to the substance of Montesquieu's thought, attention should be given to the relationship between his concept of human nature and his theory of domestic conflict. It is not surprising that he should place the clash of interest and party strife at the center of his political considerations because his psychology gives primacy to the passions. They constitute the main

59. *The Persian Letters,* tr. George R. Healy (Indianapolis, Ind., 1964), p. 232.
60. See the interesting suggestion of Kassem, op. cit., p. 204.

motive force of the human machine, a point made clear by the *Pensées* and the unpublished essay on causes.[61] "All the vices and the human virtues," Montesquieu contends, "are ordinarily the effect of a certain condition of the machine." [62] The different constitution of the human mechanism produces the different force of the passions, which vary in kind and intensity from individual to individual. The combination of passions peculiar to each determines the whole of his life, accounting for the great variety of human behavior. With his well-known theories of climate and of manners, Montesquieu allows for regularities and uniformities in human behavior dependent upon psychology and physical and social environment. The ordering of a commonwealth must rest upon an understanding of the nature and the force of the passions, and of the cardinal fact that for each individual, preservation of self is the major motive in behavior. Montesquieu does not mean self-love in any narrow sense, for it may lead us to suicide or to benevolent actions out of sympathy for the predicament of others, the very source of all social action.[63] Perhaps, because of his conception of the psyche as a crucible of energy-seeking release, Montesquieu condemns the life of ascetic withdrawal. The ideal life is one of vigor and productive activity.[64] Passions must find outlets and be safely canalized by the intervention and interaction of laws and manners in order to invigorate and strengthen the social order.

The internal dissensions, largely responsible for the Roman citizens' liberties, cannot be viewed in isolation from the passions which had set those same citizens on the road to

61. See *Oeuvres complètes de Montesquieu,* ed. André Masson (Paris, 1950), 2:149, 630; and 3:399–411, for the *Essai sur les causes.*
62. Ibid, 2:630.
63. *Considerations,* Ch. 12.
64. One of the most stimulating and revealing interpretations on much of the above is H. Barckhausen, *Montesquieu, ses idées et ses oeuvres d'après les papiers de la Brède* (Paris, 1907), pp. 18–24, 34–35. Also see Kassem, op. cit., p. 259; Cotta, loc. cit., p. 262.

world conquest. Montesquieu develops his brief reference to the importance of conflict in *Persian Letter* 136, beginning with the following opening remark in the eighth chapter of the *Considerations:*

> While Rome conquered the world, a secret war was going on within its walls. Its fires were like those of volcanoes which burst forth whenever some matter comes along to increase their activity.[65]

After citing the familiar example of the plebes and patricians, and referring to the government of England, he concludes that a free government is always "subject to agitation." [66] In the following chapter he reasons that Rome's expansionism, not social dissension, was the main factor in her decline. Conflict was inevitable because citizen-soldiers, so courageous and vigorous in the defense of the city from external foes, could not completely transform their conduct into moderation in domestic matters.[67] Boldness in war and timidity in peace are simply too much to ask of such a hardy race. Indeed, if a republic is characterized by internal tranquility, then we may be sure that the citizens have lost their liberty and vigor. Two kinds of harmony in a commonwealth must be distinguished. The first is that of the Romans: while the parts at one level are in opposition, at a higher level they cooperate for the common good. As do Aristotle and Polybius before him, Montesquieu employs the familiar analogy of musical harmony. However, he gives the musical allusion new content, because his concept of the common good entails the security and happiness of the citizens, the satisfaction of their desires instead of an absolute moral end. The second harmony is that which exists under an oriental despot, and which con-

---

65. *Considerations on the Causes of the Greatness of the Romans and Their Decline,* tr. David Lowenthal (New York, 1965), p. 83.
66. Ibid., p. 88.
67. Cf. with Cicero, above, pp, 286–87.

sists of an almost absolute quiet, the solitude of "dead bodies buried next to the other." [68] At another level, however, analysis reveals a fundamental cleavage not only between ruler and ruled, the oppressor and the oppressed, but also between each individual, so atomized has despotic society become. Unlike a republic, dissension in a despotic state will prove disastrous for the regime; rather than working to reform or change a particular law, the dissenters will unseat the despot, creating a power vacuum to be filled by another despot.

Fourteen years afterwards in *The Spirit of the Laws,* Montesquieu turns from Rome to the analysis of conflict in England. In passing, he repeats his principle that a healthy democratic republic thrives on conflict, although aristocratic republics like ancient Sparta and modern Venice do not.[69] Then in the nineteenth book he analyzes party conflict in England. The connection between this section and the comments on Roman dissension would seem self-evident, but few commentators specifically refer to it. Of the best of the traditional commentators, neither Janet nor Barckhausen makes the connection or mentions the discussion in Montesquieu's magnum opus. Shackleton discusses both, but fails to connect the two,[70] and much the same can be said of Courtney.[71] Two scholars of recent years, Cotta and Kassem, call attention to the significant relationship between the two treatments of conflict.[72] Cotta, a perceptive student of Machiavelli, refers to the ninth chapter of the *Considerations*

68. Ibid., p. 94.   69. *L'Esprit des Lois,* 2:2.
70. Op. cit., pp. 291–98.
71. J. P. Courtney, *Montesquieu and Burke* (Oxford, 1963), pp. 64–66. Although he refers to the idea of conflict in the *Considerations* in connection with Montesquieu's theory of the separation of powers, Raymond Aron does not mention the discussion of English parties. See his *Main Currents in Sociological Thought,* tr. Richard Howard and Helen Weaver (New York, 1965), 1:28–39.
72. Cotta, loc. cit., pp. 260–62; Kassem, op. cit., pp. 259, 273.

as "a new conception of political life" [73] and proceeds to discuss Montesquieu's examination of English party dissension precisely in these terms.

By designating the parties as "court" and "country," instead of by the more traditional, but for the period less accurate "Tory" and "Whig," Montesquieu proves to be an acute observer of English political life. He begins by attempting to relate the nature of the English parties to the basic separation of governmental powers between the executive and the legislative, already explained in the eleventh book. Depending upon his particular interests, a citizen is free to indicate a preference for one of the two powers, and to align himself either with the monarch or the parliament. Passions are given free reign in England; two parties, the court and country, are in constant struggle. When one party becomes too strong support may shift to the other. English politics would seem to consist of a constant circulation of supporters from one party to another, according to the power relations of the moment. Individuals may be political friends and associates one day, and enemies the next, which means that although political friendships are enfeebled, extreme political hatreds are appreciably reduced. Both sovereign and subject are in a never-ending state of political insecurity. On one day the sovereign may have to award and share confidences with individuals and groups who were his opponents of yesterday. The political friends of an individual may at any time become his opponents. All of this produces a general uneasiness, but with the salutary consequence that each individual is extremely watchful of his own liberties. A domestic threat such as the violation of a fundamental law will rally support behind the legislative, while a danger from abroad will increase the strength of the court. In what is unquestionably an allusion to the Glorious Revo-

73. Cotta, loc. cit., p. 260.

lution, Montesquieu feels that when both a domestic threat and a foreign danger occur simultaneously a revolution may take place which would alter neither the constitution nor the form of government.

The discussion of English parties is of fundamental significance. Montesquieu has provided the first effort of a political theorist, crude as it may be, to analyze a party system and to relate it to the basic structure of government. Again, he tries to explain the moderation of English politics and the stability of English government by showing that the very party system itself performs an integrating role by the reduction of extreme forms of political behavior. And finally he holds that the continuous free play of the parties is the best guarantee of the Englishman's liberties. Politics becomes a function of individual passions as they are manifested in the great social arena of clashing interests. The frenetic movement of the party struggle keeps every citizen alert, prevents indolence and social stagnation, and enhances the strength and vitality of English society.[74]

IV

What we have here considered in the thought of Machiavelli, Sidney, and Montesquieu is, in fact, the emergence of a new concept of society. Paradoxically, it is a view of society as necessarily involving asocial as well as social elements, just as man was considered to be both an asocial and a social being. The social element is necessary for men to live together; the asocial element is crucial, however, if man is to

74. Typical of Montesquieu's position on the relationship between the release of the passions through conflict and the vitality of the social order is his comment in regard to England: "All the passions being unrestrained, hatred, envy, jealousy, and an ambitious desire of riches and honors, appear in their extent; were it otherwise, the state would be in the condition of a man weakened by sickness, who is without passions because he is without strength." *The Spirit of the Laws,* tr. Thomas Nugent (New York, 1949), p. 308.

become more than an unreflective automaton of habit and tradition, as Hegel put it somewhere, a clock wound up and left to run down. Civilization implies reform and the self-conscious reflection necessary for reform. Indeed, civilization entails perpetual conflict between the old and the new in a kind of dialectical process. When this process is lacking, civilization itself is absent. Men only lifted themselves out of the primeval slime to become more than stupid, unimaginative brutes, because some individuals stood in opposition to their fellows. Modern liberalism with all its defects, has at least labored valiantly to defend the principle of opposition and conflict, particularly in the realms of thought, speech, and association. Once the principle of questioning authority and commonly accepted ends and of opposition to the established is no longer cherished or recognized, the human spirit is stifled and perishes, and society in the sense of the civilized withers away. Looking back on the modern era from his solitude in Koenigsburg, Immanuel Kant recognized something of the complex nature of society, not from a position of detachment and neutrality, but with a passionate commitment to man:

> *The means which nature employs to accomplish the development of all faculties is the antagonism of men in society, since this antagonism becomes, in the end, the cause of a lawful order of this society.* I mean by antagonism the asocial sociability of man, i.e., the propensity of men to enter into a society, which propensity is, however, linked to a constant mutual resistance which threatens to dissolve this society. This propensity apparently is innate in man. Man has an inclination to *associate* himself, because in such a state he feels himself more like a man capable of developing his natural faculties. Man has also a marked propensity to *isolate* himself, because he finds in himself the asocial quality

to want to arrange everything according to his own ideas. He therefore expects resistance everywhere, just as he knows of himself that he is inclined to resist others. This resistance awakens all the latent forces in man which drive him to overcome his propensity to be lazy, and so, impelled by vainglory, ambition and avarice, he seeks to achieve a standing among his fellows, whom he does not suffer gladly, but whom he cannot *leave.* Thus the first steps from barbarism to culture are achieved; for culture actually consists in the social value of man. All man's talents are gradually unfolded, taste is developed. . . . Without these essentially unlovely qualities of asociability, from which springs the resistance which everyone must encounter in his egoistic pretensions, all talents would have remained hidden germs. If man lived an Arcadian shepherd's existence of harmony, modesty and mutuality, man, goodnatured like the sheep he is herding, would not invest his existence with greater value than that his animals have.[75]

The thinkers who perhaps contributed most to this perspective in early modern Europe are Machiavelli, Sidney, and Montesquieu. Nor can the influential example of the English social and political experience be overlooked. If contemporary bureaucratic capitalism and communism are not to dehumanize and destroy men, more attention will have to be given to the nature of conflict and to the ways and means by which our common life can be enriched by conflict.

75. "Idea for a Universal History with Cosmopolitan Intent" (1784), in *The Philosophy of Kant: Immanuel Kant's Moral and Political Writings,* ed. and tr. Carl J. Friedrich (New York, 1949), pp. 120–21.

Contributors

Martin Fleisher, Professor of Political Science, Brooklyn College of the City University of New York, is the author of *Radical Reform and Political Persuasion in the Life and Writings of Thomas More*.

J. A. Gunn, Professor of Political Studies, Queens College, has published *Politics and the Public Interest in the Seventeenth Century*.

Harvey Mansfield, Jr., Professor of Political Science, Harvard University, is the author of *Statesmanship and Party Government* and is completing a work on Machiavelli.

Anthony Parel, Professor of Political Science, University of Calgary, has written on Machiavelli and on Indian politics and political thought.

Mark Phillips is in the Department of History at the University of Toronto.

J. G. A. Pocock, Professor of History and Political Science, Washington University in St. Louis, is the author of *The Ancient Constitution and the Feudal Law* and the recent *Politics, Language and Time*.

Brayton Polka, who teaches history at York University is completing a study of Lorenzo Valla.

Alan Ryan, Fellow of New College, Oxford University, has recently published two studies in political thought: *John Stuart Mill* and *The Philosophy of the Social Sciences*.

Sheldon Wolin, Professor of Political Science, University of California, Santa Cruz, is the author of *Politics and Vision,* among other works.

Neal Wood, Professor of Political Science, York University, wrote *Communism and British Intellectuals*. He has also written extensively on Machiavelli, including the study *Machiavelli: The Art of War*.